OUTSOURCING
WAR AND PEACE

OUTSOURCING WAR AND PEACE

Preserving Public
Values in a World
of Privatized
Foreign Affairs

Laura A. Dickinson

Yale UNIVERSITY PRESS
New Haven and London

Published with assistance from the foundation established in memory of Philip Hamilton McMillan of the Class of 1894, Yale College.

Yale University Press books may be purchased in quantity for educational, business, or promotional use. For information, please e-mail sales.press@yale.edu (U.S. office) or sales@yaleup.co.uk (U.K. office).

Set in Galliard and Copperplate type by Newgen North America.
Printed in the United States of America.

Library of Congress Cataloging-in-Publication Data

Dickinson, Laura A. (Laura Anne)
    Outsourcing war and peace : preserving public values in a world of privatized foreign affairs / Laura A. Dickinson.
        p.   cm.
    Includes bibliographical references and index.
    ISBN 978-0-300-14486-4 (hardcover : alk. paper)   1. Defense contracts—United States.   2. Private military companies—United States.   3. Contracting out—United States.   I. Title.
    KF855.D53 2011
    355.6'2120973—dc22   2010025732

A catalogue record for this book is available from the British Library.

This paper meets the requirements of ANSI/NISO Z39.48-1992 ♾.

10 9 8 7 6 5 4 3 2 1

TO PAUL AND JULIEN

CONTENTS

ACKNOWLEDGMENTS

This book is the result of ongoing research supported by multiple institutions and has benefited from the commentary and feedback of many scholars and policy makers. I completed the bulk of the work on the book during the year that I was a fellow in the Princeton Program on Law and Public Affairs, and the University of Connecticut School of Law helped to make that year possible by granting me a research leave. Arizona State University, where I am now a faculty member, has also provided generous support for my research.

I was able to gather the material in Chapter 6 only due to the generosity of the faculty of the Army Judge Advocate General's (JAG) School in Charlottesville, Virginia, which allowed me to interview JAGs studying there who had previously served in Iraq and Afghanistan and who had encountered military and security contractors during their tours of duty. I conducted additional interviews with employees of the National Committee for Quality Assurance, including Phyllis Torda, vice president for strategy. I also conducted interviews with government employees at the Department of Defense, the Department of State, and the Government Accountability Office, and with employees of contract firms and professional organizations, including Doug Brooks, president of the International Peace Operations Association.

Portions of this book were competitively selected for presentation in several forums that greatly enriched the content of the material presented. These forums include the Yale-Stanford Junior Faculty Forum, the New

Voices Forum at the American Society of International Law, the "hot topics" panel at the annual meeting of the Association of American Law Schools, and the young scholars panel of the Northeast Law and Society Association.

I am also very grateful for the comments and suggestions from participants at workshops at Arizona State University's Sandra Day O'Connor College of Law, Cardozo Law School, Columbia Law School, Duke Law School, Emory University Law School, Fordham Law School, the Georgetown University Law Center, the George Washington School of Law, Harvard Law School, New York University Law School, Princeton University, Stanford Law School, the University of Connecticut School of Law, the University of Georgia School of Law, the University of North Carolina, the University of Virginia School of Law, Vanderbilt Law School, Western New England School of Law, and Yale Law School.

More specifically, I would like to thank my cofellows from the Law and Public Affairs program and the Princeton faculty who commented extensively on the project, including Vanessa Barker, Mary Anne Case, Katherine Franke, Dirk Hartog, Stan Katz, Robert Keohane, Jamie Mayerfeld, Deborah Pearlstein, Peggy Radin, Larry Rosen, Teemu Ruskola, and Kim Lane Scheppele. My former colleagues at the University of Connecticut provided enormous support for the project as well, including, in particular, Tom Baker, Bethany Berger, Anne Dailey, Kaaryn Gustafson, Mark Janis, Richard Kay, Leslie Levin, Peter Lindseth, Alexi Lahav, Hugh Macgill, Angel Oquendo, Jeremy Paul, Peter Siegelman, Richard Wilson, Carol Weisbrod, and Steven Wilf. I am also grateful to my colleagues at Arizona State University, especially Ken Abbott, Linda Demaine, Aaron Fellmeth, Andy Hessick, Carissa Hessick, Orde Kittrie, Jonathan Rose, Mary Sigler, and Douglas Sylvester. In addition, the following individuals have given me extensive feedback at various stages of the project: Robert Ahdieh, Diane Amann, Dan Bodansky, Rosa Brooks, Phil Carter, Simon Chesterman, James Cockayne, Nestor Davidson, Larry Helfer, Scott Horton, Deena Hurwitz, Paul Kahn, Harold Hongju Koh, Kevin Lanigan, Chia Lehnardt, Janet Levit, David Luban, Sally Merry, Ralf Michaels, Jerry Mashaw, Martha Minow, Michael Newton, Hari Osofsky, Nick Parillo, Susan Rose-Ackerman, Leila Sadat, Austin Sarat, Michael Scharf, Steve Schooner, Susan Silbey, Scott Silliman, Peter Spiro, Kevin

Stack, Paul Verkuil, Kay Warren, and, last but not least, my stepfather, Robert W. Gordon, and my husband, Paul Schiff Berman.

Some of the material in this book is an expansion of articles and book chapters published over the past few years:

Military Lawyers on the Battlefield: An Empirical Account of International Law Compliance, 104 Am. J. Int'l L. 1 (2010);

Military Lawyers, Private Contractors, and the Problem of International Law Compliance, 42 N.Y.U. J. Int'l L. & Pol. 355 (2010);

Public Values/Private Contract, in Government by Contract (Jody Freeman & Martha Minow eds., Harvard Univ. Press, 2008);

Mercenarism and Private Military Contractors, in International Criminal Law (M. Cherif Bassiouni ed., 3d ed., Martinus Nijhoff Pub., 2008);

Contract as a Tool for Regulating Private Military Companies, in From Mercenaries to Market (Simon Chesterman and Chia Lenhardt eds., Oxford University Press, 2007);

Abu Ghraib, in International Law Stories (John Noyes, Mark Janis & Laura Dickinson eds., Foundation Press, 2007);

Public Law Values in a Privatized World, 31 Yale J. Int'l L. 384 (2006);

Torture and Contract, 37 Case Western Reserve J. Int'l L. 267 (2006);

Accountability and the Use of Contracts, Int'l Peace Operations Association Newsletter (2006);

Government for Hire: Privatizing Foreign Affairs and the Problem of Accountability in International Law, 47 Wm & Mary L. Rev. 135 (2005).

A great many student research assistants and research librarians helped at various stages of this project, and I am deeply grateful to all of them for their diligent work. In the preparation of this manuscript, I received important assistance from Joanne Cossitt, Beth DiFelice, Jennis Hemingway, Sakina Hussein, Virginia Iziguerre, Paul Johnson, Allison Lienau, Aparnas Patankar, Matthew Rich, Nina Robertson, Katayoun Sadhegi, Malvika Sinha, and Simren Uppal.

1

INTRODUCTION

It is the morning of September 16, 2007, and traffic clogs the crowded intersection at Baghdad's Nisour Square. Ordinary vehicles have stopped to make way for a line of gray sport utility vehicles: a diplomatic convoy is passing through. Suddenly, a fusillade of gunshots breaks through the ordinary din and bustle. Shouts and screams ring out as people run for cover. When it is over, seventeen civilians, all Iraqi nationals, are dead. The shooters are armed security guards employed by the firm Blackwater,[1] working under an agreement with the U.S. Department of State to provide protection to the department's diplomats as they travel throughout the war-torn country.[2]

According to witnesses and subsequent official reports, the deadly cascade of events began when a single bullet, apparently fired by a Blackwater guard, killed an Iraqi man driving a car that was approaching the convoy. The man's weight probably remained on the accelerator and propelled the car forward. As the car continued to roll toward the convoy, security guards responded with an intense barrage of gunfire in several directions. Minutes after the shooting stopped, the convoy opened fire on another line of traffic a few hundred yards away. One preliminary investigation concluded that at least fourteen of the seventeen killings were unjustified.[3] A military report went even further and determined that the guards had used excessive force and that all of the deaths were unjustified.[4]

Next, move seven months earlier. It is now January of 2007, and it has just come to light that the State Department paid $43.8 million to DynCorp *for operating a residential police training camp outside Baghdad's Adnan Palace grounds, a camp that has actually stood empty for months. Moreover, $4.2 million of the State Department payment has been diverted to the purchase of twenty luxury VIP trailers and an Olympic-size pool.[5] Yet egregious as this activity might be, it pales in comparison to DynCorp's previous activities in Bosnia. There, under a similar agreement, DynCorp employees working to train Bosnian police were caught running a sex trafficking ring.[6]*

Now it is April of 2006 in Iraq, and a string of stopped cars and trucks are riddled with bullets fired by another security contractor. The contractor is the shift leader of a group of guards working for Triple Canopy, a company that has entered into an agreement to protect the employees of Kellogg, Brown and Root (KBR), logistics contractors hired by the U.S. Department of Defense (DOD). According to reports from two of the other three employees on the scene, the shift leader was scheduled to return home to the United States. He declared that he was "going to kill someone today," and then proceeded to fire shots from his M4 rifle into the windshield of a stopped truck, and later into a stopped taxi.[7] The third employee in the group, a Fijian national, went further and reported that after the shift leader had fired his gun all three of the others laughed, and one said to the shift leader, "Nice shot."[8] Whether anyone died in the incident is unknown.

And of course there is Abu Ghraib, two words that have become shorthand for the abuses committed by U.S. forces in Iraq. But though those abuses are widely known, less recognized is the involvement of contract interrogators and translators at Abu Ghraib. According to military investigators, these contractors were inadequately trained and supervised and were responsible for some of the worst abuses at the prison.[9] Thus Abu Ghraib is not only a story of military personnel run amok but of the sometimes unhealthy mixing of uniformed soldiers and private contractors.

Together these various incidents reveal one of the most remarkable facts about the U.S. conflicts in Iraq and Afghanistan: alongside the men and women in uniform who are risking their lives each day to protect the United States and bring peace, security, and the rule of law to Iraq and Afghanistan, there is another fighting force. The members of this second force also are putting their lives in jeopardy. They too are attempting to bring peace and security to the region. Yet they are not wearing uniforms, and they are not subject to military discipline or the chain of command. Rather, they are working as private contractors, employed by companies that have entered into contracts with the DOD, the Department of State, and other U.S. government agencies operating in conflict zones. There are at least as many of them as there are uniformed soldiers: more than 225,000 by mid-2009.[10] And, while the incidents described above may not be typical, these contractors are, at least on occasion, taking actions that threaten core public values, including a fundamental respect for human dignity—human rights, human security, and the idea that the use of force has certain limits, even during armed conflict—transparency, and public participation.

This book grapples with the implications of this profound shift in the way the U.S. government projects its power overseas. Most fundamentally, the book closely examines the impact of our growing use of private contractors on these core public values. Outsourcing our foreign affairs and security work overseas threatens such values in significant part because the legal and regulatory framework we have used to protect them was designed in an era when governmental officials were the ones who primarily carried out this work. Though it is debatable whether this framework was even adequate in a prior era, there can be little doubt that it cannot cope with the new way that we are conducting our affairs abroad. And yet, at the same time, it will be insufficient to merely protest this privatization trend or call for its reversal. For better or worse, privatization is likely to be a fact of life for twenty-first-century military activity. Accordingly, if we want to protect core public values, we need to radically rethink and rebuild our regulatory architecture.

A Breathtaking Shift

States and international organizations have, over the past ten years, shifted a surprising range of foreign policy functions to private contractors. While they have done so quietly and with little fanfare, the extent of this shift is truly breathtaking: working for both for-profit companies and nonprofit organizations, these contractors are delivering aid, negotiating peace settlements, and fighting wars. In the military arena the scope of this trend is perhaps most surprising, as private actors have assumed roles considered (at least in the past seventy-five years) largely within the exclusive province of state bureaucracies.[11] Indeed, private contractors are even being used to conduct intelligence operations abroad in areas officially off-limits for spying.[12] Precise figures on the size of the military services industry are difficult to obtain, but its scope is clearly vast. Experts offer estimates of the industry's annual revenue that range from $100 billion to a more conservative, but still sizable, $20 billion.[13] The U.S. government alone has spent nearly $100 billion on contracts in Iraq. The numbers of personnel that the firms employ, and the ratio of such personnel to uniformed troops, are also striking. Recent reports indicate that 190,000 government contractors are operating in Iraq, resulting in a ratio of contractors to troops that exceeds one to one. During the first Gulf War, by contrast, the U.S. military hired only 9,200 contractors, and the ratio of contractors to troops was one to fifty-five.[14]

In addition to the United States and other developed countries,[15] governments around the world have employed these contractors. Weak states or states embroiled in civil war have in many cases turned to companies that provide training and combat services. For example, the government of Sierra Leone hired Executive Outcomes to fight back rebels who were terrorizing the country. The firm is widely credited with winning the civil war and bringing peace.[16] An even broader array of developing countries—including many with functioning militaries—rely on contractors for logistics support and weapons maintenance, as their own forces lack the technical skills to fulfill such functions.[17] The United Nations and other international organizations have used contracted military services as well, particularly for logistics and training.[18] And while proposals to use private contractors to conduct direct peacekeeping have thus far been rejected,[19] it may only be a matter of time before the privatization trend reaches such activities.

In Iraq, the U.S. government has used private security companies and other contract firms to perform a wide variety of functions that involve the potential use of force. Private contractors have provided security for housing and work areas, including the U.S. military installations themselves. In this capacity, they guard entrances and exits, station sharpshooters on perimeter towers, conduct roving patrols, and provide security screening of visitors. Likewise, they serve as the security detail for high-ranking U.S. officials and Chief of Mission personnel, security escorts for U.S. government employees moving through the country, convoy security, and security advisers and planners. This is all in addition to the contract interrogators and translators operating in detention facilities around the country, as well as the vast number of contractors involved in reconstruction aid projects and other logistical operations.[20] Thus, the scope of private activity is broad, and the possibility that contractors could be involved in questionable (and violent) activity is real indeed.

As to the firms themselves, although many are incorporated in the United States, the United Kingdom, and other Western countries, they are located around the world, and even companies based in the West hire *employees* of multiple nationalities. Indeed, a recent government report indicates that only 5 percent of the employees of private security contractors in Iraq are U.S. citizens, and fully 77 percent are not Iraqi either.[21] Thus, military privatization is truly a worldwide phenomenon.

Although it has received less attention, the same privatization trend can be seen in the realm of foreign aid.[22] From emergency humanitarian relief, to long-term development assistance, to postconflict reconstruction programs, private actors under contract with the United States, other governments, and international organizations are taking a larger and larger role. The most dramatic surge in privatized aid has involved emergency humanitarian relief. The United States, for example, has contracted with private companies such as KBR to build refugee camps,[23] and with nonprofit nongovernmental organizations (NGOs), such as Save the Children, to deliver relief, supplies, and medical services.[24] For fiscal year 2008 the USAID Office of U.S. Foreign Disaster Assistance spent 55 percent of its nearly $740 million budget through NGOs.[25] Other countries and international organizations are similarly turning to NGOs to deliver humanitarian aid.[26] Longer-term development aid has followed a similar trend. Beginning in the mid-1980s, development agencies shifted their focus from general funding for foreign governments to more targeted direct support both to grassroots organizations helping to eradicate poverty and to other civil society institutions seen as necessary for democracy and development.[27] In the United States, for example, the government now uses both international and foreign NGOs to deliver much of its aid overseas, rather than providing aid directly to foreign governments.[28] As the cases of Iraq and Afghanistan make clear, privatization is also taking place in the arena of postconflict reconstruction, with multimillion-dollar contracts and grants awarded to private aid providers.

In addition, while nonprofit organizations such as Oxfam and C.A.R.E. receive much of the aid funding, in recent years for-profit companies have begun to receive an increasing share of aid contracts, either directly from governments or as subcontract work from nonprofit organizations. Indeed, in Iraq and Afghanistan for-profit companies have actually predominated. Moreover, many of the same companies that provide military sector services are also involved in aid delivery. For example, Dyn-Corp has received U.S. government contracts to train police in Iraq and Afghanistan, while Military Professional Resources, Inc. (MPRI) trains other security services there. KBR has built refugee camps in the Balkans and elsewhere. Other military contractors, such as International Charter Incorporated and Evergreen Defense and Security Services, transport humanitarian relief supplies around the world. It has, accordingly, become increasingly difficult to draw boundaries between foreign aid and military services.

Although foreign affairs outsourcing is not completely new—mercenaries have appeared throughout history[29]—this trend does represent a substantial shift from the large bureaucratized military and foreign policy apparatus that characterized states in the twentieth century. Indeed, the government's monopoly on violence and the conduct of foreign affairs has often been assumed to be a quintessential feature of the modern liberal democratic state.[30] We have therefore entered a new era, and it has taken us almost by surprise.

A Burgeoning Literature

Over the past seven years, scholars have begun to recognize this privatization trend and grapple with its implications. In 2003, P. W. Singer wrote the first comprehensive account of military privatization. In *Corporate Warriors: The Rise of the Privatized Military*, Singer assembled voluminous data demonstrating the scope of military privatization.[31] And though not himself a lawyer, Singer expressed concern that established international and domestic legal norms might be insufficient to provide accountability in this new era.

While Singer's work mostly sought to ring alarm bells, political scientist Deborah D. Avant, in her book *The Market for Force: The Consequences of Privatizing Security*, turned the conversation to an analysis of the political, sociological, and regulatory preconditions necessary to ensure both efficiency and accountability.[32] As she put the question, "[Under what conditions will] the political changes introduced by privatization engender needed capabilities governed by acceptable political processes that operate according to shared values?" This framework allowed Avant to focus attention on the wide range of potential mechanisms that impact compliance with norms. Thus, Avant argued that we must consider whether "consequential mechanisms" such as screening and selection, monitoring, and sanctioning, can be joined with "mechanisms for transmitting appropriateness," such as norms, standards, training, and industry practice. By emphasizing both formal and informal factors, Avant usefully expanded the analytical playing field.

Paul R. Verkuil's *Outsourcing Sovereignty: Why Privatization of Government Functions Threatens Democracy and What We Can Do About It* was the first book-length analysis of military privatization written by a legal scholar.[33] As his title suggests, Verkuil argued that military security is an inherent part of governmental sovereignty and should not be privatized. According to Verkuil, privatization undermines the capacity, effectiveness, and morale of governmental officials. Focusing on domestic U.S. constitutional and administrative law, Verkuil presented arguments aimed at protecting the public role in exercising military authority.

As the potential threats posed by private contractors entered the popular consciousness, journalists began turning their attention to the issue. In 2007 Jeremy Scahill published *Blackwater: The Rise of the World's Most Powerful Mercenary Army*,[34] and in 2010 David Isenberg published *Shadow Force: Private Security Contractors in Iraq*.[35] Although these books usefully document important problems caused by the deployment of contractors, they are not focused principally on legal and public policy reforms that might increase accountability.

In addition to these monographs, two collections of essays—*From Mercenaries to Market: The Rise and Regulation of Private Military*

Companies[36] and *Government by Contract: Outsourcing and American Democracy*[37]—have tackled issues raised by military outsourcing from a wide variety of disciplinary perspectives. Though these essays cannot, because of their length, offer the sort of extended analysis afforded by the monographs, the breadth of the essay collections makes clear that foreign affairs outsourcing is one of the defining trends of the first part of the twenty-first century and one that needs further scholarly and policy attention.

This book builds on these pioneering studies, but turns the focus to the necessary next step: How do we build a comprehensive legal, regulatory, and institutional architecture that will begin to respond to the threats posed by security outsourcing?

The Threat to Public Values

In order to begin to craft such a response, we need to be clear just what threats we are addressing. As the incidents described at the outset of this chapter starkly illustrate, outsourcing our foreign affairs work implicates what we might call core public law values. To be sure, while these incidents have garnered significant media attention, they may not be typical. And contractors themselves are risking their lives to bring peace and security to Iraq—more than a thousand have died in Iraq since the conflict began[38]—so we need not demonize these private contractors. But even if these incidents are not the norm, they nonetheless illustrate the extent to which our public values are at risk.

These values include:

- the fundamental respect for human dignity enshrined in public international law, including norms of human rights, human security, and the idea of rule-bound warfare, with its protections for non-combatants and wounded soldiers;
- public participation in decision making; and
- transparency and anticorruption.

Take the Blackwater Nisour Square shooting as an example. If Blackwater guards did indeed spray multiple rounds of ammunition on a crowd of civilians in the square, without provocation, those actions undermine a central value that undergirds much of the law of armed conflict. A core principle embedded in the Geneva Conventions of 1949—which govern both international and internal armed conflict—is that the use of force has limits: warring parties or occupying powers may not target civilians or take actions that disproportionately harm civilians.[39] This is also a key principle the U.S. military aims to follow. As one uniformed military lawyer put it, "When [your] job is to fight and kill, you try to do it with some sense of integrity . . . you want the Army to be able to say that."[40] Similarly, another stressed, "We can only fight the global war on terror by holding onto our core values, [and by] establishing the rule of law."[41]

Next, consider the example of the DynCorp contracts to train police and build facilities in Iraq and Afghanistan that ended up in millions of dollars of overcharges and unauthorized projects. Here, we need to think not about human rights values but the value of public participation, which is a critical element of the democratic political process. Yet, even members of Congress had little awareness of, or input into, the decision to award the contract in the first place. Moreover, members of Congress could not scrutinize many of the contract terms, because they were not publicly available. And of course there was no scrutiny by the general public at all. Meanwhile, contract managers from the State Department, the agency that entered into the agreements with the firm, were missing in action in Iraq. Their poor oversight of the agreements, and failure to report on progress to Congress, contributed to the waste and abuse. Thus, neither Congress nor the public at large was able to meaningfully participate in the decisions being made about how to train police forces in Iraq and Afghanistan. And this is to say nothing about possible opportunities for input by populations within Iraq and Afghanistan, which were, of course, nonexistent.

Throughout this book, I explore ways in which we might try to protect the core public values of human dignity, public participation, and transparency in an era of military outsourcing. Of course, some might object to my labeling these values as "public." Indeed, over the past fifty years many values and rights have been reframed or redefined so that they apply well beyond the traditionally public sphere. Thus, for example, drawing on legal realism, many scholars and lawmakers in the civil rights era reconceived certain antidiscrimination rights as belonging to individuals regardless of whether the infringer was a policeman or a restaurateur. Thus, it might seem anachronistic to try to privilege certain rights or values as quintessentially public.

By using the term "public values," however, I certainly do not intend to reinscribe a sharp or essential division between public and private spheres or to argue that the values shift from sphere to sphere. To be sure, in the international realm, the values I describe as public have often been identified with governmental actors. For example, human rights norms have principally been applied to curtail abuses committed by governmental officials—the government security forces who beat and kill protesters, the prison guards who torture detainees, and so on. But one of the core points of this book is that these public values ought to govern even when those acting are not governmental employees or representatives. Thus, it is my position that the values remain core public values and that those values can and should be applied, regardless of whether the actor in question is public or private.

An Outmoded Legal Architecture

These core public values are at risk in large part because the legal, regulatory, and institutional architecture we have constructed over the past century to protect these values was built in an era when governmental actors fought our wars, delivered our aid, and rebuilt failed states. The laws and agency rules that we have used to ensure that we respect those values when we act overseas were designed primarily to constrain *governmental* actors. For example, the primary treaty that prohibits torture only bans the practice when a "public official" commits it, or someone acting under that official's supervision.[42] Likewise, various rules designed to ensure greater transparency and governmental accountability often do not apply to private contractors.

A significant reason for this outmoded legal and regulatory framework is the quiet way that foreign affairs outsourcing has grown. Despite the potentially profound impact of such outsourcing, it has happened mostly under the radar, and scholars and policy makers have barely begun to address its consequences. To be sure, in the domestic setting, commentators have debated the implications of governments' increasing use of private actors to run prisons, provide health care, manage schools, and deliver welfare.[43] Yet this debate has generally not focused on the foreign affairs arena at all.[44]

Indeed, international law scholars have not addressed outsourcing in a comprehensive way, let alone considered its implications or the lessons that might be learned from the domestic debate. These scholars have long considered how to apply international legal norms to nonstate actors in general.[45] But "nonstate actors" is too broad a category because a private contractor is very different from, say, a guerrilla soldier. In particular, because outsourcing involves an increasing contractual relationship between governments (or international organizations) and private actors, contractual mechanisms for importing public accountability are potentially available with regard to outsourcing, whereas they obviously are not relevant to other nonstate actors. Nor have international law scholars and policy makers much considered applying to the foreign affairs setting some of the tools used to try to tame privatization in the domestic context.

Constructing a New Regulatory Architecture for an Era of Privatization

To the extent that international law scholars and policy makers have proposed solutions to potential problems created by outsourcing, these proposals fall far short. For example, some argue that the best response to privatization is simply to oppose it.[46] However, as noted previously, this is unrealistic given that the trend toward outsourcing is probably irreversible, at least in the foreseeable future. Indeed, in testimony before Congress in January 2007, General David Petraeus made clear that the U.S. military would not be able to function in Iraq at all without contract security personnel.[47] Thus, although *specific* activities—military interrogation, for example—may pose such acute risks that they should never be privatized, that is a far cry from simply opposing privatization *in toto*. Other critics assume that private actors with significant impact in the international sphere inhabit a regulatory void and must therefore be brought more formally within the normative framework of international law.[48] These critics therefore conclude that the principal (or only) possible response is the creation of new treaties to address private contractors so that they may be tried before international courts. Yet, even if states expand the norms of international law to apply to the broad range of outsourced activities, and even if the international courts can be established to enforce these norms, such tribunals will never have the capacity to address more than a few cases. Accordingly, while these approaches are important, we need alternative mechanisms for controlling private contractors and implementing core public law values in the international sphere.

This book explores such mechanisms, providing a comprehensive account of the problems posed by foreign affairs outsourcing as well as offering concrete solutions. Such outsourcing presents a series of crucial questions. How can we make private security forces accountable, and to whom? And if complete accountability is not possible, might we at least be able to harness mechanisms of constraint that will help deter private contractors from committing abuses? How can people whom contractors harm seek either redress or at least an opportunity for criticism or feedback? How can the government agencies for which contractors work supervise, monitor, and control their actions, while punishing them for misconduct? How can the organizational structure and culture of private military firms be reformed to try to ensure greater respect for public values? How can the media, public-interest monitors, NGOs, and the foreign citizens affected by contractors find out what contractors are doing and make such activities known to audiences who would care? And are certain types of privatization more likely to result in abuse and fraud than others?

In order to address such questions, we must think in terms of mechanisms for achieving greater *accountability* and *constraint*. Accountability is often thought to be limited only to post hoc mechanisms that allow actors to hold other actors to a set of standards, to judge whether they have fulfilled their responsibilities in light of these standards, and to impose sanctions if they determine that these responsibilities have not been met. Thus, we tend to think of accountability only in terms of criminal or civil penalties against those who break the law. However, this sort of formal sanctioning law is only one way in which we might seek greater control over contractors, and it is a central premise of the book that we need to expand our inquiry to include a broader range of mechanisms. Accordingly, I speak not only of legal accountability but of various other kinds of constraint as well.

The book surveys four distinct mechanisms of accountability or constraint, each of which may be used as a means of controlling foreign affairs contractors and trying to ensure that they will respect the core public law values delineated above: human dignity, public participation, and transparency:

(1) *Pursuing litigation under international and U.S. domestic law and possibly changing existing statutes.* I suggest that existing law provides more of a framework than current scholarship suggests, though I agree that it must be expanded, and enforcement remains a problem.

(2) *Reforming both the contracts themselves and the entire contract oversight and enforcement regime.* I argue that we can use the contractual agreements that are the very engine of privatization to build in a variety of substantive requirements. In addition, there could be increased domestic and transnational efforts to develop private monitoring and accreditation regimes to try to differentiate among contractors.

(3) *Fostering public participation.* I lay out both regulatory and contractual reforms that could help create opportunities for increased public participation regarding privatization activities.

(4) *Addressing organizational structure and culture.* I outline ways we might reform the organizational structure and culture of private firms to mirror some of the ways in which military lawyers in the Judge Advocate General's (JAG) Corps contribute to the creation and development of internal organizational constraints.

Thinking more broadly about all of these mechanisms of accountability allows us not to be limited to formal legal solutions. Indeed, especially in the privatization context it may be that alternative mechanisms offer at least the potential for greater constraint. Intriguingly, however, just as the increasing scope of privatization has challenged a legal architecture premised on governmental actors, so too does privatization pose challenges to these alternative mechanisms of accountability and constraint. For example, though in theory we could impose oversight constraint by reforming the privatization contracts and monitoring them better, our current contracting and monitoring regimes were developed in an era when the government primarily contracted for goods, such as airplanes. In a world of complex services contracts, where private contractors guard

Army troop commanders, use deadly force, and conduct interrogations, contract monitoring takes on a whole new dimension, one we are as yet unequipped to deploy effectively. Likewise, although we might seek to impose greater transparency and democratic accountability, we must also recognize that privatization tends to remove governmental action from the direct control of governmental actors, thereby making traditional forms of democratic accountability more difficult. Finally, with regard to organizational structure and culture, uniformed military lawyers have generally embraced the values embedded in the law of armed conflict, and they play a significant role by helping to inculcate those norms within the military more broadly. The private firms that provide security lag far behind the uniformed military in having a structure or culture that would be likely to transmit those values.

Thus, the expansion of privatization in the military and foreign aid arenas places significant pressures on the whole panoply of constraint mechanisms we might seek to deploy. Accordingly, our conceptions of all four of these mechanisms must be changed in order to keep pace with the sweeping changes that privatization has brought. And while this task is daunting, I argue that each of these mechanisms can be strengthened in order to provide better constraint, and operating together they can provide some capacity to help tame outsourcing and even perhaps harness some of its potential. Throughout, I draw on lessons that might be learned from the privatization of domestic governmental functions in the United States, though I also suggest the limits of such lessons in the more complex foreign affairs context. And, though space considerations force me to focus principally on the means of constraining U.S.-based contractors, at least some of the lessons I draw are likely to be applicable to foreign affairs privatization in other countries as well.

In the end, we shall see that although privatization may put public values at risk, the very fact of outsourcing—with its hybrid public-private character—may actually open up some new avenues for effectuating and embedding these values and perhaps even extending their reach. And, as we seek these better accountability mechanisms, we must look not only to reforms of formal legal frameworks but also to a wide variety of approaches that harness potential changes in accreditation regimes, political structures, and organizational cultures. Significantly, these approaches do not necessarily rely on governmental action; many can be undertaken by nongovernmental organizations, both domestically and transnationally.

Two Background Premises

At the outset, I should note that this book rests on at least two fundamental premises. The first is that public values matter when we are acting overseas. When we go to war to protect our security, for example, we also strive to maintain a respect for human dignity and abide by the principle that there are limits on the appropriate use of force during armed conflict. At the same time, even during wartime, we aim to include the public in key decision-making processes. Similarly, when we seek to rebuild a society that has been consumed by war and ethnic or political conflict, we do so in a way that aims to maintain the ability of our own citizens to participate meaningfully in the policy-making decisions about how we provide aid.

Some scholars and policy makers have argued that when we conduct foreign affairs, and in particular when fighting a war, raw interests are all that matter and further that these interests are limited to providing physical security and material resources to our own citizens. Such foreign policy "realists" tend to believe that power politics alone dictate states' behavior in the international arena,[49] and indeed that power politics alone are all that *should* matter. This view appeared to dominate in the administration of President George W. Bush, most notably in the policies advocated by Vice President Dick Cheney, Bush's secretary of defense Donald Rumsfeld, and Bush's White House counsel and later attorney general Alberto Gonzales, particularly with regard to the treatment of detainees. Cheney, Rumsfeld, and Gonzales made it clear in their public statements that they viewed international law rules such as the prohibitions on torture and other protections for detainees as cumbersome fetters on the hard-headed actions needed to combat terrorism, with Gonzales famously observing that the Geneva Conventions themselves had become merely "quaint" relics of a bygone era.[50]

Yet, unbridled power is not the only possible perspective. Indeed, even within the Bush administration this view was not monolithic, as we saw, for example, when Secretary of State Colin Powell argued in favor of applying international laws of war to detainees.[51] And from the administration of President Eisenhower, to that of the first President Bush, to that of President Clinton and that of President Obama, another view has often been ascendant: the idea that public values matter. They matter in part because they actually advance our interests. In the words of President Clinton's second secretary of state, Madeleine Albright, "We have an abiding political interest in supporting democracy and respect for human rights and the rule of law . . . because stability and prosperity ultimately depend on it."[52] But they also matter because they reflect, importantly, who we are. As President Ronald Reagan noted when commemorating the signing of the Helsinki Final Act, an agreement to observe and protect human rights, "The values enshrined in the Act . . . are fundamental to our way of life and a source of inspiration to peoples around the world."[53] In this book, I do not rehearse this debate but rather start from the premise that public law values both do and should matter.

Second, as noted previously, this book also starts from the premise that foreign affairs outsourcing has become so entrenched that we cannot completely eliminate it. To be sure, we may be able to roll back some specific forms of outsourcing. For example, we may decide that contract interrogators may pose such serious risks to human dignity, and the regulatory possibilities for warding off those risks may be so weak, that we seek legislation to ban the outsourcing of interrogation functions in particular. But overall, we have shifted such a significant array of foreign affairs functions to private contractors that it would be difficult, if not impossible, to curtail the trend, at least for the foreseeable future. To use one example, the U.S. Army announced in April 2008 that it had awarded LOGCAP IV, its enormous, core logistic contract, to three companies: DynCorp, Fluor Intercontinental, Inc., and Kellogg, Brown and Root. The contractors will deliver food and supplies, run dining, laundry, and housing facilities, manage waste, provide morale and recreation activities, and build and maintain facilities. Worth up to $15 billion per year, the contract extends for ten years into the future.[54] Likewise, a report of the Special Inspector General for Iraq Reconstruction, issued on April 24, 2009, notes that the DOD agreements with security contractors have been "streamline[d] . . . in anticipation of an increased need for these services in Iraq."[55] As a prominent U.S. Army commission headed by Dr. Jacques Gansler, former undersecretary of defense, recently concluded, "Whatever threats the Army next faces will be different from the last, but they are likely to be expeditionary and likely to involve high numbers of contractor personnel."[56] The privatization train thus has not only left the station, it is so far down the track that it cannot return for a very, very long time. Moreover, private contractors can sometimes be used in pursuit of humanitarian aims, and we should not assume that all use of contracted labor in the foreign affairs context is necessarily suspect. If we want to protect public values, therefore, our best hope is not to resist privatization altogether, but to rethink how to embed those values into the privatization framework.

Structure of the Book

The remainder of the book proceeds as follows. Chapter 2 offers a brief recent history of privatization and situates the current outsourcing trend within a broader analysis of the public-private divide. I look back at contracting during the Vietnam War to show the dramatic contrast between the relatively low level of contracting in that period and the levels we see during the conflicts in Iraq and Afghanistan. At the same time, I suggest that the practices in Vietnam sowed the seeds of our current contracting explosion. I then outline key points on the path of that explosion through the administrations of Presidents Ronald Reagan, George H. W. Bush, Bill Clinton, George W. Bush, and Barack Obama. I suggest that while a desire to circumvent rule-of-law values in the conduct of our foreign affairs may have motivated some of the turn to the private sector, a broader political ideology of privatization and generalized faith in the market were also significant factors. This political context facilitated innumerable small decisions that paradoxically increased the reach of the government even as it reduced the number of government employees on the payroll.

Indeed, I suggest that the turn to private organizations has fundamentally altered the very nature of the modern liberal democratic state. And although some might see in this privatization trend a decline in state power, I argue that the state is not disappearing but, rather, fundamentally changing. As the tasks of large state bureaucracies shift to private contractors, the state is hollowing out but may actually (in partnership with the private sector) be extending its power even as it loses its core. At the same time, the boundaries between public and private are blurring. In this new context, core values of the liberal democratic state—values that we have in the past identified as the values embedded in public law and that have been enforced by and against the state—remain important. The rest of the book therefore turns to consider ways we might reform a broad range of potential constraint mechanisms, both formal and informal, in order to help protect these core values.

Chapters 3 through 6 discuss each of the mechanisms of accountability and constraint identified above. Chapter 3 focuses on *legal* accountability and assesses the extent to which private contractors might be amenable to criminal prosecution or civil suit in international or domestic legal forums. I address the various immunity and jurisdictional issues involved and I conclude that, though far from perfect, some legal avenues do exist, at least in theory, to hold contractors accountable through either domestic criminal prosecutions or civil suits. Thus, it would be a mistake to assume that privatization removes the possibility of legal accountability altogether. Indeed, while significant gaps persist in existing criminal and civil law, I conclude that the problem of legal accountability is not as much a deficiency of law on the books as it is a failure of law in action. Accordingly, I argue that rather than focusing on writing new laws, we should devote our energy to redesigning our institutions of enforcement.

Nevertheless, because legal accountability is weak in the foreign affairs context with regard to either state or nonstate actors, I suggest alternative mechanisms of control. Chapter 4 considers *contractual* accountability and constraint. As scholars have pointed out in the domestic setting, government contracts could be reformed to include provisions that would help to ensure greater adherence to public law values. I draw on my study of all the publicly available military and reconstruction contracts between the U.S. government and companies working in Iraq, and I compare them to contracts between state governments and companies performing roughly analogous domestic functions, such as prison management, health care, and so on. The Iraqi contracts fall far short. They could do better, I argue, by explicitly extending the norms of public international law to contractors (thereby addressing any potential "state action" problems in international law), providing more specific terms (such as training requirements and performance benchmarks), assuring better monitoring and oversight, requiring contractors to submit to outside accreditation by third-party organizations, and offering better enforcement mechanisms, such as third-party beneficiary suits.

Chapter 5 turns to the knotty problems of *public participation* as a mechanism of constraint, as well as a value in its own right. Here, I do not refer solely to the process of voting. Rather, I seek a variety of ways to create effective communication between an entity engaged in an activity and those most affected by that activity. In the context of foreign affairs outsourcing, such public participation is complicated by the fact that the communities directly affected will often have only minimal ability to influence the distant government overseeing the contract or its polity. Thus, it is especially important to build into the privatized relationship itself mechanisms that will require contractors to consult with affected populations concerning the design of projects and to offer opportunities for feedback or the filing of grievances concerning implementation. And while such consultation and feedback might not always be feasible in the military context, most foreign aid projects could usefully employ such mechanisms for fostering at least a limited form of public participation.

Finally, Chapter 6 suggests that more attention be paid to *organizational* constraints. I use organizational theory to explore ways in which governmental and private entities (both for-profit and not-for-profit) develop internal norms of behavior that render them more or less likely to conform to various public law values. For example, in the years following Vietnam, the U.S. military built a culture of respect for the values embedded in international law, including those rules addressing the treatment of detainees and limits on the use of force during armed conflict.[57] The military achieved this goal in part through organizational structure, by increasing the role and authority of uniformed judge advocates in the field. Despite actions by civilian officials within the Bush administration aimed at weakening that commitment, the uniformed leadership persisted in its efforts to protect those values. Yet the use of private military contractors—especially interrogators and security contractors—has effectively weakened that culture on the ground. Indeed, according to the military's own internal report, contracting out interrogation at Abu Ghraib contributed to an environment of lawlessness that resulted in torture.[58]

And interviews with uniformed judge advocates about the growing role of security contractors shows how the rise of such contractors threatens the judge advocates' ability to protect public values on the battlefield. Use of military contractors also muddies command lines of authority in theater and creates conflicts between uniformed personnel and their more highly paid private counterparts. Finally, the contract firms themselves do not have the robust organizational infrastructure of the U.S. military or the equivalent of judge advocates who can help to inculcate rule-of-law values within the firms. Perhaps these are arguments not to outsource. Yet, the power of organizational structure and culture might also be harnessed as a mode of controlling private military companies. Security firms could be better integrated into the military's judge advocate system, for example, or firms might implement organizational reforms that could mitigate some of the problems.

There are, of course, potential difficulties with all four mechanisms of accountability and constraint that I discuss, and throughout I seek to address the variety of objections that might be raised. One objection, however, should be considered at the outset. It might be suggested that any of the reform proposals I recommend regarding privatization are inherently unrealistic because one of the main reasons governments privatize is precisely to *avoid* the kinds of constraints that I seek to impose. Yet governments are not monolithic, and there are undoubtedly many people within bureaucracies, such as contract monitors, who honestly wish to do their jobs and would therefore welcome (and lobby for) mechanisms that increase accountability. In addition, legislatures sensitive to public opinion may be able to play an increased oversight role, and NGOs and international organizations can sometimes pressure states to adopt at least some of the regimes I discuss. Moreover, even when states fail to act, NGOs can take actions on their own—such as adopting accreditation and rating schemes—that may have significant impact. And such efforts may occur domestically or through transnational legal and political processes. Finally, once the focus moves beyond simply trying to impose direct legal liability, governments may be more willing to consider alternative contract language, internal organizational structure, and public participation values in drafting and awarding contracts in the first place. The problem is that neither policy makers nor scholars have sufficiently focused on privatization or the alternative mechanisms of constraint that the privatized relationship itself opens up.

Most importantly, while it is of course true that these various mechanisms of constraint will not "solve" the problems posed by privatization, either separately or in combination, it is not as if even *non*-privatized foreign affairs activity is subject to sufficient mechanisms of accountability or constraint. And in any event, given that foreign affairs privatization is probably here to stay, those who care about human dignity, public participation, and transparency values will need to think creatively about a variety of plausible means to constrain privatization; we will not be able to simply resist the privatization trend altogether. In addition, once we seek to constrain privatization, rather than eliminate it outright, we may find that while outsourcing sometimes threatens these values, it does not always do so. Indeed, the very fact of privatization may actually create some interesting and surprising spaces where public law values may be protected, and perhaps even expanded.

Throughout, this book is not only a story about the particular problems posed by privatization. At the same time, I aim to tell a broader tale about how the law works (or fails). An important part of this story is the fact that the law in action matters just as much as, if not more than, the law on the books. Thus, when State Department officials can plausibly argue that federal laws do not explicitly allow U.S. federal courts to try State Department contractors for crimes they commit overseas, Congress should enact new legislation to make it clear that those contractors are subject to U.S. criminal law. But the institutional and organizational arrangements to ensure that those laws are enforced—the ability of Congress to scrutinize the Department of Justice, the expertise and incentives of the lawyers within the Department of Justice, and the ability of the Department of Justice to gather evidence overseas—are just as significant as the formal legal rules. Indeed, the intangible norms of a particular organization's culture—as the uniformed judge advocates' commitment to the principle that the use of force is limited during armed conflict powerfully attests—are perhaps the most significant factor of all. This book therefore seeks to bring to the surface these often hidden and intangible elements in addressing the particular challenges that arise from foreign affairs privatization.

In the end, the book seeks to focus attention on privatization in the international realm as a crucial field of study, to call for dialogue among international and domestic scholars, advocates, and policy makers concerning appropriate responses, and to suggest that more attention be paid to the possibility of using a variety of mechanisms to constrain contractor malfeasance and hold private actors more accountable both to those affected by their activities and to those footing the bill. In the coming years we shall need to think broadly about how best to respond to the threats posed by the outsourcing of governmental functions to nongovernmental entities. Only through such efforts will we be able to find ways to protect crucial public law values in the era of privatization that is already upon us.

2

KEY MOMENTS IN U.S. MILITARY AND SECURITY OUTSOURCING, FROM VIETNAM TO IRAQ

While it is certainly true that private contractors—or mercenary soldiers—have been a fixture of warfare throughout history, the turn to military contractors in the United States over the past few decades (and particularly the past few years) represents a dramatic shift from our practice at least in the first part of the twentieth century. Indeed, as we shall see, as recently as the Vietnam War contractors were a relatively small part of the U.S. force. So, one logical starting point in any discussion of contracting is: How did we get here? What were the steps in the progression to the current reality of one contractor for every uniformed soldier? And can we tease out some of the reasons why this shift has occurred?

This chapter does not purport to provide a comprehensive history of military outsourcing in the United States. Instead, I offer a snapshot of outsourcing during the Vietnam War period and then again some forty years later in Iraq, while also noting some key developments between the two wars that contributed to the expanded use of contracting. This brief discussion reveals two key points. First, even as far back as the Vietnam War period, the outsourcing of military operations appears to have been a way for government officials to try to evade accountability by decreasing outside oversight of military and intelligence operations. Second, although this desire to avoid accountability is one likely driver of the outsourcing trend, perhaps an even more important causal factor has been a more general "ideology of privatization" that has, since at least 1980, encouraged government to privatize many functions, both in the domestic and in the foreign affairs areas. Thus, at least some of the rise of military privatization is simply a path-dependent outgrowth of the belief that private entities are inherently more efficient than governmental ones.

Contractors During the Vietnam War: Planting the Seed

Official military histories report that nine thousand U.S. citizens served as civilian contractors in Vietnam during the height of the troop buildup in 1969, alongside 540,000 troops, a ratio of one to sixty,[1] though this probably understates the number of contractors, because it excludes Vietnamese and third-country nationals.[2] These contractors operated power plants, constructed bases, transported materials by truck and barge, maintained equipment, cleaned troops' laundry,[3] and provided other ancillary "support" functions.[4] And though both the amount of contractor activity and its scope were far less significant during the Vietnam War than in Iraq, it is useful to examine the Vietnam experience because we can see the beginning of the move toward greater use of contractors. As Lieutenant General Joseph Heiser observed in an official postwar assessment of U.S. Army logistic support during Vietnam, "The use of contractor services for trucking, terminal and marine purposes provided the extra punch needed in these operations, and provisions should be made to include in future planning consideration for use of contractors when the opportunity arises."[5]

In providing support to troops, some of the Vietnam contractors caused problems that are now all too familiar. One general, in conducting a postwar analysis of contractors, wrote that "many of the contractor employees who flooded the country were drawn by the prospect of easy money and an exciting, unrestricted life." His survey focuses on instances of unauthorized transfers of merchandise, currency manipulation, "rowdyism," and both drug use and trafficking in marijuana and opium.[6] Nevertheless, it is significant that this list does not include even more serious abuses, such as unprovoked attacks on civilians, most likely because contractors were not placed in the sorts of combatlike roles we have seen in Iraq.

The portrait of contractors in Vietnam grows a bit more complex if we consider the tens of thousands of Vietnamese and other nationals, essentially hired by U.S. authorities to conduct defensive, offensive, and counterinsurgency operations. One such group was the Civilian Irregular Defense Group (CIDG), organized by the U.S. Special Forces, the Green Berets. Under this program, Green Berets—serving officially as advisers to Vietnamese Special Forces—helped to train local villagers to defend their homes against the Vietcong and engage in other counterinsurgency and offensive operations. In this capacity, the Green Berets advised both volunteer "hamlet militias" as well as a paid "strike force" to fight off the enemy. Many of the Vietnamese recruited into this program belonged to the distinct ethnic Montagnard minority,[7] but they also included ethnic Cambodians and Chinese. The CIA reportedly initiated the program in 1962 and operated it through Green Berets specialists in counterinsurgency warfare on loan from the U.S. Army. But approximately two years later, "when the mission became too big and too expensive for the CIA to hide, it was turned over entirely to the Special Forces and run openly under U.S. Army financing."[8] By December of 1963, Special Forces detachments, "working through counterpart Vietnamese Special Forces units, had trained and armed 18,000 men as strike force [paramilitary] troops" and even more volunteer "hamlet militia." By 1967, there were more than forty thousand paramilitary troops.[9] During this period, the height of their operations, the Special Forces ran more than sixty remote posts or camps of these CIDG forces along the border with Laos and Cambodia.[10] Their principal focus was to watch Vietcong infiltration routes along the border "for enemy activity and occasionally to attack small enemy forces in South Vietnam."[11] Many CIDG forces died while fighting.

Initially designed to provide a cohesive unit of strike troops to defend their local villages, the program grew beyond its local focus as the Special Forces moved the CIDG troops to camps around the country. In addition, the activities of the group extended beyond defensive operations to offensive actions in enemy territory. The CIDG program was terminated in 1970 as part of the overall Vietnamization program that ended the war, and many of the CIDG members became part of the Vietnamese regular forces.[12] Others, particularly those of Cambodian origin, were flown off to Cambodia and fought in the escalating conflict there. Indeed, some reports suggest that the United States recruited and sent thousands of ethnic Cambodians back to Cambodia after training and arming them.[13]

In some ways, the members of the CIDG resembled contractors. In theory, the Green Berets were to serve only as advisers to the Vietnamese Special Forces, who had official control over the program. Yet in practice the Green Berets often wielded control: they ran the training exercises, directed the operations, supplied the CIDG members with weapons, and paid them.[14] Accordingly, there was substantially more military oversight and direction than we see in modern-day military contracting. Nevertheless, cost cutting appears to have been a primary motivation then as well. Thus, Colonel Harold R. Aaron, the commander of all Special Forces in South Vietnam in 1968, reported that "we put them in the field for six bucks a day. It costs a lot more than that to put a South Vietnamese solider in the field. And they figure about $30 a day for an American soldier."[15]

The highly controversial Operation Phoenix was another program through which the U.S. government trained and paid a cadre of Vietnamese nationals to engage in counterinsurgency tactics.[16] The program, begun as a CIA operation, was designed to "neutralize" the South Vietnamese Vietcong political infrastructure (VCI) in an effort that was parallel to the conventional war against the Vietcong guerrillas and troops. The CIA trained and paid Vietnamese nationals, primarily of Chinese Nung and Cambodian ethnicity, and organized them into Provisional Reconnaissance Units (PRUs) whose task was to gather intelligence on Vietcong political authorities within local villages and "neutralize them." Neutralizing reportedly involved outright killing in some cases.[17] In others, it involved capture, interrogation, and handover to Vietnamese police for detention and trial.

The U.S. government greatly expanded the program in 1968, transferring it from CIA ownership to military control. An "intelligence coordination program" was "designed to identify VCI targets for the PRUs."[18] The coordination program involved collaboration between U.S. military advisers and Vietnamese authorities,[19] and the U.S. component came to be known as ICEX (Intelligence Coordination and Exploitation) and eventually Operation Phoenix. The Vietnamese component was called "'Phung Hoang,' after an all-seeing mythical bird, which, condor-like, selectively snatches its prey."[20] By 1969, ICEX became CORDS (Combined Operations for Revolutionary Development Support), and CIA support and personnel gave way to U.S. Army advisers and a few civilians. The CIA, however, continued to pay and control the PRUs, which were sometimes directed by Navy Seal advisers assigned to the CIA. While the cost of the program is impossible to pin down, estimates range between $80 and $100 million in total costs.[21]

Often described in the press as an "assassination" program, Operation Phoenix methods reportedly ranged from "after-dark assassination strikes by small killer squads to battalion-sized cordon and search efforts."[22] The PRUs and others also reportedly tortured many suspects, in addition to killing others. *Newsweek*, for example, ascribed to Operation Phoenix "the techniques of intimidation, torture, and outright murder."[23] Moreover, the targets of Operation Phoenix activities were often villagers whose connection to the Vietcong was tenuous.

But even as some "attacked Phoenix as an instrument of mass political murder," such "sinister descriptions" were not often heard in Vietnam, where Phoenix had "the reputation of a poorly plotted farce, often with tragic overtones."[24] Thus, other critics pointed not to sinister effectiveness but to woeful *ineffectiveness.*[25] In this view, Phoenix conducted too many "cordon/search" operations that alienated villagers, without producing real results. According to such accounts, "dozens of soldiers would sweep or cordon an area and detain every adult they came across." These suspects "would sit for hours while their ID cards were compared against a cumbersome 'blacklist' which was never up to date." And these searches resulted in the capture of only very few VCI officials. Those who were captured often eluded punishment because they would be released after passing through the ineffectual Vietnamese legal system. Moreover, after Operation Phoenix was brought under the control of the U.S. Army, the Army's unquenchable thirst for statistics and quotas resulted in mounds of paperwork and false reports that VCI were "neutralized" even when they ultimately were released from Vietnamese prison. One civilian adviser who worked in the Phoenix program has argued that, in the end, Phoenix served more as a tool for the South Vietnamese authorities to exercise a domestic program of general political repression than as a targeted program that eliminated VCI.[26]

Eyewitness accounts of Phoenix cordon/search operations give a sense of both the nature of the program and the role of the Vietnamese PRU forces run by the CIA. According to one *Wall Street Journal* report, for example, two refugees from the village of Vinh Hoa told Phoenix authorities in 1969 that the village housed a large number of VCI officials and had become a secure VCI bastion. Based on these reports, a joint team of U.S. and Vietnamese authorities planned a cordon/search of the village. Approximately forty PRUs were assigned to the mission. They included men such as a former Vietcong who apparently had spent years in the brush conducting a "private vendetta" against the Vietcong and was seeking to "kill more VCs." Due to the large number of people involved in the planning, by the time U.S. and Vietnamese troops arrived (several hours later than planned), most of the Vietcong guerrillas and political officials had fled. But a team of PRUs captured and questioned a man identified by the refugee informants. The interrogation turned brutal, as several PRUs "yank[ed] his hair and kick[ed] his head." By the end of the day, he had been killed. Meanwhile Vietnamese troops and PRUs looted some houses, burned down a hospital they determined to be a Vietcong haven, and rounded up some villagers. Those fingered by the informants were brought to prison. U.S. Army personnel do appear to have killed a few Vietcong guerrillas as they were fleeing the village. But, according to the *Wall Street Journal* account, the result of the operation was "eight kills, one after torture. Seven prisoners taken for interrogation. One war memorial dynamited. One hospital burned."[27]

A final category of quasi-contractors might be the uniformed troops from the Philippines, the Republic of Korea, and Thailand who fought in Vietnam under the More Flags program. Initiated in 1964 under President Lyndon Johnson, the program began as a Vietnamese aid effort coordinated by the United States. Soon, however, the United States was paying these countries by various means to send troops to fight in Vietnam. The Johnson and Nixon administrations sought to keep the payments secret through various devices, including allowing the governments to sell U.S. food aid for profit.[28] The United States also gave military assistance directly to the governments sending troops. For example, in 1966 the United States spent $39 million to send a Filipino construction battalion to South Vietnam, and paid four times as much as the Philippine government to support the battalion.[29] When the press and Congress caught wind of the program, such troops were denounced as "mercenaries,"[30] and in June of 1970, the Senate voted after a long debate and filibuster to approve a statutory provision that would have prevented such funding to foreign troops sent to Cambodia without the knowledge and consent of Congress.[31] Known as the "anti-mercenary" provision of the Cooper-Church Amendment, which more broadly sought to cut off funding for U.S. troops and advisers in Cambodia, the provision did not pass in the House. The following year, however, Congress did enact a similar, watered-down version of the amendment that did not contain the "anti-mercenary" language.[32]

The Vietnam experience with contract labor of various types thus provides a useful starting point for our story about how we have come to rely so heavily on contractors on the battlefield. On the one hand, the military (and CIA) use of contractors in Vietnam stands in sharp contrast to the current experience in Iraq and Afghanistan. Even including the local nationals hired by corporations working under agreement with the U.S. military, the ratio of contractors to troops is not even close to the numbers we currently see in Iraq and Afghanistan. If one adds the CIDG troops paid and managed by the Green Berets and the PRUs paid and directed by the CIA and Navy Seals the numbers are much higher, but in those cases there was no corporate intermediary. Moreover, for the corporate contractors the primary types of misconduct at issue—currency manipulation, drug use, crimes unrelated to the conflict—did not involve abuses of force in the conduct of the war itself.

Yet on the other hand, the seeds of the current framework can be seen in Vietnam. Official military reports after the war make the case for continued and increased use of contractors to provide logistical support on the battlefield.[33] Moreover, it appears that PRU and CIDG tactics were especially brutal, which may in part have stemmed from the nature of these troops essentially as contract labor. Although they did not work for corporations and were in fact trained by U.S. forces or CIA, they did not benefit from the same institutional checks on abuse of force that the U.S. military would have. To be sure, the uniformed military committed gross abuses in Vietnam, both at My Lai and elsewhere. And, as I discuss in Chapter 6, the military established many of its institutional checks on abuse in response to the Vietnam experience. Thus, one might say U.S. troops committed atrocities even apart from atrocities of

Vietnamese "contractors." Moreover, any abuses by the contractors, who were after all fairly closely controlled by the U.S. forces, should arguably be attributed to the United States rather than to anything inherent in the contractual relationship. Nevertheless, the CIDG troops and PRU, while trained by U.S. troops (and the CIA), most likely did not receive the sorts of training on limits in the use of force that was mandated for troops even then. And of course the mere fact that these foreign fighting forces were not literally U.S. troops helped the U.S. government distance itself from their actions, rendering abuses more likely, and legal and democratic checks less so. This is a pattern that has continued to the present.

The "Privatization Revolution"

In the 1980s and 1990s, many government agencies with a domestic focus downsized and outsourced jobs in the face of a political mood for smaller government and the widespread belief that the practices of the private sector, when applied to fattened government bureaucracies, could trim waste and save the taxpayers money. This "privatization revolution," which swept through the country in the 1980s during the presidency of Ronald Reagan, dramatically shifted the way governments provided domestic services, such as health care, prison management, welfare, and education. Others have recounted this story: how policy makers and commentators became captivated by the idea that market forces could provide services more cheaply than the government and that it would therefore be better for governments to downsize.[34] Some privatization advocates sincerely believed that the market could provide better, more efficient services. Others had more ideological reasons for pursuing the change: either they had a faith in the market that was not always founded on evidence, or they wanted to oust government civil service employees (who were considered more liberal than contract labor), or they wanted to break the already weakened labor movement, with its stronghold among federal and state employees.[35]

As the work of Paul Light and others has shown,[36] the massive privatization trend in this period did not in fact shrink government; instead, it expanded it. Whether measured by number of workers or amount of money expended, the downsizing and outsourcing movement in fact led to a larger governmental workforce. And while studies suggest real efficiency gains and innovations in some areas,[37] in many cases actual cost savings from outsourcing remains elusive. Moreover, the market has not always functioned well. Indeed, a case could be made that there is no really competitive market for many government contracts.

If the Reagan and George H. W. Bush presidencies saw the advent of a new era of privatized *domestic* government, the foreign policy government sector was still largely immune from this trend. During the first Gulf War, for example, the use of contractors remained ancillary. Indeed, the ratio of contractors to troops (one to fifty-five) was even lower than in Vietnam.[38] To be sure, this was partly because of the nature of the conflict, with only a swift "tip of the spear" attack by conventional forces and no lingering "postconflict" period. Nonetheless, the fact that contractors played such a minor role is significant and highlights the fact that the ideology of privatization had not yet dramatically altered the shape of the military.

Privatization of Defense Department Operations

It was not until the presidency of Bill Clinton that privatization began to penetrate deeply into the corridors of the Pentagon and other foreign policy agencies. Through the reinventing government program of Vice President Al Gore, the Clinton administration accelerated the privatization pace across all governmental sectors. But what is significant for our purposes is that in this period the foreign policy sector was also part of the privatization trend.

At the DOD, Secretary William Cohen was a key figure. Caught between escalating price tags for weapons systems and political pressure to cut costs in the post–Cold War era without weakening the military's capabilities, Secretary Cohen turned to the private sector for advice. During the summer of 1997 he assembled a committee that included leading executives from private industry to offer their wisdom about the road ahead. Cohen then proceeded to pursue a reform path that aimed to modernize defense by embracing the rhetoric, practices, and methodologies of American businesses.[39] This embrace is perhaps most apparent in his Defense Reform Initiative, which he launched in the fall of

1997 as an effort to "aggressively apply to the Department those business practices that American industry has successfully used to become leaner and more flexible in order to remain competitive." The four pillars of the initiative included the following practices: "(1) *reengineer* by adopting the best private sector business practices in defense support activities; (2) *consolidate* organizations to remove redundancy and move program management out of corporate headquarters and back to the field; (3) *compete* many more functions now being performed in-house, which will improve quality, cut costs, and make the Department more responsive; and (4) *eliminate* excess infrastructure."[40] To further these goals, Secretary Cohen proposed reductions of 33 percent in the number of employees in the Office of the Secretary of Defense, 29 percent in the Joint Staff, 10 percent in military headquarters, 21 percent in defense agencies, and 36 percent in departmental field activities.[41] He also sought to make at least thirty thousand DOD positions subject to competition with the private sector each year for five years, outsourcing those that the private sector could perform better—dwarfing any previous outsourcing efforts.[42] Thus, he sought to implement the troika of practices that had become the buzzwords of American industry in the 1980s and 1990s: downsize, compete, and outsource.

While Secretary Cohen cut many civilian employees, Pentagon officials downsized troops and closed military bases, replacing uniformed soldiers with contractors for certain support roles. In the words of one senior DOD official, "The peace dividend requirement forced us to downsize. We had to reduce Army divisions from 18 to 10. But we didn't cut all types of troops proportionally. We didn't want to take the risk on the combat side. We took the risk on the support side. In 1991 we had 56 combat brigades. We cut the number down to 46. But if we had taken it down proportionally, we would have taken it down to 36."[43] Thus, the Pentagon increasingly came to rely on contractors to supply food, build bases, deliver latrines, and perform other support roles.

Yet, at the same time, DOD cut its acquisitions staff by 38 percent.[44] As a senior DOD official later noted, "Where we screwed up was not to cut the guys who buy the tanks and the big equipment; instead, we cut the guys who do nuts, bolts, supplies and so on—these were the guys who we were going to need as we turned more and more to service contractors."[45] Thus, at the very moment that the military was turning increasingly to contractors to provide support services to troops, the Pentagon, under pressure from Congress, cut back severely on the acquisitions workforce that would become increasingly necessary to manage those contractors. Yet such cuts were politically much easier to make because, as Steven Schooner has argued, there is no natural political constituency for the acquisitions workforce.[46]

Conflict in the Balkans: Setting the Stage for Iraq and Afghanistan

Thus, by the time of the conflict in the Balkans in the late 1990s, all the elements were in place for a sharp escalation in the use of contractors. Troop cuts and steep reductions in the civilian workforces at the foreign policy agencies meant that government personnel simply were not available to perform—or supervise—critical tasks. Faced with an urgent need on the ground and no political appetite for increasing the government workforce, it was much easier for government officials to turn to the private sector.

During the initial fighting in Bosnia, the United States did not directly employ contractors—indeed, the United States did not send troops at all—but instead gave a nod and a wink to a U.S. company, MPRI, which trained the Croatian Army.[47] As P. W. Singer and others have documented, the United States encouraged MPRI (even without paying the company directly), in part because MPRI may have served as a means for the United States to weaken the Serbs by strengthening the Croat forces.[48] Although MPRI disputes the nature of the support it provided the Croatians,[49] claiming it provided only strategic planning and not direct combat reinforcement, some have argued that MPRI actually assisted troops on the ground.[50] Moreover, allegations have surfaced that MPRI may have facilitated, or at least looked the other way, regarding Croatian troops' abuses of the law of armed conflict.[51]

By the end of the Bosnian conflict, it was clear—given the fragile peace agreement—that a large police force would be needed to keep the peace. Yet the United States simply could neither provide such a force directly nor manage one. As one Foreign Service officer present at the talks observed,

"We just could not do this ourselves."[52] State Department officials thus suggested that they run the operation through a contract with a private corporation, DynCorp, which was already providing support to the U.S. military. DynCorp contributed hundreds of police officers, some of whom later were implicated in the sex trafficking ring alluded to in Chapter 1.[53]

The Kosovo intervention marked another significant moment in the foreign policy agencies' deployment of contractors. Determined to halt ethnic cleansing in Kosovo, the Clinton administration was nevertheless haunted by the specter of U.S. soldiers being dragged through the streets in Somalia during Clinton's first venture in committing U.S. forces to humanitarian intervention, and so the political pressure on Clinton to minimize U.S. casualties was particularly high. Thus, in addition to deploying an air attack that put virtually no troops on the ground, Clinton decided to rely as much as possible on contractors, whose deaths arguably would not carry the same political costs as troop deaths.

By the end of the conflict in the Balkans, estimates suggest that the ratio of contractors to troops had surged to one to one.[54] DynCorp contractors hired by the State Department kept the peace in Bosnia and trained local police officers. Meanwhile, Kellogg, Brown and Root (KBR) contractors hired by the U.S. military built bases and refugee camps and supplied troops.

The use of contractors during the Balkan conflict shows how privatization, once set in motion, can accelerate. Significantly, this increase in contracting activity does not appear to have resulted from a grand political strategy. Although Secretary Cohen did support outsourcing in general as a means of saving money, there was no high-level process, either within each agency or at the interagency level, to develop or assess outsourcing policies.[55] Instead, outsourcing happened quietly, with little fanfare, one position at a time. Due to the continuing political hunger for smaller government, when a need arose to project a U.S. presence overseas it was much cheaper politically to staff the operation with contract labor, and to create any new positions needed in Washington through outsourcing rather than through expanding the civil service workforce. As one senior official at the U.S. Government Accountability Office (GAO) observed, "It always was much easier to add contractors" because funding was much more readily available. Moreover, this official observed that in filling the position fewer rules applied, so "you could hire someone much more quickly."[56] Nevertheless, even as the use of contractors increased, there were few incentives to create more contract management positions.

In addition, once a position was turned over to the private sector, it was difficult to bring it back into the bureaucracy. Nick Parillo has recently told the story of how, in the nineteenth century, the U.S. government did in fact "deprivatize" many tasks, taking functions performed by private actors and bringing them within the responsibility of government officials.[57] Yet in recent years, there are very few cases in which a government agency has assumed responsibilities for tasks that had previously been handed over to private contractors.[58] The return of airport security to Transportation Security Agency employees may be the one notable exception.

And while agency officials quietly transformed civil service jobs into private sector ones, Congress did nothing to halt the trend. Rather, these decisions for the most part fell below the radar of Congress and the general public. For its part, the GAO issued numerous reports in the 1990s warning that increased military outsourcing posed severe management challenges due to the lack of acquisitions staff to monitor and supervise contractors.[59] Yet, there was little, if any, public discussion or debate in Congress about the wisdom of outsourcing various military functions.

Other factors drove the military outsourcing trend. For example, contractors were seen as having greater expertise in servicing the increasingly complex weapons systems the military was deploying. Because contractors generally continue in the same position for longer periods than troops, there is less need for constant retraining.[60] Thus, for some highly technical positions, contractors may be more cost-effective (though it is important to emphasize that this claim of cost savings has never been rigorously assessed). In addition, agency officials within the DOD have argued that contractors can staff a mission in a matter of weeks, while the Army process can take months or more.[61]

Meanwhile, the companies themselves responded to the increased demand and sought to create path dependencies by developing niche services. KBR specialized in logistical support, Vinnell Corporation and Bechtel focused on military infrastructure, CACI International, Inc., developed its intelligence gathering operations, DynCorp established itself as the provider of police training and security services, and so on.

The Iraq War and the Expansion of the Privatized Military

As we have seen, by the time the United States invaded Iraq the conditions were in place for a radically different kind of war and postwar occupation. First, as with Operation Phoenix and the Kosovo intervention, nongovernment labor was likely useful to military leaders and policy makers in part because the activities of such units could more readily be hidden from view. Indeed, just as the use of "black sites" outside the territorial borders of the United States was at least in part an effort to evade accountability under U.S. and international law,[62] so too the use of contractors may have been attractive as a way to shield interrogation, detention, and security practices from greater scrutiny. And though hard evidence of such motivation is difficult to come by, at least one FBI interrogator has asserted that contractors did in fact tend to push the envelope concerning such practices. This interrogator reported to Congress, for example, that he was actually removed from the interrogation of one suspect in favor of a contract interrogator who then ratcheted up the abusive techniques.[63] Similarly, a military report on the abuses at Abu Ghraib pinned at least some of the responsibility on the use of untrained contract interrogators.[64] Nevertheless, whether the use of abusive interrogation techniques was deliberately outsourced to contractors to shield these acts from scrutiny or whether the abuses were simply the result of inadequate training and oversight is difficult to say for certain.

But in addition to possible efforts to avoid oversight, it seems clear that a large part of the turn to contractors in Iraq was fueled simply by the preconditions that already existed at the time of the intervention, all of which tended to push in the direction of greater privatization. As a recent Congressional Budget Office Report on contracting in Iraq makes clear, the drastic increase in the number of contract security personnel is directly attributable to broader trends that had forced reductions in the size of the post–Cold War military and that had pushed the U.S. government to outsource any activity not deemed inherently governmental.[65] Thus, the privatization movement of the 1990s had reshaped the Pentagon and other foreign policy agencies, increasing the contract workforce and decreasing the acquisitions staff charged with monitoring that workforce. At the same time, political currents made outsourcing and downsizing the default position, and small decisions over time had increasingly turned over government jobs to the private sector. The military's use of more complex weapons systems further fueled the trend, as did the perception that private companies could mobilize more quickly than the government. And corporations had grown to fill these niches, creating an easy path for government agencies seeking to off-load projects. Finally, as one senior DOD official noted, "No one expected we'd be in Iraq for so long."[66] Accordingly, there was insufficient troop strength to support the occupation that occurred. Indeed, the U.S. governmental officials, who initially were protected by troops, came to feel that troop protection was insufficient. According to one military lawyer, it was a "bone of contention" among "the State Department people" that they didn't have "enough security," because only the high-level officials were getting protection. And when the military provided security, officials had to comply with strict military rules; for example, they had to plan specific trip movements in advance and could not easily change the itinerary. Private security therefore offered greater flexibility.[67] All of these factors joined to create the impetus for a massive private military presence.

And that is precisely what occurred. Indeed, by the summer of 2007, the number of contractors in Iraq likely had exceeded the number of troops. Contractors from the DOD alone made up a workforce that was roughly 90 percent of the size of the uniformed forces on the ground,[68] a percentage that one senior DOD official has said "is likely to persist."[69] In April 2007 the U.S. Central Command census reported that the DOD supported and funded 128,888 contractor personnel, while 140,000 uniformed soldiers were on the ground in Iraq.[70] And this figure does not include the number of contractors working for other agencies, such as the Department of Justice,[71] the Department of State (including USAID), and the CIA.[72] The total dollar value of these contracts is enormous: more than $16 billion dollars for the 2007 DOD contracts alone.[73]

Thus, in sheer numbers alone we've obviously come a long way since Vietnam. Moreover, contractors are performing a much wider array of functions than they have in the past. In Vietnam, contract labor was mostly limited to building power plants and transporting weapons, food, fuel, and other materials on trucks and barges. In Iraq and Afghanistan contractors are carrying out a much broader group of logistics and infrastructure tasks. Thirty-five years ago, uniformed troops would have cooked and served food, serviced latrines, and laundered uniforms. Now, contractors are performing all these roles. In addition, contractors are filling many jobs that go far beyond logistics. They are fixing weapons and teaching troops how to use them. In some cases, they help troops aim bombs at targets. They also guard diplomats, convoys, and other sites, they gather intelligence, and they conduct interrogations.

To be sure, the picture changes somewhat if we consider the Green Berets' CIDG troops or the CIA's PRUs. Trained, armed, and paid by Green Berets, the CIDG troops were Vietnamese nationals who scouted out enemy routes and fought the Vietcong. Similarly, the PRUs, made up of Vietnamese nationals, paid and supervised by the CIA, gathered intelligence and conducted interrogations. Accordingly, we might count these groups as quasi-contractors. Yet, unlike the Iraqi contractors in Iraq, the Vietnamese nationals working for the Green Berets and the CIA did not answer to corporate managers and directors. Nor did they act pursuant to formalized contractual agreements. Thus, while we might see them as a precursor to the current contracting regime, what we have now is a much more formal, organized system in which corporations are handed the reins to manage contractor employees.

Finally, although one response to this trend is simply to oppose it and seek to roll back military privatization altogether, such efforts seem destined to failure. Certainly there might be sufficient political will to declare some limited types of activities "unprivatizable." For example, the military currently draws the line at direct combat, and some might argue that interrogation should never be contracted. But contractors are now serving such a great variety of roles and are supporting the military and other foreign policy actors to such an extent—they are so intertwined with the U.S. foreign policy apparatus projecting itself overseas in contingency operations—that they are likely to be here for a long time to come. Indeed, the 2006 DOD Quadrennial Defense Review includes contractors as a core category of the "total force" that also includes active duty military troops, reservists, and civilian government personnel. According to the review, "the Department's policy now directs that performance of commercial activities by contractors, including contingency contractors and any proposed contractor logistics support arrangements, shall be included in operational plans and orders" issued by combatant commanders.[74] Similarly, as noted in Chapter 1, the U.S. Army issued an umbrella logistics support contract in 2007, LOGCAP IV, which designated three firms to provide ongoing logistics support for $150 billion over ten years.[75] Clearly, the military is planning to use contractors for a long time to come.

Moreover, it would be naïve, I think, to assume that, with the change in administrations, outsourcing will suddenly be scaled back dramatically. To the contrary, if President Obama is to make good on his campaign pledge to draw down the U.S. military presence in Iraq, it is almost certain that security contractors will be needed as the uniformed troops recede. Indeed, all the evidence so far indicates that the Obama administration will rely on contractors at least as much as the administrations that preceded it. A recent report counts approximately 240,000 contractors in Iraq and Afghanistan employed by the DOD alone as of the end of 2009.[76] Thus, military privatization is a reality we will need to address for the foreseeable future, and instead of (or at least in addition to) railing against it we need to seek multiple forms of accountability and constraint in order to rein in its worst excesses. The remainder of this book considers such modes of accountability and constraint.

3

TOO MANY GAPS?
CATCHING PRIVATE CONTRACTORS
IN THE WEB OF LITIGATION

It is the fall of 2003. Military reservists guarding detainees at Abu Ghraib prison in Iraq are beating and sexually humiliating Iraqi detainees. Yet not all of the abusers are in uniform. Some of the men supervising the guards are civilian contractors, hired by CACI International Corporation under an agreement with the Department of the Interior and essentially loaned out to the military for interrogation work. Others are working as translators, hired by the Titan Corporation. One of these contractors reportedly questions an Iraqi detainee while a soldier holds his hands over the detainee's mouth, preventing him from breathing for several seconds. The soldier then uses a collapsible nightstick to push and possibly twist the detainee's arm, causing pain. When the soldier leaves the room, the contractor tells the detainee he'll bring the soldier back if the detainee refuses to answer questions.[1]

Some of these contractors are even more directly involved in abuse. According to the military's subsequent investigation, one contractor reportedly grabbed a detainee from a truck, dropped him on the ground, and dragged him into an interrogation booth. "When the detainee tried to get up to his knees, [the contractor] would force him to fall." Another contractor reportedly threatened detainees with dogs and encouraged others to do so as well.[2] Yet another contractor, an interpreter, reportedly sodomized a juvenile male detainee. One contractor confessed during a polygraph test to kicking detainees in the head while he was wearing boots.[3] Many of these contract interrogators and translators lacked training in standard interrogation techniques, let alone instruction in the rules regarding the use of force.[4] *Indeed, one former employee asserted that the firms essentially just hired anyone they could find, regardless of prior experience or training.*[5]

If, as we have seen so far in this book, the use of private military contractors is on the rise and unlikely to be eliminated in the near future, the obvious question is: How can these contractors be regulated and restrained? Even if the kinds of abuses described above are not typical, what mechanisms of accountability might be available when such incidents do occur, and how effective are these mechanisms likely to be? Each of the next four chapters examines a different possible mechanism of accountability and constraint and assesses its efficacy. Let us begin with the most obvious such mechanism: the use of formal legal regulatory systems, either criminal or civil, to hold contractors accountable for the wrongs they commit.

This focus, in turn, leads to a new set of questions: What laws regulate these contractors? Might international or domestic law be applied to prohibit states from hiring private contractors altogether? Alternatively, assuming states do privatize, what laws exist to hold these actors in check? And finally, what accountability mechanisms can be used to enforce these laws, and how effective are they? This chapter answers these questions in ways that may be surprising to some. Contrary to the claim often made that private military contractors inhabit a virtual regulatory void,[6] I argue that they are in fact subject to a broad legal and regulatory framework that seeks to control their behavior. To be sure, this framework has holes that need plugging. But perhaps even more important, privatization poses challenges to the organizational and institutional apparatus used to *enforce* existing laws and regulations. Thus, if we want to strengthen our legal and regulatory framework, we need to look beyond writing new treaties, statutes, and agency rules, and focus more attention on finding better ways to ensure that these treaties, laws, and rules have force on the ground.

To begin, it is important to recognize that international law does not pose an outright bar to the use of contractors, at least in most circumstances.[7] Protocol I to the Geneva Conventions, drafted in the 1970s, does seek to punish mercenaries somewhat, by denying them prisoner-of-war status.[8] But even this protocol defines mercenaries narrowly[9] and else-where both extends protections to indigenous guerrillas and preserves the rights of foreign military forces fighting on their behalf, clearly reflecting postcolonial debate and biases regarding the use of mercenaries in struggles for liberation.

The International Convention Against the Recruitment, Use, Financing and Training of Mercenaries (drafted between 1980 and 1989) goes further, because it imposes criminal liability on mercenaries, accomplices to mercenaries, and anyone who "recruits, uses, finances, or trains" them.[10] In addition, the convention seeks to impose an affirmative duty on states to prohibit, and perhaps prevent, mercenarism.

Nevertheless, the convention on mercenaries, like the protocol, defines "mercenary" narrowly, requiring, for example, proof that the contractor was motivated by financial rather than ideological gain.[11] Moreover, it is significant that, even with such limitations, the treaty took quite some time (until 2001) to enter into force—when Costa Rica became the twenty-second state to ratify it—and it still does not enjoy particularly widespread support. Likewise, though some countries, such as South Africa, forbid the use of military contractors as a matter of domestic law, such provisions are not common. And, of course, none of these provisions—international or domestic—would bar the use of contractors in the foreign aid context.

Although states are therefore unlikely to be barred from privatizing altogether, both international humanitarian law and human rights law, as well as domestic criminal law and tort law, do place important limitations on contractors. And while this regulatory framework is more of an uneven latticework than a solid wall, I argue that the architecture is there, and it can potentially be used more aggressively in the future to better deter and punish abusers. On the criminal side, the problem is not so much an absence of applicable law (though there are holes that need filling) but rather the mobilization of sufficient political will to actually enforce the laws that exist by making important organizational reforms or through other means. On the civil side, although some important threshold questions remain unresolved, contractors could potentially be *more* subject to accountability through the tort system than are comparable governmental actors.

This chapter is divided into four parts. The first part discusses the general international humanitarian and human rights law governing the use of force and prohibiting serious human rights abuses. Here, I address the extent to which this law applies to private military and security contractors and can therefore be used to place limits on their behavior. The second part surveys domestic law potentially applicable to private military contractors, focusing primarily on the United States. The third part examines the organizational and institutional apparatus used to enforce this legal framework, and shows how privatization poses particular challenges for enforcement. The fourth part then analyzes how useful this international and domestic legal framework is actually likely to be in holding private actors to account. Using the contractor abuse story from Abu Ghraib as an example, I discuss the various possible means of subjecting these contractors to criminal or civil actions. I conclude that, although international criminal prosecution is unlikely, the legal framework for domestic criminal prosecution is in place if U.S. government officials are willing to use it. Moreover, domestic tort suits are at least a possibility. Thus, while the mechanisms of legal accountability over contractors could certainly be improved, we should not leap to the conclusion that the mere fact of privatization eviscerates all legal oversight. To the contrary, as we shall see with regard to civil suits under ordinary domestic tort law, legal actions against contractors may sometimes have greater chances of success than similar suits against government or military actors.

This does not mean, of course, that the existing legal and regulatory framework merely requires minor adjustments in order to cope with the growing use of contractors. Rather, my argument is that, contrary to what some have suggested, and contrary to the dominant frame in the popular press, we cannot solve the accountability problem simply by enacting more federal statutes to allow for criminal prosecution of contractors. Congress has already provided a legal framework for holding contractors criminally accountable, either in civilian or in military courts, when they commit abuses—but this framework does not work. To be sure, as discussed in more detail below, there are some jurisdictional holes in the law, and Congress could, and should, address these deficiencies. But the real problem is that neither civilian nor military prosecutors have thus far done much to *enforce* these statutes. As we shall see, prosecutors probably could have indicted the contractors implicated at Abu Ghraib under existing law—but they did not. This failure is evidence of a lack of political will, but it also suggests an absence of the critical organizational and institutional structures necessary to foster meaningful enforcement. Thus, the point of this analysis is not to say that the legal framework is sufficient and therefore we have no problem but to say that we should not be focusing exclusively on how to solve the supposed legal gaps regarding contractors. Instead, real accountability for contractors requires organizational and institutional arrangements that would encourage enforcement and help mobilize political will: law in action is as important as the law on the books.

International Law

Despite the loopholes noted above in the various treaties that seek to forbid (or criminalize) mercenarism outright, other bodies of international law do regulate the activities of private military companies and their employees. Specifically, both international humanitarian law—which protects civilians during armed conflict and sets limits on the permissible use of force—and international human rights law—which protects the rights of individuals from certain serious abuses—constrain the activities of military and security contractors in some circumstances. And though these bodies of law admittedly have gaps and uncertainties in their application to such contractors, they do provide mechanisms for potentially reining in some of the worst abuses private contractors might commit.

International Humanitarian Law (the Law of Armed Conflict)

International humanitarian law, also known as the law of armed conflict, restricts a broad range of actors from committing atrocities on the battlefield, though the precise reach of this body of law over private military and security companies and their employees is unsettled. The most significant humanitarian law treaty regime—the four Geneva Conventions negotiated shortly after World War II[12] and the two Additional Protocols[13]—outlaws certain categories of extreme abuse, such as torture, executions, and other "grave breaches." In addition, although, as we shall see, application of some legal regimes varies depending on whether contractors are classified as governmental employees or nonstate actors, key provisions of international humanitarian law apply regardless of classification. More specifically, Common Article 3, a provision identical in each treaty, criminalizes these acts, whether committed in international or in internal armed conflict,[14] and provides that "all parties to the conflict" are bound to refrain from such acts.[15] The provision thus clearly applies to nonstate actors, which is not surprising given that the drafters of the provision constructed it with nonstate guerrilla movements in mind.[16] Moreover, Additional Protocol II explicitly applies to armed conflicts that "take place in the territory of a High Contracting Party between its armed forces and dissident armed forces *or other organized armed groups* which, under responsible command, exercise such control over a part of its territory as to enable them to carry out sustained and concerted military operations and to implement this Protocol." Accordingly, nonstate actors during internal armed conflict are clearly governed by this Protocol.[17]

Courts have also held that nonstate actors may be held criminally and civilly accountable for committing war crimes. For example, in the proceedings at Nuremberg following World War II, the tribunal convicted several corporate managers for such crimes, including the makers of the Zyklon B gas that the Nazis used for mass killings.[18] The International Criminal Tribunal for the Former Yugoslavia has stated in dicta that there is no "state action" requirement for war crimes, including torture, even though international human rights law defines torture as actions committed only by "official" actors.[19] And in a civil suit brought against self-proclaimed Bosnian-Serb leader Radovan Karadžić in U.S. court under the Alien Tort Statute (which permits aliens to sue in U.S. federal courts for alleged violations of international law),[20] the court allowed a war crimes claim (among others) to proceed without requiring plaintiffs to show that Karadžić was a state actor, concluding that "private persons may be found liable under the Alien Tort Act for acts of genocide, war crimes, and other violations of international humanitarian law."[21] Likewise, in a case against Blackwater and several affiliated firms, a U.S. district court has made clear that corporations can be held liable for war crimes without a showing of state action.[22]

Two other crimes that stand at the intersection of international humanitarian and human rights law—genocide and crimes against humanity—

even more explicitly apply to nonstate actors. The Genocide Convention provides that "persons committing genocide . . . shall be punished, *whether they are constitutionally responsible rulers, public officials or private individuals.*"[23] Likewise, the statute of the International Criminal Court designates certain acts as crimes against humanity so long as they are committed as part of a "widespread or systematic attack directed against any civilian population, with knowledge of the attack." This provision therefore contains no state action requirement. Moreover, the statute elsewhere defines "attack" as a series of acts "pursuant to or in furtherance of a State *or organizational policy.*"[24] Accordingly, so long as nonstate actors are following some type of organizational policy, international law would prohibit them from committing a crime against humanity.

International humanitarian law thus exerts some control over private military contractors, at least as a formal matter. Moreover, even if a particular crime were interpreted not to apply to nonstate actors directly, private military contractors might still face criminal liability if they were deemed sufficiently intertwined with the state so as to be considered governmental actors. On the other hand, it is less clear whether international humanitarian law could be used against the corporate entity as a whole, as opposed to individual employees.[25]

International Human Rights Law

International human rights law also constrains private military contractors, though its effective reach in this context is more unsettled than that of international humanitarian law. This is because much of international human rights law contains state action requirements that ostensibly permit liability only for abuses by state actors. For example, although the Torture Convention broadly defines torture as "intentionally inflicted" acts of "severe pain or suffering" for the purpose of obtaining information from, punishing, intimidating, or discriminating against the victim or third person, such acts must be "inflicted by or at the instigation of or with the consent or acquiescence of a public official or other person acting in an official capacity."[26] Similarly, many of the rights defined in the International Covenant on Civil and Political Rights (ICCPR)—such as the right to be free from summary execution and to be imprisoned without charges[27]—are generally conceived as rights only against misconduct by official governmental actors.

To be sure, *states themselves* may sometimes be deemed responsible for abuses committed by nonstate actors, if those actors are sufficiently linked to the state. The ICCPR, for example, imposes obligations on states not only to "respect" but also to "ensure" the protection of human rights.[28] Regional human rights treaties contain similar terms,[29] which tribunals have interpreted to hold states liable for the actions of death squads and armed militias that are not technically state actors.[30] Likewise, courts and tribunals have at times held states liable for the actions of companies that were effectively controlled by those states.[31] The United Nations' recent Draft Articles on Responsibility of States for Internationally Wrongful Acts aims to make these principles clear, asserting that the "conduct of any State organ shall be considered an act of that State under international law," and that a person's conduct shall be attributed to the state if he or she is acting on the state's instructions or under the state's direction.[32]

At the same time, courts and tribunals have permitted cases to proceed against nonstate actors. Some have done so on the ground that, as with international humanitarian law, violations of certain international human rights, such as torture, do not require a nexus to state action.[33] But even courts that do not go that far have used various theories that link those actors to the state, such as conspiracy or aiding and abetting.[34] And at least one federal circuit, in considering violations of international law brought under the Alien Tort Statute (ATS), appears to construe the state action requirements in international human rights law in a broader way than it would in considering claims of domestic constitutional rights that also have a state action requirement.[35] The discrepancy is particularly striking because, although the court purports to use the U.S. constitutional test for measuring state action in the international law context, it seems to be applying that test in a way that is more likely to result in a finding of state action.

For example, in *Abdullahi v. Pfizer* Nigerian citizens brought an ATS suit against the pharmaceutical company Pfizer for using a new antibiotic drug Trovan to treat Nigerian children suffering from meningitis and other diseases. They alleged that Pfizer was essentially using Nigerian children (many of whom died) as subjects to test the drug's effectiveness, and that these actions violated various provisions of the ICCPR. The U.S. Court of Appeals for the Second Circuit determined that plaintiffs had made sufficient allegations of state action.[36] The court applied the test from domestic constitutional jurisprudence that private activity can become actionable misconduct when "there is such a 'close nexus between the State and the challenged action' that seemingly private behavior 'may be fairly treated as that of the State itself.'"[37] It further found that a nexus may exist "where a private actor has operated as willful participant in joint activity with the State or its agents."[38] The court then reasoned that such a nexus existed (assuming the complaint's allegations were true) because the Nigerian government allegedly sent a letter to the Food and Drug Administration requesting that the agency authorize Trovan's export, arranged for Pfizer's accommodation in a Nigerian hospital, backdated an approval letter to the U.S. government, and silenced Nigerian physicians critical of the test. This degree of government involvement would arguably fall short of state action in a domestic constitutional case applying the very same test. Indeed, in contrast to *Abdullahi*, the U.S. Supreme Court has held, in *American Manufacturers Mutual Insurance Co. v. Sullivan*, that the government entity must actually participate in the "specific conduct" in question for state action to be found.[39] Knowledge of the activities and background assistance of the sort deemed sufficient in *Abdullahi* therefore appears to be insufficient to support a finding of state action in the domestic context.

Likewise, the Second Circuit permitted ATS claims to proceed against Shell Oil Co. and individual defendant employees of Shell. The plaintiffs, members of Nigeria's Ogoni ethnic group, alleged that Shell had instigated and supported a Nigerian government campaign of repression against the Ogoni people, who were protesting Shell's activities in Nigeria. Plaintiffs' complaint contained allegations of numerous international human rights violations, including torture, cruel, inhuman, and degrading treatment, summary arrest and arbitrary detention, and interference with the right of peaceful protest, all of which the district court concluded were claims that required a showing of state action. Unlike in *Abdullahi*, the involvement of the Nigerian government was not in question, as the complaint alleged that Nigerian officials had directly tortured, attacked, and killed plaintiffs. Rather, the issue was whether Shell and its employees were sufficiently involved in the Nigerian government's actions. Applying the state action test from U.S. constitutional law, the district court explicitly rejected an interpretation of *Sullivan* that would have required actual corporate knowledge of, or participation in, each instance of abuse.[40] Again, the Second Circuit permitted the case to go forward using an expansive interpretation of state action.

Nevertheless, the substantive scope of the ATS itself is uncertain. In 2004 the U.S. Supreme Court narrowed the types of international human rights violations that may be subject to suit under the ATS.[41] In the wake of that decision, one district court dismissed torture claims against private contractors on the ground that the scope of the ATS only applies to "official" torture, and the U.S. Court of Appeals for the D.C. Circuit affirmed that decision.[42] Moreover, in a bizarre sort of Catch-22, the court ruled that, if the plaintiffs could show that the contractors were sufficiently tied to the state so as to render the actions "official," the ATS claims would again be barred because then the suit would be tantamount to suing the government itself, thereby violating sovereign immunity. This reasoning will undoubtedly be tested in the future. After all, there is no reason to believe that the ATS state action inquiry and the sovereign immunity determination must necessarily be tied together in this manner. Indeed, just because a contractor is sufficiently linked to the government to overcome state action requirements does not necessarily transform the suit into one against the government itself. In contrast with the D.C. Circuit decision, the Second and Eleventh Circuits, along with several district courts, have interpreted the ATS more broadly and permitted it to be used in suits against nonstate actors in a variety of contexts. However, even if the D.C. Circuit's reasoning were ultimately followed by other courts, it would not, in any event, bar claims based on other international law provisions, domestic statutes, or common law torts that do not require state action.

Domestic Law

In addition to international law constraints, domestic law also can impose obligations on private military contractors. Contractors are potentially subject both to the law of the country in which they are operating and the law of their home state. However, because contractors are often deployed to unstable regions, such as Iraq or the Balkans, the local law will usually be unsettled, and local prosecutors or courts will likely face challenges in pursuing either criminal or civil actions.[43] Thus, as a practical matter the only viable form of domestic law enforcement is likely to be in the home country of the contractor firm or employee. Accordingly, because many (though by no means all) military contractor firms are based in the United States, I will analyze the possibilities for criminal and civil suits in the United States, while recognizing that a complete picture would require analysis of the legal regimes of other countries as well.

Criminal Law, Military and Civilian

Contractors employed by the U.S. government may be subject to federal criminal law. Although the U.S. Supreme Court has historically prohibited military trials of U.S. civilians absent a declaration of war,[44] contractors could be prosecuted in federal courts under the Military Extraterritorial Jurisdiction Act (MEJA) if they commit acts abroad that would qualify as federal crimes. Indeed, Congress enacted MEJA precisely because U.S. military courts were not an option for private actors, and this law specifically allows criminal charges to be brought against U.S. contractors working for the Department of Defense (DOD).[45] On the other hand, the statute does *not* clearly apply to the many contractors who operate under agreements with other government entities, such as the State Department, CIA, or Department of Interior.[46] An amendment to the statute expanded its reach, applying it to contractors from other agencies whose employment relates to "supporting a Department of Defense mission,"[47] which could, of course, apply even to contractors from other agencies. A bill that would have closed the loophole more clearly passed overwhelmingly in the House of Representatives, but stalled in the Senate.[48] The USA PATRIOT Act, however, does address this gap to some extent by expanding the United States' special maritime and territorial jurisdiction (SMTJ) to include any facilities run by the United States overseas, regardless of the agency in control.[49] Thus, a prosecutor could bring charges against private military contractors mistreating detainees or others overseas if the abuses were committed within a U.S. facility. Indeed, a federal court convicted a private contractor working for the CIA for felony assault committed within the SMTJ, based on allegations that he abused detainees at a U.S. facility in Afghanistan.[50] Prosecutions are also possible under federal statutes that criminalize war crimes[51] and extraterritorial torture,[52] though these statutes probably require a sufficient nexus to state action.

Finally, in 2007 Congress amended the Uniform Code of Military Justice (UCMJ) to bring military contractors "serving with or accompanying an armed force in the field"[53] under the jurisdiction of military courts, not only during a time of declared war but also during "contingency operations."[54] Senator Lindsay Graham quietly slipped the provision into the Defense Appropriations Authorization Act in order to impose the same standards on both contractors and troops and thereby provide "uniformity [with regard to] the commander's ability to control the behavior of people representing our country."[55]

Tort Law and Other Civil Law Remedies

Tort suits, brought under the law of the contractor firm's home state, are also a possibility. These suits may take a number of different forms. First, foreign victims of contractor activities may file suit, assuming domestic law provides them standing.[56] Second, we may see suits brought by contractor employees against their employers.[57] For example, one still-pending wrongful death action against Blackwater arises from the murder and mutilation of four of its employees in Fallujah, Iraq,[58] and another alleges that Halliburton knowingly used one convoy as a decoy for a second, resulting in the deaths of at least six drivers and injuries to eleven others.[59] Third, domestic actors harmed by private contractors abroad may seek redress, as in the variety of actions that have been brought by U.S. military personnel killed or injured in accidents involving airplanes and trucks operated by contractors.[60]

Nevertheless, all three types of suit must potentially surmount two threshold obstacles. First, courts may refuse to hear such suits by invoking the political question doctrine. Yet, although courts have in fact dismissed suits against contractors on this ground,[61] it may well be an inappropriate use of the political question idea. After all, the doctrine is only meant to exclude from judicial review "those controversies which revolve around policy choices and value determinations constitutionally committed for resolution to the halls of Congress or the confines of the Executive Branch."[62] As one court held in refusing to dismiss a case against a contractor on political question grounds, "Controversies stemming from war are not automatically deemed political questions merely because militaristic activities are within the province of the Executive. . . . Tort suits are within the province of the judiciary, and that conclusion is not automatically negated simply because the claim arises in a military context, or because it bears tangentially on the powers of the executive and legislative branches."[63] Thus, the political question doctrine seems to be a dubious rationale for dismissing tort suits against contractors.

A second obstacle derives from the federal government's sovereign immunity. The Federal Tort Claims Act (FTCA) seeks to balance the need of government employees to do their work without fear of litigation against the rights of individuals to seek compensation when government actions injure them. Accordingly, the act allows plaintiffs to sue the government, but only when government employees are negligent and when a private person would be liable under similar circumstances.[64] Even then, however, governmental employees may benefit from additional enumerated immunity provisions. Thus, for example, the act provides immunity when a claim arises out of a government employee's exercise of (or failure to exercise) discretion, or when a claim arises out of combatant activities. In these circumstances, the federal immunity preempts any tort claims based in state law.

The extent to which contractors can invoke the FTCA's immunity framework is in flux and the subject of considerable litigation.[65] At least one court has strongly suggested that contractors could never invoke immunity to shield themselves from claims arising out of gross human rights abuses.[66] In addition, a plausible argument can be made that the FTCA simply does not apply to contractors, or if it does, it only reaches procurement contractors supplying weapons and other materials, not contractors who provide services, particularly where the contractor exercises a wide degree of discretion.[67]

To give a sense of how these distinctions can be drawn, consider a federal district court in the District of Columbia that allowed a case to proceed against contract interrogators implicated in the abuses at Abu Ghraib prison, but not against the Abu Ghraib contract translators. The court reasoned that the plaintiffs' ability to sue depended on the degree to which the contractors were integrated into the military command structure: whether the military had direct command and exclusive operational control. Because there was undisputed evidence that the military had incorporated contract translators within its chain of command, and the contractors essentially stood in the shoes of government actors, the court dismissed the suit against them. But because there was at least some evidence that the contract interrogators took orders from managers within their company, and not solely from government officials, the court determined that the case against them could proceed.[68]

This seems to be a reasonable basis for determining potential tort immunity for contractors, and it may gain traction. However, the U.S. Court of Appeals for the D.C. Circuit has, at least for the moment, adopted a broader test that would give far more sweeping immunity to contractors. The appellate court concluded that the key test was not whether the military had exclusive control over the contractors but rather whether, "during wartime, . . . a private service contractor is integrated into combatant activities over which the military retains command authority." Thus, the court adopted a surprisingly broad definition that would immunize contractors whenever the military has overall command authority for a conflict (seemingly regardless of whether the military has control over the particular contractors being sued). Ultimately, the court concluded that because both the contract interrogators and the translators were integrated into combat activities at least to some degree, the federal immunity preempted any claims under state (or foreign) law against either group of contractors. According to the majority, allowing such claims to proceed would improperly interfere with the military's conduct of war, and would set perverse incentives because contractors would "obviously be deterred from reporting abuse to military authorities if such reporting alone is taken to be evidence of retained operational control."[69]

Yet, as the dissent observed, the reach of the Federal Tort Claims Act immunity provisions to contractors should be narrow, as the statute does not explicitly apply to contractors at all but rather is designed to safeguard *governmental* immunities. Here, the military did not dispute that the contractors fell outside the chain of command, as numerous contractual provisions, DOD regulations, and military rules made clear. Moreover, the U.S. government did not authorize, and indeed expressly prohibited, the abuse in question. Finally, the concern about interference in the military's conduct of war seems unwarranted. After all, courts could wait to hear suits until after hostilities concluded or could simply apply normal privileges and rules to prohibit gathering or presenting evidence in such a way that would harm national security.

Thus, unless the D.C. Circuit's rule is broadly adopted, civil suits remain a possible avenue for vindicating the values embedded in international human rights and humanitarian law.[70] Other circuits may take a more expansive approach to tort liability,[71] and Congress could also step in to define a role for tort litigation against military and security contractors. And as we shall see in the next chapter, another possibility is a suit to enforce the contractual terms under which the private firms operate. Currently, only the government itself or specific classes of contractors can bring such claims, but Congress could act to expand the possibility of third-party-beneficiary suits.

Enforcement Regimes

While the formal legal framework is important, it is only one piece of any legal accountability regime. Indeed, although there appear to be sufficient legal mechanisms for holding contractors criminally liable for abuses, the actual feasibility of criminal accountability is not a matter of the law that exists on the books but rather of how the law is (or is not) actually applied in practice. In this regard, the structure, number, and type of organizations involved—as well as the relationships among them and the way authority is delegated within them—are perhaps just as significant. As we shall see in Chapter 6, organizational structure and culture can be powerful tools to enhance (or weaken) compliance with legal rules and respect for public values. The broader political context also plays a key role.

If we take as an example the efforts to hold contractors criminally responsible for serious abuses committed in the conflict zones of Iraq and Afghanistan, we can see in painful detail that the enforcement regime for contractor accountability has lacked bite. The chaotic environment on the ground in a war zone always makes accountability difficult, and the lack of political consensus around certain core values—such as the right of detainees to be free from abuse and the need to hold abusers accountable for their actions—very likely had a significant impact. But a close examination of the organizational and institutional context suggests that privatization and outsourcing strained existing enforcement mechanisms because of the way the act of privatization changed and fragmented the responsibilities of organizations and because the lines of authority within those organizations were blurred. Thus, if we want to protect public values in an era of foreign affairs privatization, we need to realign the way that agencies interact with one another, as well as with Congress.

To date, very few contractors have faced criminal proceedings of any kind, despite numerous incidents of reported abuse. The most notable case involved David Passaro, a CIA contractor who reportedly beat and interrogated a war on terror detainee for two days and nights in Afghanistan. According to reports of soldiers who witnessed the events in the detention facility, Passaro allegedly kicked the detainee in the groin hard enough to lift him off the ground and jabbed him in the abdomen with a two-foot-long flashlight. The detainee ultimately died, and the U.S. attorney for the Eastern District of North Carolina filed assault charges in federal court invoking the special maritime and territorial jurisdiction. A jury convicted Passaro in August 2006, and he was sentenced to eight years in prison.[72] Other than Passaro, however, few contractors have faced even the prospect of trial. In February 2007, Aaron Langston, a resident of Snowflake, Arizona, working for Kellogg, Brown and Root in Iraq, was indicted in federal court under MEJA for stabbing a fellow contractor.[73] The only other successful prosecution of a contractor under MEJA was the conviction in May 2007 of a DOD contractor in Baghdad who pleaded guilty to possession of child pornography.[74] Federal authorities did in the end indict some of the Blackwater guards implicated in the Nisour Square shootings, although the indictments were ultimately dismissed because they improperly relied on compelled statements made by defendants during a prior State Department inquiry.[75] Finally, the military successfully prosecuted Alaa "Alex" Ali Mohammed, a dual citizen of Iraq and Canada working as a translator for the U.S. Army under a contract with L-3 Communications Titan Group. Mohammed pleaded guilty in a court-martial proceeding to stabbing a fellow L-3 Titan interpreter at a remote U.S. military base in Al Anbar province and was sentenced to five months' imprisonment.[76]

Compared to the likely overall number of incidents of contractor abuse, however, these efforts to hold contractors accountable are few and far between. The total number of cases of abuse is of course difficult—if not impossible—to measure, but available reports raise serious concerns. For example, one congressional report on State Department security contractors indicated that guards working for Blackwater were involved in at least 168 "escalation of force" incidents just between January 2005 and April 2007, an average of 1.4 shooting incidents per week. Moreover, the report concluded that Blackwater guards fired the first shot in 85 percent of those incidents. Although the report notes that the Blackwater guards rarely remain on the scene after such an incident, the firm's internal records reported sixteen casualties in that time period and 162 incidents of property damage. According to the same congressional report, DynCorp guards were involved in 102 incidents and Triple Canopy guards in thirty-six, and the guards working for these two firms fired first in 62 percent and 83 percent of the incidents, respectively.[77] To be sure, the guards were working in a dangerous conflict zone. Still, these figures are troubling, particularly because in many instances the guards appear to have initiated fire despite the fact that their role—guarding diplomats— was primarily defensive in nature.

The congressional report is consistent with interviews of uniformed military lawyers who observed security contractors in Iraq during this same period. For example, one judge advocate who served in Baghdad in 2005–2006 said that there were problems with security contractors using force "on a weekly basis if not more," including "shootings at checkpoints" and other incidents that suggested a "reckless disregard for Iraqi civilians." Not surprisingly these incidents left the Iraqi civilians "very angry, and they came to us." The problem, according to this judge advocate, is that the contractors, unlike uniformed troops, "didn't hesitate to shoot."[78] Another judge advocate who served in Baghdad in 2007 referred to the infamous Nisour Square shootings incident involving Blackwater and emphasized that "that stuff happened frequently." As this judge advocate noted, "I saw Blackwater use warning shots to clear traffic. That's not something our troops do. People get hurt, property gets damaged, people get killed." Moreover, in this judge advocate's view, "contractors don't care, and they don't stop and ask questions." As a result, "my soldiers are stuck with the consequences." Indeed, according to this advocate, "once or twice a week, there would be an incident involving the use of force by a contractor, or a contractor killing someone. . . . Were the rules regarding the use of force violated? Yes."[79]

Despite the indications that contractors are involved in more possibly unjustified use of force incidents than uniformed troops are, it appears that contractors are investigated for such incidents far *less* frequently. For example, according to one study of detainee abuse cases, one-third of the uniformed military personnel implicated in abuse were recommended for court-martial or other disciplinary proceedings, and most of those received some kind of criminal or administrative penalty. While the report criticizes the military for not punishing more soldiers, and for failing to punish high-ranking officers, the comparable percentage of contractors held accountable is much lower—only 5 percent: of twenty contractors implicated in the cases documented in the report, only one contractor faced criminal punishment.[80] The case of Abu Ghraib prison in Iraq illustrates the point perhaps even more starkly. To date, military authorities have punished twelve soldiers for their role in the abuses at the prison.[81] Yet although a military report found that there was contractor involvement in fourteen incidents of abuse at Abu Ghraib prison, to date neither military authorities nor civilian prosecutors at the Department of Justice have indicted any contractors for their participation in these incidents.[82]

Why have so few contractors faced punishment for serious abuses? Part of the problem is that the same executive branch that may have authorized actions leading to abuse in the first place is then responsible for pursuing prosecutions. For example, stories abound that many case files concerning contractor abuses occurring during the administration of George W. Bush languished for years in the U.S. Attorney's Office for the Eastern District of Virginia because there was, apparently, no political will within the Bush Justice Department to pursue the cases.[83] Overcoming this lack of political will is not easy. With respect to the treatment of detainees in particular, members of the George W. Bush administration were bitterly divided about a host of issues, including whether extreme interrogation tactics such as waterboarding were immoral or illegal, whether international or domestic law even applied to detainees, and whether U.S. courts had jurisdiction to consider cases involving noncitizens detained outside the territorial United States. Even in clear cases of abuse—such as the many incidents of sexual humiliation, beating, and other acts that took place at Abu Ghraib prison—differences persisted about whether those involved should be held accountable at all, or what form accountability should take. Critics of any punishment would often point to the terrorist "ticking time bomb" scenario, in some cases arguing that the need to obtain information to thwart terrorist attacks could justify even the most brutal interrogation tactics.[84] Within the Obama administration, Attorney General Eric Holder and CIA director Leon Panetta have reportedly butted heads over whether to criminally prosecute CIA agents (and possibly contractors) for cases of extreme detainee abuse,[85] and President Obama has issued somewhat conflicting statements on the subject.[86] To some extent, then, the failure to hold contractors accountable for serious abuses can be seen as part of a broader lack of political consensus or political will to address abuse across the board.

But even if a lack of political will can explain a failure to move forward on cases generally, it cannot explain the accountability gap between uniformed soldiers and contractors. Here, it appears that the practice of outsourcing has changed the way in which multiple agencies and organizations interact in conflict zones, contributing to a fragmentation of authority that has weakened enforcement.

Particularly in the early years of the conflicts in Iraq and Afghanistan confusion about supervision and oversight of contractors—indeed, what appears to have been sheer chaos on the ground—seriously hampered any efforts to hold contractors accountable for abuses. Many contractors working on military bases, for example, essentially had two chains of command: nominal oversight by contracting personnel and limited control by the commander in charge of the base. However, neither chain of command provided adequate supervision. As we shall see in the next chapter, the contracting personnel were often overtaxed or simply missing in action. And the authority of commanders was actually quite limited and did not include the ability to modify contractual terms.[87] In many cases—when security contractors were guarding governmental employees working for other agencies, for example—a commander might not even know that a group of contractors was present. As one uniformed military lawyer put it, "We didn't know what they were doing when they came through our area."[88] Indeed, during the first several years of the conflict, the DOD did not even have the ability to count and keep track of contractors from the Department of State, and as recently as February 2008 had still not fully entered the State Department contractors into the DOD tracking database.[89]

Equally lacking was any system for tracking incidents in which contractors used excessive force or committed other abuses. Indeed, the DOD ultimately hired a security contractor—Aegis Corporation—to monitor these incidents! Begun in 2004, this system was designed primarily to reduce conflict and enhance coordination among troops and contractors, not to track abuse cases. As a report by Human Rights First put it, "There is nothing to suggest that the system was designed to be particularly useful for monitoring, reviewing, or investigating contractor use of force."[90] State Department systems for tracking abuses were even worse. A State Department report issued in the wake of the September 2007 Nisour Square shootings observed that "the lack of specific identifiers for many private security contractors operating in Iraq has led to confusion about responsibility for reported incidents and complicated the task of determining accountability."[91]

Adding to the difficulty of investigating abuse incidents is the fact that contractors generally leave the scene before any investigation can commence. As one congressional report noted, for example, "In the vast majority of instances in which Blackwater forces engage in weapons fire, the Blackwater shots are fired from a moving vehicle and Blackwater does not remain at the scene to determine if their shots resulted in casualties."[92] And as one uniformed military lawyer put it more bluntly, it was to the contractor's "advantage to fly under the radar."[93]

With contractors fleeing the scene and such poor systems in place for tracking incidents, investigation proved difficult, to say the least. Military lawyers and investigators were typically the first to respond. As one uniformed lawyer put it, with the contractor often gone, it was "our job to respond, to take the flak from families," and further, "to clean it up, conduct an investigation."[94] But it was nearly impossible to gather evidence without any ability to locate the contractors. Indeed, Army Criminal Investigative Division reports reveal case after case in which investigators could not interview contractors, because the contractors could not be found.[95]

Even when contractors were available for questioning, they did not always cooperate with military lawyers and investigators, in part because of unclear lines of authority. For example, a uniformed lawyer who served in Baghdad in 2005 and 2006 described an incident in which a contractor killed an Iraqi Army lieutenant at a checkpoint. The contractor refused to talk to military investigators or turn over a videotape he had retained documenting the incident. According to the judge advocate investigating the incident, the contractor instead retorted: "What authority [does the military] have to require me to provide a sworn statement?"[96] And, in truth, the military investigators themselves were not at all clear that they did indeed have the authority to investigate.

Moreover, even when military investigators and lawyers did gather evidence that could lead to prosecution, there was little follow-up, because of poor interagency communication channels and weak incentives to pursue cases within other agencies. For example, in one case involving suspected extortion, the military sent a report to the Department of Justice, but nothing further happened. As the uniformed lawyer on the case noted, "We were aware of [the Military Extraterritorial Jurisdiction Act], but who do you call? We were never told 'here's the person you can call to help you.'" Accordingly, "ultimately we dropped it all . . . we weren't going to force it . . . we weren't going to keep calling."[97]

Even for more high-profile incidents, such as the Nisour Square shootings, investigators were often slow to the scene. For example, FBI agents arrived to investigate the Nisour Square case a full two weeks after the incident and therefore could not reconstruct the crime scene. In addition, by that time the State Department had already conducted its own investigation, an investigation that, as noted previously, elicited many statements that were ultimately deemed to violate the Fifth Amendment's prohibition on self-incrimination, thereby scuttling subsequent efforts by the Department of Justice to secure a conviction.[98] Accordingly, this case highlights the inadequacies of the existing investigatory apparatus and the urgent need for well-trained in-theater investigative units that can properly gather evidence so that prosecutions, if necessary, can be effectively pursued.

To be sure, U.S. federal agencies operating overseas have improved their enforcement efforts since the early period of the wars in Iraq and Afghanistan. The DOD and the State Department, in particular, have made some strides in monitoring the activities of private security contractors, tracking incidents of abuse and coordinating responses to such incidents. In 2008 the DOD created Contractor Operations Cells to be in charge of coordinating security contractor missions and placed these cells within the regional tactical command centers throughout Iraq. Accordingly, security contractors working for the DOD must now report any serious incidents to the Contractor Operation Cells that have been established, as well as to commanders of any units to which they are assigned. Military units are also required to report such incidents to the Contractor Operation Cells. In addition, the Armed Contractor Oversight Division was created to report, track, and investigate serious incidents[99] and to detail any response by commanders or civilian prosecutors.[100] Meanwhile, the State Department assigned responsibility for tracking security contractor activities to the U.S. Embassy's Regional Security Office, and private security contractors must now report serious incidents to this office. In addition, an incident review board with representatives from both the Department of State and the DOD meets quarterly to review incidents and trends, make recommendations, and communicate them to the contractors.[101]

The agencies have also now clarified the process for investigating and prosecuting incidents. For example, the secretary of defense issued guidance in March 2008, providing that, if there are reasonable grounds to believe that a contractor has committed a criminal act, the DOD must notify the Department of Justice to give the Justice Department the "opportunity to pursue prosecution in federal district court" under MEJA or some other statute. The DOD general counsel is also required to confer with the Justice Department, and the DOD inspector general is required to report to the attorney general whenever there are reasonable grounds to conclude that a contractor has violated federal criminal law.[102] If the Justice Department refuses to pursue a case, the DOD may now choose to pursue prosecution in military courts under the UCMJ's expanded jurisdiction over contractors, discussed previously. Furthermore, the 2008 guidance clarifies the authority of commanders to act if contractors commit offenses, noting the "broad scope of command authority to act whenever criminal activity may relate to or affect the commander's responsibilities."[103] DOD officials claim that the new system has reduced the number of serious incidents involving the use of force. According to department officials, since the Armed Contractor Oversight Division began to monitor such incidents in October 2007, weapons discharges by private security contractors have decreased approximately 60 percent.[104]

Despite these encouraging steps, serious problems remain. The most significant of these is that the new tracking systems instituted by the DOD and the State Department fail to capture all of the serious incidents that are occurring and therefore, in the words of the Special Inspector General for Iraq Reconstruction (SIGIR), "do not present a complete picture."[105] For example, the SIGIR report concluded that the database maintained by the Armed Contractor Oversight Division included only 264 of 618, or 43 percent, of the total number of serious incidents committed during the period of May 1, 2008, through February 28, 2009.[106] In addition, SIGIR concluded that, even by its own more narrow definition, the DOD was underreporting incidents and not properly investigating those incidents that were reported.[107]

In addition, the State Department and the DOD define "serious incident" differently, with the DOD adopting a broader view. Also, each agency maintains a different database for tracking the incidents, and even within the DOD different entities use different databases that contain different information. Meanwhile, some of the State Department security contractors report both to the DOD and to the State Department, but others do not. Finally, it is unclear whether security contractors working for other agencies are even covered by this oversight regime. And subcontractors for all the agencies seem to fall through the cracks.[108]

Thus, organizational structure plays a key role; current lines of authority within and among agencies impede accountability, and reforms might address these problems, even to the extent of overcoming weak political will. For example, in order to create a more regularized mechanism for mobilizing pressure to spur prosecutorial action, Congress could require the Department of Justice to establish a dedicated office within the department itself, rather than fragmenting prosecutorial authority over contractor abuse cases across all the U.S. attorneys' offices around the country. In addition, this office could work with an FBI in-theater investigative unit that could collaborate with military investigators to gather evidence in a timely and legally sound manner. Such a central office would help build up expertise, since extraterritorial prosecutions require special skills that most U.S. attorneys' offices lack. The work of this office might also go at least part way toward addressing the problem of political will. The current arrangement leaves no one with a particularly strong incentive to prosecute, because U.S. attorneys tend to place the highest priority on prosecuting cases of local significance. Moreover, the existence of a centralized office would be "information forcing": Congress could more easily demand information and perform its oversight role because legislators could require the head of such an office to report regularly on the status of contractor prosecutions generally. To be sure, the existence of such an office would not itself cure the problem of political will, and the actual autonomy of even such a nominally independent office would always be precarious, given that the Department of Justice resides within the executive branch. But creating this unit would at least channel information flows and help to build up a group of actors with experience and the incentive to prosecute contractor abuse cases, which might help to build political will over time.

Another avenue is for the military to pursue contractor cases under the UCMJ and thereby bring contractors more clearly within the organizational culture of the military. As discussed previously, the U.S. military has initiated one such case, against "Alex" Ali Mohammed, for a stabbing,[109] but further prosecutions are possible. To be sure, the UCMJ expansion raises serious constitutional concerns because the U.S. Supreme Court, in a series of cases from the 1950s and 1960s, struck down a similar UCMJ provision purporting to confer military jurisdiction over civilians overseas.[110] These decisions, however, did not squarely address the constitutionality of asserting military authority specifically over contractors serving with or accompanying armed forces in the field. Moreover, the current Supreme Court may be more likely to allow limited use of military jurisdiction for civilian contractors than in decades past, because the military justice system itself has been reformed during the intervening years and now more strongly resembles the regime applied in civilian federal courts, particularly with regard to the rights of the accused.[111]

Assuming this new UCMJ provision withstands constitutional scrutiny, it might help rein in contractors by potentially subjecting them to court-martial for crimes that would be prohibited under ordinary federal criminal law, such as murder, assault, and rape.[112] The provision thus could effectively bring contractors within military commanders' authority, rather than leave them to the separate control of their contracting officers, as has been the practice. Under the previous framework, for example, a military commander arguably could not order a security contractor to hold his or her fire on civilians, but rather had to await contract officer approval. As few contract officers travel to Iraq, let alone accompany the security employees on dangerous missions, such an arrangement is hardly ideal. Likewise, contractor employees who have made allegations of rape by co-workers have often been required under the terms of their contracts to submit their complaints to arbitration.[113] Given the difficulties of pursuing federal criminal actions in such cases, UCMJ jurisdiction would create a venue outside the arbitration process for pursuing such allegations.

Of course, even apart from the constitutional concerns, UCMJ jurisdiction poses some difficulties. One problem is that military courts could end up deciding cases involving the many foreign employees of security contractors working for the U.S. government. The Bush administration did not hesitate to subject noncitizen terrorism suspects to military tribunals, even ones that curtailed the rights of the accused to a much greater degree than the courts established in the UCMJ.[114] But other countries may protest the imposition of military justice on their citizens, particularly when those citizens are not accused of terrorism. Additional challenges stem from the sometimes byzantine nature of the military command structure. In certain instances, it may prove unjust to subject unschooled civilians to this authority. And of course the military is subject to political control from the executive branch, just as is the Department of Justice. In any event, the military has only possessed this new statutory authority over contractors for a relatively short time, so we will need to wait for further developments to determine both whether the provision is deemed constitutional by the courts and, if so, whether it is ultimately effective in constraining contractor abuse.

Holding Employees of CACI and Titan Accountable for Abuses at Abu Ghraib

Let us now return to the story of prisoner abuse at Abu Ghraib recounted at the outset of this chapter. By surveying the various possible avenues by which CACI and Titan employees may be held accountable for their role in the abuse, we may get a better sense not only of which legal regimes are applicable in theory but also of what the actual likelihood of accountability is in practice.

Perhaps the most obvious place to vindicate the values embedded in international law would be international courts and tribunals. Yet in many instances there will simply be no realistic international forum for imposing either civil or criminal liability under international law on an individual private contractor, the private contracting firm, or a government actor employing the firm. In many cases the courts simply do not have jurisdiction. For example, the International Criminal Court has no jurisdiction over Iraq.[115] And even if it did, under the complementarity principle any credible domestic U.S. investigation or prosecution would defeat jurisdiction.[116] No other international criminal tribunal has jurisdiction, either. In addition, even if a tribunal had jurisdiction, that tribunal would never be able to handle more than a handful of the most egregious cases.

Civil liability or another form of accountability in an international venue is equally unlikely. Iraq could theoretically bring a complaint against the United States before the Human Rights Committee, the treaty-monitoring body charged with monitoring implementation of the International Covenant on Civil and Political Rights.[117] A complaint against the contract firm (or the individual contractor) would not be possible, as the venue considers only claims against states. Moreover, state-to-state complaints in such a venue are extraordinarily rare,[118] and it seems unlikely that, given Iraq's continuing dependence on U.S. support and aid, the Iraqi government would risk souring that relationship by bringing such a complaint at any point in the near future. A suit in the International Court of Justice, while conceivable, is unlikely for the same reason. And here, too, at most the claim would be against the U.S. government rather than the contract firm or the individual contractors.

Suits, whether criminal or civil, are also unlikely in Iraq, either under international law or under Iraqi law. Although criminal or civil proceedings could theoretically be brought locally, the U.S. Coalition Provisional Authority granted immunity to U.S. and other foreign actors in Iraq.[119] It is, of course, an open question whether such an immunity provision can effectively shield individuals from accusations of gross human rights violations. And, under the new Status of Forces Agreement, the United States lifted that immunity moving forward.[120] But regardless, the Iraqi legal system is not in any condition to consider such cases.

Finally, the prospects of either a civil or a criminal case in a third-party state are also slim. For example, though a group of Abu Ghraib victims filed an action for war crimes in Germany under that country's universal jurisdiction statute,[121] the statute requires approval from the chief German prosecutor before jurisdiction can be exercised, and the prosecutor declined to move forward with the case,[122] most likely because of its politically sensitive nature.

Thus, we must turn to domestic U.S. venues for legal accountability. To begin with, the CACI and Titan employees could be criminally prosecuted in U.S. courts for violating international law norms that have been incorporated into U.S. law, assuming, of course, that sufficient evidence of criminal activity could be gathered. Indeed, the domestic statutes criminalizing war crimes and torture are almost certainly applicable, given that a sufficient nexus to state action is not difficult to establish in the Abu Ghraib case. In addition, as discussed previously, contractors can be subject to prosecution for committing ordinary domestic crimes abroad at a U.S. facility or in support of a U.S. DOD mission. Thus, because Abu Ghraib was a U.S. facility, crimes such as assault, battery, and murder would likely fall within the special maritime and territorial jurisdiction.

However, the prosecution of military contractors under these provisions did not occur during the Bush administration because, of course, such cases would have had to be brought by the same executive branch that authorized the activities of these contractors in the first place. Indeed, the Bush administration was reluctant even to characterize abuses committed at Abu Ghraib as torture or war crimes; it was therefore, not surprisingly, reluctant to initiate prosecutions of contractors implicated in the abuse. And, as noted above, though numerous case files concerning abuse at Abu Ghraib were opened, there was little political will in the Bush Justice Department actually to pursue any such cases.

Beyond the lack of political will, as discussed above, the way in which outsourcing has fragmented responsibilities for contractor oversight and prosecution has further undermined the prospect of accountability. It is, of course, possible that outside pressure could prompt more prosecutions, and the Department of Justice did finally seek criminal indictments of five Blackwater guards implicated in the Nisour Square shootings (although, as previously discussed, those indictments were later dismissed). In addition, the Obama Justice Department may take a more aggressive approach to accountability issues concerning Abu Ghraib or other abuses allegedly committed by contractors. The military might also now be able to try contractors who committed abuses (assuming such military jurisdiction over private contractors is ultimately deemed constitutional), but so far these possibilities remain unrealized.

As to domestic tort suits against contractors, the big question will be whether plaintiffs can overcome the threshold obstacles of the political question doctrine and sovereign immunity, or walk the fine line between sovereign immunity and state action in Alien Tort Statute claims. As the stark divisions within the D.C. Circuit indicate, these issues are likely to percolate throughout the federal (and state) courts for some time. At a minimum, despite the D.C. Circuit decision putting the brakes on such an approach within that circuit, suits against contractors are more viable than similar suits against government employees, who are protected by more robust immunity doctrines.

In the end, though the prospects are far from perfect, the potential for holding contractors legally accountable does exist. Although international criminal accountability is unlikely, there are clear legal mechanisms for pursuing criminal actions in U.S. domestic courts, assuming there were political will to pursue prosecutions. Organizational reforms, such as creating a dedicated Department of Justice office with reporting requirements to Congress, along with a special FBI in-theater investigative unit, might help pave the way for better evidence gathering and more prosecutions. In addition, if plaintiffs can defeat dubious applications of the political question and immunity doctrines, then civil tort suits are also a viable alternative, one that is not usually available against government actors who commit similar torts. Thus, although the avenues for legal accountability could certainly be improved, we should not assume that contractors necessarily inhabit a regulatory void where traditional legal mechanisms of accountability cannot reach. Accordingly, the real work to be done in this area is not only in enacting more statutes to close supposed legal "gaps" but also, perhaps just as important, developing an organizational and political infrastructure to make it more likely that we will see actual enforcement of existing law.

4

THE UNEXPLORED PROMISE OF CONTRACT

It was in the early days of the effort to rebuild Iraq. U.S. forces had felled Saddam Hussein's brutally repressive regime, after a swift and stunning "shock and awe" campaign that showcased U.S. military might. Yet chaos reigned on the ground. An entity largely created by the United States, the Coalition Provisional Authority (CPA), had taken the reins in May 2003 and was attempting to govern the country. L. Paul Bremer, appointed by President George W. Bush and Secretary of Defense Donald Rumsfeld, was serving as the CPA's chief administrator. The overwhelming majority of those working for the CPA were U.S. employees or civilian contractors—though there were a few representatives from Australia, Spain, the United Kingdom, and a handful of other countries that had joined the coalition occupying Iraq.[1]

The prevailing mood was, in the words of former CPA official Franklin Willis, like the "Wild West." The CPA had disbanded the Iraqi Army, and so crime and violence were rampant. CPA officials struggled to do their work. As Willis has observed, a "lack of security, restricted meetings, [and] difficulty of communication[] made every task longer and slower— in short [it] severely inhibited out [sic] ability to do our job." This difficulty was "compounded by the fact that we had to meet face-to-face with our counterparts to accomplish anything because the telecommunications system was for all practical purposes inoperable." Most significant of all, perhaps, "security was simply a black hole."[2]

Into this black hole stepped the newly minted security and reconstruction firm Custer Battles, one of many companies seeking to make a profit as part of the Iraqi reconstruction effort. Founded in 2002 and managed by two former U.S. Army Rangers, Scott Custer and Michael Battles, the firm described itself as a "leading international risk management firm with extensive experience assisting large organizations reduce and manage risk in extremely volatile environments." Custer Battles quickly secured several lucrative contracts, including one for $15 million, beginning in August 2003, to help manage logistics and security for a program to introduce a new Iraqi currency.[3]

The country was awash in loose cash, which set the scene for danger and corruption. There was no banking system, and Iraqi dinars and American dollars circulated freely. As Willis has noted, American dollars, "often crisp, new $100 bills, were found throughout Iraq in large amounts by our armed forces as we completed sweeps across the country." CPA officials then apparently stashed the money in a vault in the basement of CPA headquarters—which at times may have contained more than $3 billion in cash— releasing wads of the bills from time to time to pay contractors for services and to fund Iraqi salaries.[4]

In these heady times, it certainly appears—from the public record, at least—that Custer, Battles, and some of their employees committed improprieties. Under its currency contract, the firm agreed to build, equip, and service three hubs, located in Baghdad, Mosul, and Basra. At these locations, the old Iraqi currency, the dinar, was to be exchanged with a new dinar that did not bear the portrait of Saddam Hussein. The contract was issued on a "cost-plus" basis, which meant that Custer Battles would be reimbursed for actual expenses plus 25 percent of these expenses "to cover overhead and provide a profit."[5]

By October 2003, problems arose with the currency contract, and officials from the CPA and the U.S. military called for a meeting with Custer and Battles. At the meeting, Battles by accident left behind a document that a federal court of appeals panel has since described as no less than "astonishing." In it, one column listed the "actual cost" of items used by the firm to manage the contract, while another column listed much higher amounts "invoiced" for the items. For example, at the Baghdad hub Custer Battles provided two flatbed trucks, for which it paid $18,000 but invoiced

$80,000, and generators that cost $74,000 but were invoiced at $400,000. Moreover, the firm "improperly received the difference between the actual costs and the inflated invoiced amounts and also 25% of the inflated invoiced amounts." Thus, Custer Battles apparently received millions of dollars more than it was actually owed under the contract.[6]

As with many debates about legal reform, most discussions about holding private military and security contractors accountable for abuse typically begin and end with the legal frameworks of criminal and tort law described in Chapter 3. There are, however, a variety of other potential mechanisms of accountability and constraint that deserve consideration. Indeed, in light of the difficulties government officials and private actors have faced as they have tried to invoke and enforce criminal and tort rules, these alternative mechanisms may sometimes provide more effective pathways to reform than their more frequently mentioned counterparts. The next three chapters, therefore, consider some of these alternatives. And, as in the previous chapter, we will always look beyond the formal rules on the books to the broader context and environment that gives these rules meaning and force (or hinders their enforceability) in actual practice.

In this chapter, we take up the possibility that contractual agreements between governmental entities and private organizations providing services can themselves serve as vehicles to promote public law values. Contractual reform is particularly important in the foreign affairs context because many of these contracts are negotiated in secret, without competition, based on exceptions to the normal contracting requirements.[7] For example, with respect to the U.S. government's foreign affairs contracts in Iraq, in many cases it is impossible for the public or a watchdog group even to obtain the text of the contracts, either because government officials have kept them secret for security reasons[8] or because the contractors have exercised what is essentially a veto, under the Freedom of Information Act (FOIA), for certain types of commercial information.[9] Problems posed by secrecy are reinforced by problems of conflict of interest because many of the contracts are awarded to firms run by former government personnel. Indeed, a 2003 study by the Center for Public Integrity reports that 60 percent of the companies that received early contracts in

Iraq or Afghanistan "had employees or board members who either served in or had close ties to the executive branch for Republican and Democratic administrations, for members of Congress of both parties, or at the highest levels of the military."[10] Thus, it is essential that, at the very least, the contracts themselves incorporate public values.

Nevertheless, government contracts are not a particularly sexy area of the law or of government employment. Law schools offer few courses in the topic (though George Washington University Law School's rich program in the area is a notable exception). In the military, where the need for contract specialists has skyrocketed, the prestige and value of personnel overseeing contracts has not. As the Commission on Army Acquisition and Program Management in Expeditionary Operations lamented in its hard-hitting report from 2007, the Army's culture "does not sufficiently value or recognize the importance of contracting, contract management, and contractors in expeditionary operations."[11] Uniformed military lawyers have noted that many do not specialize in contracting because it is not considered to be a high-status area with sufficient opportunities for career advancement. Yet not only do contracts for goods and labor now make up an enormous share of U.S. government activities overseas, the contracts themselves can be a vehicle for conveying the kinds of values we typically expect of governmental actors. Contractual terms can specify norms and can help structure the privatization relationship in ways that spur contractors to implement those norms. Thus, although typically conceived as the quintessential private law form, contracts used in this way might be a tool to instill broader public values—in short, to "publicize" the process of privatization.[12]

Scholars and policy makers in the field of administrative law have developed this insight in the domestic context. Most notably, Jody Freeman has suggested that states "could require compliance with both procedural and substantive standards that might otherwise be inapplicable or unenforceable against private providers." And in some cases, this insight reflects real reforms, as when state governments' contracts with privately run nursing homes mandate hearings and oversight procedures.[13] Yet this scholarship has focused on privatization of health care, welfare, and prison administration in the United States and has not generally addressed privatization of military, security, and foreign aid functions. Meanwhile, as noted in the Introduction, until recently few if any international law scholars, policy makers, or nongovernmental organizations (NGOs) have considered the possibilities of using contractual terms in the international context.[14] Accordingly, this chapter seeks to bridge the gap between domestic administrative law and international law scholarship by exploring a variety of contractual mechanisms that might be used to extend public law values to privatized foreign affairs.

Specifically, I discuss four contracting practices that government officials and contractors could deploy in the foreign affairs arena: (1) explicitly incorporating public law standards in contractual terms, including references to specific legal frameworks and provisions for training; (2) enhancing contractual monitoring and oversight, including contractual terms providing for performance benchmarks and self-evaluation, as well as increased staffing and training of contract management personnel; (3) requiring that contractors receive accreditation from independent organizations; and (4) expanding contractual enforcement options. All four of these reforms could be implemented through contracting regulations at the agency level, or they could be terms imposed by Congress through legislation.

In considering these possibilities, I use Iraq as a case study, examining all of the publicly available contracts the U.S. government negotiated to support the U.S. military or to provide for foreign aid to Iraq during the early period of the war, through 2005. This period was in many respects a low point for the oversight of contractors, and both Congress and the foreign affairs agencies have implemented some reforms since then. Yet further reform is still desperately needed, and this period offers a clear window into the kind of problems we face when we use contractors to such an extraordinary degree. Moreover, the principles we might derive from this setting could also apply to other types of contracts negotiated by states or international organizations with contractors providing a variety of foreign affairs functions. I conclude the chapter by revisiting the Custer Battles contracts in Iraq, to highlight the deficiencies and show how the kinds of reforms I describe might have improved these agreements.

Nevertheless, it is important to recognize at the outset the significant obstacles to contract reform. Indeed, even in the domestic setting, scholars have questioned the extent to which government is likely to prove willing to engage in close monitoring or to provide greater contractual oversight. As noted in Chapter 2, there is no natural political constituency for better contract monitoring, which makes implementing such monitoring regimes very difficult. And the politics of privatization have created incentives to cut civil service jobs—including those of contract monitors—while adding contract labor, thereby creating a monitoring crisis. In addition, if governments privatize in part to *avoid* oversight, it might be difficult to prod them to reinscribe oversight provisions into the contracts themselves. Moreover, the nature of monitoring in contingency operations—the difficulties in giving monitors sufficient incentives to serve in a war zone, the high turnover, and the poor training of monitors—present special challenges. Finally, it may be especially difficult to monitor discretionary functions that require complex judgments and balance competing values. Accordingly, functions requiring less complex judgments (serving meals to soldiers as opposed to providing private security) may be more susceptible to effective monitoring.

These are important considerations, to be sure, but they merely highlight the need to engage in the debate about contract reform more directly. Indeed, I think we should pursue this debate without cynically assuming at the outset that governments would necessarily be resistant to all forms of greater contractual monitoring. Governments are not monolithic, and there are many actors within the bureaucracy who are interested in this issue and ready to lobby for and adopt reforms. Moreover, at least within the United States, there is a new appetite for contractor reform both in the executive and legislative branches and even from within the industry itself. For example, over the past few years, I have participated in several working groups of contractors, high-level agency officials, and congressional staff members, during which policy makers from multiple governments and members of the private military contractor industry were very eager to discuss and implement contractual reforms of the sort I suggest. I therefore believe we have a window of opportunity in the wake of the various contractor scandals of the past few years to build momentum for such reforms within Congress. The Obama administration may also be more open to such reforms, though it remains to be seen whether the professed interest in reform is more rhetoric than reality. Finally, as I discuss below, some reforms could be pursued by NGOs, even if governments are reluctant to act. In any event, even if it is not a panacea, trying to reform the foreign affairs contracts along the lines I suggest below is certainly a necessary part of any comprehensive response to the privatization trend.

Including Public Law Standards in Contractual Terms

First, of course, the contracts could explicitly require that the contractors obey the norms and rules that implement public law values. For example, the terms of each agreement could identify the relevant legal frameworks and provide that private contractors must abide by the applicable legal rules within those frameworks. Similarly, the contracts could provide for specific training of contractors that would better enable the contract employees to abide by those rules.

Ensuring That Contracts Incorporate Specific Legal Frameworks

In the domestic setting, contractual provisions that lay out specific legal regimes and bind the contractor under those legal regimes, either by referring to existing legal frameworks or by laying out specific rules or standards in the contracts themselves, are commonplace. As a term in their contracts with privately run prisons, for example, many states demand that contractors comply with constitutional, federal, state, and private rules and standards for prison operation and inmates' rights.[15] In addition, contractual agreements may specify that contractors must hold hearings and review contractor actions when aggrieved parties lodge complaints.[16]

The U.S. government's military and foreign aid contracts in Iraq, by contrast, have been strikingly inadequate on this score, and were particularly lacking in the early days of the Iraq war. Of the sixty Iraq contracts publicly available as of 2005,[17] none apparently contained specific provisions requiring contractors to obey human rights, anticorruption, or transparency norms.[18] The agreements between the U.S. government and CACI International Corporation to supply military interrogators starkly illustrate this point. The intelligence personnel were hired pursuant to a standing "blanket purchase agreement" between the Department of the Interior and CACI, negotiated in 2000.[19] Under such an agreement, the procuring agency need not request specific services at the time the agreement is made but rather may enter task orders as the need arises. In 2003 eleven task orders, worth $66.2 million, were entered (none of which was the result of competitive bidding).[20] The orders specified only that CACI would provide interrogation support and analysis work for the U.S. Army in Iraq, including "debriefing of personnel, intelligence report writing, and screening/interrogation of detainees at established holding areas."[21] Significantly, the orders did not appear to expressly require the private contractor interrogators to comply with specific international human rights or humanitarian law rules such as those contained in the Torture Convention or the Geneva Conventions. Likewise, although the contractors were subject to international and domestic laws prohibiting the bribery of government officials,[22] as well as the general terms of applicable contracting statutes and regulations,[23] none of the contracts specifically prohibited the contractors themselves from accepting bribes, an area that remains ambiguous under domestic and international law. Similarly, the contracts did not appear to include terms making it clear that FOIA was applicable to contract activities, a provision that would have helped to make contractor activities more transparent.

It might at first seem surprising that these contracts would not contain, as a matter of course, provisions requiring compliance with specific international law rules (or standards). However, as we saw in Chapter 2, the move to outsourcing occurred through hundreds of small decisions made in different agencies, and until now there has been no high-level analysis or public discussion of how these contracts should be framed. In addition, at least during the George W. Bush administration, there was antipathy toward international (and even many domestic) legal regimes, and outsourcing was used as one way to circumvent these regimes. Finally, although many foreign affairs contracts could fall within the purview of the military judge advocates, overseeing contractors has historically had a low status among military lawyers, and the contracts have not typically received approval or input from the judge advocates in advance. This is in sharp contrast, as we shall see in Chapter 6, with the very active role military lawyers play in advising uniformed commanders on the ground. Thus, the primary military body institutionally committed to a culture of respect for rule of law values has not historically been involved in the drafting and oversight of contracts. Now that the potential problems of the contracting regime have come to light, however, there may be a possibility for institutional change in this regard.

To be sure, the Department of Defense (DOD) and State Department officials have now acknowledged serious missteps during the early stages of the conflicts in Iraq and Afghanistan. For example, testifying in 2008, Jack Bell, then deputy undersecretary of defense for logistics and materiel readiness, emphasized that, "faced with this unprecedented scale of dependence on contractors, we have confronted major challenges associated with visibility, integration, oversight, and management of a large contractor force working along side our deployed military personnel that, frankly, we were not adequately prepared to address."[24] Secretary of State Condoleezza Rice, testifying in the wake of the September 2007 Blackwater Nisour Square incident described in the Introduction, acknowledged that the State Department should have acted earlier to rein in the security firm: "I certainly regret that we did not have the oversight that I would have insisted upon."[25]

Officials have also taken steps to improve contractual language. For example, the DOD finally, in 2005, issued a document providing general instructions on contracting practices that required contractors to comply with existing law and policy.[26] By the end of 2007, the DOD Joint Contracting Command for Iraq and Afghanistan included the more sweeping requirement that all contracts had to include a provision mandating that contractors, subcontractors, and personnel "comply with all existing and future U.S. and host nation laws, federal and DOD regulations, and U.S. Central Command [CENTCOM] Orders and directives, including rules on the use of force . . . applicable to personnel in Iraq." Moreover, individual contractor and subcontractor employees were required to "provide written acknowledgement that they understand the penalties for noncompliance, [which] include criminal and civil actions, revocation of weapons authorization, and contract termination."[27] Thus, not only does this provision include a broader reference to future laws, regulations, and directives, it includes subcontractors as well as prime contractors, makes specific reference to rules on the use of force, and mandates that contractors affirm their understanding of these rules.

Despite these reforms, significant problems remain. As late as September 2007, four years after the beginning of the Iraq War and six years after the beginning of the conflict in Afghanistan, the DOD and the State Department had strikingly different contracting practices. Indeed, a 2007 report produced by the Secretary of State's Panel on Personal Protective Services in Iraq observed starkly after two weeks of on-the-ground interviews that security contractors in Iraq were still operating "in an environment that is chaotic, unsupervised, deficient in oversight and accountability, and poorly coordinated." Moreover, the report noted a lack of "parallelism" with the CENTCOM rules on the use of force by contracted security in Iraq, and in particular urged the State Department to revise its rules to clarify that "if an authorized employee must fire his/her weapon, he/she must fire only aimed shots; fire with due regard for the safety of innocent bystanders; and make every effort to avoid civilian casualties."[28] Since then, the DOD and the Department of State have hashed out a Memorandum of Agreement[29] to harmonize their approaches to standards for private security contractors as well as contract management more broadly. This effort has earned the praise of watchdogs such as the Government Accountability Office (GAO)[30] and the Special Inspector General for Iraq Reconstruction (SIGIR).[31] Yet the fact that the rules regarding the use of force for contractors were so different for so long is troubling. In addition, the Memorandum of Agreement covers only security contractors and not other contractors, such as interrogators, translators, or logistics contractors who carry weapons for self-defense, and who therefore might use force. Moreover, the contract language remains relatively broad and vague. More useful terms would refer to particular obligations under international law, such as specific human rights or humanitarian law treaties, as opposed to the general command to obey applicable law. Furthermore, although setting forth principles regarding the use of force for contractors is critical, principles on their own are insufficient without including the legal frameworks that spell out those principles. References to specific bodies of law would therefore be especially useful.

In addition to laying out a specific set of legal rules (or standards) for the contractor to follow, more specific and comprehensive contractual terms would have the added benefit of clarifying that certain legal regimes would indeed bind the contractors, regardless of ambiguities in the legal regimes themselves. For example, as discussed in Chapter 3, certain legal norms, both under international and under domestic law, may not apply to private contractors because the so-called state action doctrine and other similar doctrines render a variety of norms only enforceable against governmental entities. Thus, as we have seen, the Convention Against Torture bans all torture but defines torture as consisting of certain acts committed at the "instigation of or with the consent or acquiescence of a public official or other person acting in an official capacity."[32] Accordingly, explicit contractual terms applying the norms of the convention would obviate the need to show that the private actors were functioning as an extension of government so as to satisfy any state action requirement. Instead, the norms applicable to governmental actors would simply be part of the contractual terms, enforceable like any other provisions, regardless of state action.

Requiring That Private Contractors Receive Training

Foreign affairs contracts could also explicitly require that contractors receive training in activities that would promote public law values. Such training, as a contractual requirement, could help instill in contractor employees a sense of the importance of these values. At the same time, training could provide employees with concrete recommendations about how to implement these values in specific, challenging situations.

Again, in the domestic setting such training provisions are commonplace. A standard term in state agreements with companies that manage private prisons, for example, requires companies to certify that the training they provide to personnel is comparable to that offered to state employees.[33] Such training would normally include instruction concerning legal limits on the use of force and examples of what those limits mean in circumstances likely to arise in the prison setting.

As of 2005, none of the publicly available Iraq contracts appeared to mandate such specific training. Indeed, although a few of the agreements required contractors to hire employees with a certain number of years' experience,[34] none apparently specified that the contractor must provide any particular training at all. For example, the U.S. government's agreement with Chugach McKinley, Inc., to screen and hire a broad range of military support personnel—from doctors to "special mission advisers"—said nothing about whether such personnel were to receive training in applicable international law standards, even though such personnel were often placed in a position where abuse might occur.[35] The U.S. government's agreements with CACI to provide interrogators were likewise apparently silent on whether interrogators were to receive education in international humanitarian and human rights law, training that U.S. military interrogators would normally receive.[36] This omission is particularly glaring given the highly volatile Iraqi interrogation environment. In testimony as part of litigation arising out of the abuses at Abu Ghraib prison, Torin Nelson, one of the contract interrogators hired by CACI, asserted that he received little, if any, training in the applicable law. When asked, "Was there any direction given to you from CACI about what legal regime applied to interrogation?" he responded flatly, "No."[37] Indeed, as noted previously, a military investigation of the abuses at Abu Ghraib prison found that "integration of some contractors without training, qualifications and certification created ineffective interrogation teams and the potential for non-compliance with doctrine and applicable laws." The report concluded that 35 percent of the contract interrogators lacked formal military training as interrogators. In addition, the technical training requirements of the contract were deemed "not adequate" because they did not "list specific training," such as "tests on interrogation and the Geneva Conventions." According to the report, "numerous statements indicated that little, if any, training on Geneva Conventions was presented to contractor employees."[38]

Government officials have improved contractual training requirements and policies somewhat, but there is far more that could be done. Uniformed military lawyers have reported that contract interrogators now generally participate in government training programs, which include classes in the Geneva Conventions and other applicable rules,[39] along with mock incidents to test students' ability to apply the rules in specific scenarios based on actual incidents. And the 2005 DOD instructions require contractors to document that they have received training in the appropriate rules regarding the use of force.[40] Yet in 2007 a State Department report suggested that the training that security contractors received concerning the limits on the use of force was deficient. The report noted that while the U.S. Embassy "provides comprehensive guidance on permissible uses of deadly force and the circumstances under which deadly force can be used," that guidance "is less explicit on *how* deadly force should be used."[41]

In a 2009 assessment the SIGIR and the State Department Inspector General jointly reported that the State Department's security contract with Blackwater required the company to screen and train personnel, and that the State Department had approved the company's training facility. Yet while this assessment noted that the training included "organization of a protective service detail, terrorist operations, motorcade operations, radio procedures, emergency medical care, and firearms shooting proficiency," the report did not mention training in the Geneva Conventions or applicable law, raising serious questions about the adequacy of such training.[42]

Anticorruption training would also be useful for foreign affairs contractors generally, and for contracts in Iraq specifically. Iraq ranks among the worst countries in the world on Transparency International's corruption index,[43] and it is no surprise that such corruption reaches U.S. contractors operating there. Yet such contracts, at least early on, said little about training for contractors in practices to avoid corruption. And while training requirements undoubtedly would increase the cost of the contracts, the fraud and waste that could be deterred with better training might well offset such increases.

Enhancing Contractual Monitoring and Oversight

Provisions could also be made for increased contract monitoring, which would help ensure an important additional check on abuses. Such monitoring should include, to begin with, sufficient numbers of trained and experienced governmental contract monitors.[44] At the same time, other governmental personnel who interact with the contractors, such as commanders and other uniformed military personnel, must understand the contractors' roles and in some cases have their own oversight capability. In addition, governmental ombudspersons—leaders of independent offices charged with providing enhanced oversight—serve as an important supplement to the contract monitors. Thus, at a minimum, it is essential that government agencies devote enough resources to ensure that these requirements are implemented in a meaningful way. In addition, outside independent NGOs, both for-profit and nonprofit, can serve an important function by monitoring contracts. Finally, contractual terms, such as mandatory contractor self-evaluation and performance benchmarks, can increase the impact of monitoring.

Increasing the Number, Training, and Effectiveness of Contract Monitors and Other Oversight Personnel

Contracts for services in the domestic context regularly include a three-tiered monitoring structure: government personnel assigned as contract monitors, supplemented by other agency actors such as ombudspersons, further supplemented by independent outside groups. In the privatized health care context, for example, where private nursing homes receive Medicaid funding and private hospitals receive Medicare and Medicaid support, the trend is toward agreements that require a state-appointed contract manager.[45] Federal agencies such as the Department of Health and Human Services (whose inspector general issues reports on contracts with private hospitals that receive public funding)[46] and the Health Care Financing Administration (which exerts fairly tight control over private nursing homes receiving Medicaid funding)[47] also have significant oversight authority. In addition, third-party independent organizations play an important role. For example, the Joint Commission on Accreditation of Healthcare Organizations (JCAHO), a private organization of professional associations, certifies health care institutions for compliance with federal regulations and state licensure laws.[48]

Foreign affairs contracts provide for far less monitoring. To be sure, the statutory and regulatory scheme includes provisions for governmental contract monitors, including the contract officers' representatives (CORs). In most cases, these CORs are supposed to oversee the contracts on the ground, and they are supplemented by inspectors general of the respective agencies responsible for the contracts,[49] and independent private accounting firms that audit the contracts.[50] Yet in practice this regime has failed in significant—and in some cases spectacular—respects.

The virtual lack of oversight of the Iraq contracts in the early stages of the war provides a salient example. The government agencies with responsibility for the contracts—primarily USAID, the DOD, and the now dismantled CPA—devoted extraordinarily minimal resources to monitoring.[51] For example, early on in the conflict USAID had responsibility for approximately $3 billion in reconstruction projects,[52] but for some time the agency had only four contract monitors on the ground. In fact, due to the difficulties of monitoring contracts with so little staff, USAID determined to contract out the monitoring function itself![53] Likewise, a DOD Inspector General study conducted early in the Iraq reconstruction effort concluded that more than half of the Iraq contracts had not been adequately monitored.[54] This fact is not surprising given that, as discussed in Chapter 2, DOD reduced its acquisitions workforce by more than half between 1990 and 2001, while the department's contracting workload increased by more than 12 percent. In addition, those who were assigned to monitor contract performance were often inadequately trained.[55] A 2007 report on contracting by the Army concluded that Army contractors experienced a 600 percent increase in their workload and performed increasingly complex tasks, while the number of Army civilian and military employees had either remained static or declined because of congressional direction to the DOD and the Army to make significant cuts in the acquisition workforce.[56] Finally, in an ironic twist, government officials often hire private contractors to write the procedural rules governing contracting and monitoring protocols, thus leading to further conflict-of-interest problems. Indeed, one of DOD's principal military contractors drafted the DOD handbook on the contracting process.[57]

The lack of oversight begins with the way in which the contracts are awarded in the first place. Many of the procedural requirements tend not to apply in emergency situations, which are, of course, precisely the occasions when military intervention or humanitarian relief efforts and postreconstruction aid are most likely. Thus, ordinary contracting procedures, such as competitive bidding, are often waived.[58] In addition, as with the Custer Battles contract described above, many of the contracts are written as cost reimbursement contracts, often termed "cost-plus" agreements, under which the government reimburses the contractor for costs incurred in providing a service, plus a fee that is calculated as a percentage of the cost.[59] Though often criticized as leading to waste and abuse,[60] such contracts become the norm in emergency situations, rather than the exception. Acknowledging these problems, President Obama issued a July 29, 2009, Memorandum instructing government agencies to reduce the number of cost reimbursement contracts issued,[61] but it is unclear whether the Memorandum will have significant long-term effect. At the same time, too few contract monitors are appointed, those who are appointed lack expertise, and ombudspersons are not given the resources they need to do an effective job.

But even more than hasty drafting, one of the biggest reasons for the lack of oversight is that the contract monitors themselves are simply missing in action. For example, General George Fay observed in his report on the Abu Ghraib prison abuses that, "as learned in the current situation, it is very difficult, if not impossible, to effectively administer a contract when the COR [contract officer's representative] is not on site." As General Fay further noted, "Meaningful contract administration and monitoring will not be possible if a small number of CORs are asked to monitor the performance of one or more contractors who may have 100 or more employees in the theater, and in some cases, perhaps in several locations (which seems to have been the situation at Abu Ghraib)." In these situations, "CORs do well" simply "to keep up with the paperwork" and "have no time to actively monitor contractor performance." In General Fay's assessment, at Abu Ghraib prison "there was no credible exercise of appropriate oversight of contract performance."[62]

In the case of the CPA, whose contract oversight lapses were particularly blatant, a sheer lack of oversight staff was a main factor. A report notes that the CPA failed to keep accounts for the hundreds of millions of dollars of cash in its vault, had awarded contracts worth billions of dollars to American firms without tender, and had no idea what was happening to the money from the Development Fund for Iraq (DFI) that was being spent by the interim Iraqi government ministries.[63] One former CPA official has observed that "contracts were made that were mistakes, and were poorly, if at all, supervised [and] money was spent that could have been saved, if we simply had the right numbers of people."[64] For example, even devoting a single staff person to the Custer Battles contracts might have saved at least $4 million.[65]

Those contract officials that have been on the ground often lack sufficient training and in any event do not focus on a wide enough range of issues. For example, many of the existing monitors see their role as only keeping track of money and auditing for fraud and bribery. As we have seen, contracts say little specifically about human rights norms, and governmental contract monitors and ombudspersons are not ordinarily focused on these values when scrutinizing contractors.[66] Indeed, as General Fay lamented in his report in the aftermath of the detainee abuses at Abu Ghraib prison, many of the contract monitors themselves lack training in the legal rules that apply to contractors: "Training is required to ensure that the contract officer's representative is thoroughly familiar with the contract and gains some level of familiarity with the Geneva Conventions standards. It needs to be made clear the contractor employees are bound by the requirements of the Geneva Conventions."[67] Furthermore, to the extent that independent third-party groups are empowered to monitor under the contract, they similarly tend to be auditing firms, whose expertise lies in financial matters, not in international human rights or humanitarian law. Foreign affairs contracts rarely, if ever, provide for monitoring by independent groups with expertise in this area.[68]

An added difficulty has been the lack of clarity of roles among the contract monitoring personnel and others, such as the commanders on the ground and other uniformed military actors. The situation at Abu Ghraib prison during the period of abuses there spotlights this problem. As General Fay reported, "No doctrine exists to guide interrogators and their intelligence leaders (NCO, Warrant Officer, and Officer) in the contract management or command and control of contractors in a wartime environment." As a consequence, "these interrogators and leaders faced numerous issues involving contract management: roles and responsibilities of [prison] personnel with respect to contractors; roles, relationships, and responsibilities of contract linguists and contract interrogators with military personnel; and the methods of disciplining contractor personnel."[69]

Agencies have improved contract monitoring to some degree since the early days of the conflict in Iraq and Afghanistan. Indeed, the GAO concluded in 2009 that the "DOD and the State Department have improved oversight and coordination" of security contractors. For example, in 2007 the DOD established a new unit, the Armed Contractor Oversight Division, to monitor security contractors. As noted in Chapter 3, this division has improved tracking of serious incidents involving armed security contractors, and has increased accountability. Furthermore, military units are now "more responsible for providing oversight" including "reporting and investigating as well as contract management." Thus, according to the GAO, on-the-ground military units are no longer working in ignorance of the contracts, or even worse, at cross-purposes with the contract monitors. And the State Department has increased oversight of security contractors by placing diplomatic security agents in each security contractor motorcade, and has increased the number of governmental security agents more broadly.[70]

Yet significant challenges remain. For example, even in praising the DOD and the State Department for their increased contract monitoring, the GAO questioned whether the agencies had enough personnel in place to make the increased monitoring effective. As the GAO put it, "It is not clear whether the [DOD] can sustain this increase [in staffing]." Indeed, according to the report, the Army "lacks the leadership and military and civilian personnel to provide sufficient contracting support to either expeditionary or peacetime missions."[71] In a separate 2009 audit of the State Department security contracts with Blackwater, the SIGIR found that the contract officer representatives for the contract were severely overtaxed: "Since the COR duties are collateral and are assigned to special agents who spend most of their time planning and executing their own protective missions, the special agents have little time for contract administration or monitoring."[72] These reports strongly suggest that contract management remains a side job that gets short shrift in the face of other, overwhelming duties. Even the DOD's recent commitment to hire twenty thousand new contract-monitoring personnel by 2015,[73] though a step in the right direction, is probably insufficient given the huge growth in contract labor over the past decade.

Improving Interagency Coordination

Complicating oversight matters further, an alphabet soup of agencies oversees agreements with contractors who work in conflict and postconflict zones. From the State Department, to the U.S. Agency for International Development, to the DOD, to the CIA, to the Department of the Interior, each agency has different rules for contractors and different approaches. This dispersal of authority across multiple agencies creates interagency communication problems and conflicts of interest that

impede oversight.[74] For example, officials at different agencies use different methods to calculate the costs of contracts, and these methods may
also vary from those used by the companies themselves.[75] In addition,
because agencies can earn fees for facilitating other agencies' contracts
but are not adequately held to account for monitoring those contracts,
agencies have incentives to sponsor other agencies' contracts but little
incentive to supervise them.[76] These arrangements can lead to abuse, as
occurred in the case of the Department of the Interior sponsorship of the
DOD's task orders for intelligence services at Abu Ghraib prison under
an existing contract between CACI and the Interior Department.

As discussed in Chapter 3, for most of the past decade the State Department and the DOD have apparently had different rules regarding
the use of force. Moreover, officials from different agencies have failed to
communicate with each other about the activities of contractors working
for their respective units. For example, uniformed military lawyers have
noted that at times commanders were not aware when State Department
security contractors entered their areas of control.[77] Such problems arose
in part because the agencies used different databases to track their contractors; indeed, the DOD has long been unable even to count the number of State Department security contractors in Iraq. Thus, as one report
observed, "the process for coordination and sharing of information between the Embassy and the Multi-National Force-Iraq is not sufficiently
robust to ensure mutually beneficial situational awareness and knowledge
of the particulars . . . that could potentially affect U.S.-Iraqi relations."
The report thus concluded that "improvements are necessary to address
shortcomings in coordination and oversight that have undermined con-
fidence in the operation of the security program on the part of the U.S.
military command and the Iraqi government and public."[78]

Since 2007 the DOD and the State Department have made significant
strides in increasing coordination, but serious problems persist. Thus, as
noted earlier, the agencies signed a Memorandum of Agreement in December 2007 to improve coordination over security contractors. They
have worked to develop consistent standards, including rules regarding
the use of force. They have put in place liaison personnel from both agencies. For example, the State Department liaison briefs the Multinational
Force staff daily on State Department security contractor movements.

Meanwhile, the DOD has established a unit to monitor incidents involving security contractors, including certain categories of State Department security contractors.[79] Yet not all security contractors appear to be covered, and not all agencies participate in the coordination effort. Furthermore, these efforts, while important, do not appear to extend beyond security contractors. Arguably, much more comprehensive coordination is needed, perhaps in the form of an interagency working group at the National Security Council.

Laying Out Clear Performance Benchmarks

Of course, to some degree increased contract monitoring can only be effective to the extent that the contracts lay out clear benchmarks against which to measure compliance. In the domestic context, commentators and policy makers have long urged that contracts must include benchmarks, and rigorous performance standards regularly appear in contracts.[80] Scholars have argued that, ideally, performance-based contracts should "clearly spell out the desired end result" but leave the choice of method to the contractor, who should have "as much freedom as possible in figuring out how to best meet government's performance objective."[81]

State contracts with companies that manage private prisons implement these ideas. For example, under the model contract for private prison management drafted by the Oklahoma Department of Corrections, contractors must meet delineated standards for security, meals, and education. They must also certify that the training provided to personnel is comparable to that offered to state employees.[82] In Texas, contractors must abide by similar terms and, in addition, must "establish performance measures for rehabilitative programs."[83] The American Correctional Association is revising its accreditation standards to include performance measures, and the Office of Juvenile Justice and Delinquency Prevention is developing performance-based standards for juvenile correctional facilities.[84] Commentators have noted, further, that performance measures for private prison operators could include both "process measures such as the number of educational or vocational programs, or outcome measures such as the Logan quality of confinement index, the number of assaults, or the recidivism rate. . . . Because no single statistic adequately captures 'quality,' and because focusing on any single measure could have perverse effects, performance-based contracts should tie compensation to a large and rich set of variables."[85]

Privatized welfare programs have also experimented with performance measures as a means to improve quality. In 1996 Congress authorized the implementation of welfare programs "through contracts with charitable, religious, or private organizations."[86] Since then, states have increasingly contracted with such organizations,[87] and many of these contracts contain performance benchmarks and output requirements.[88] For example, under a performance-based system, a welfare contractor might receive financial rewards for increasing the percentage of program participants who receive job placements.[89]

The foreign affairs contracts are notably less rigorous in providing for performance measures. Although military service contracts are difficult to evaluate because so many of them are not publicly available, contract officers familiar with the contracts have remarked on their generally vague terms.[90] And the fact that they are often so-called indefinite delivery/indefinite quantity contracts adds to their open-ended quality.[91] Under this structure, the government awards a contract that does not specify how many services or goods will be necessary or the dates upon which they will be required.[92] These additional details are specified in subsequent task orders, which themselves are often vague because the task orders need not pass through the same degree of supervision as the initial contract award.[93] Of course, such contracts may sometimes be necessary, because the government cannot know in advance precisely what will be required or for how long.[94] Yet the lack of any administrable standards in these contracts can lead to significant abuses.[95]

Of the publicly available Iraq contracts for military services, it is striking that none contains clear benchmarks or output requirements. Instead, these contracts are phrased in amorphous language that provides little opportunity for compliance evaluation. For example, a contract between the U.S. government and Military Professional Resources, Inc. (MPRI) to supply translators for government personnel simply states that interpreters will be provided. The agreement says nothing about whether the interpreters must be effective or how effectiveness might be measured.[96] Similarly, the CACI task orders for interrogators specify only that CACI will provide interrogation support and analysis work for the U.S. Army in Iraq, including "debriefing of personnel, intelligence report writing, and screening/interrogation of detainees at established holding areas."[97] The task orders offer little more than these broad goals. To be sure, security concerns may require some degree of vagueness. Nonetheless, the task orders could be much more specific about training requirements, standards of conduct, supervision, and performance parameters.

Certainly performance benchmarks that are too strict can pose problems. As scholars of domestic privatization have noted, discretion can serve useful goals; indeed, discretion is in part what makes privatization desirable, as private contractors have more flexibility than rule-bound bureaucratic actors to pursue innovative approaches.[98] Output requirements that preserve flexibility about the means to achieve those results are therefore the most effective.[99] But even carefully tailored output requirements can go awry, as when, for example, private welfare providers "cream" those accepted into their programs in order to increase the percentage of those who receive job placements.[100] Moreover, output requirements can sometimes give contractors tunnel vision, leading them to focus only on the benchmarks, thereby missing opportunities to achieve wider benefits. A recent study of the enhanced "auditing" that accompanied privatization in Thatcherite Britain, for example, suggests that narrow output requirements steered organizations and individuals away from broader, more diffuse, social goals.[101]

In addition, by their very nature results-based contracts raise difficult questions about how best to measure output. Creating benchmarks may be relatively straightforward if the project at issue involves simply building a bridge or dam, but it is very difficult to measure intangibles, such as fostering human development or building civil society. Likewise, short-term results, such as whether food aid was delivered, are much easier to measure than longer-term systemic efforts to alleviate poverty, provide education, and so on. As a consequence, results-based contracts tend to put more emphasis on short-term delivery of services rather than longer-term impact.[102] Finally, contractual output requirements do not, of course, necessarily ensure compliance, because contractors may simply fail to meet their goals. In addition, even the most detailed performance requirements and standards inevitably leave considerable discretion to the contractor.[103]

Nonetheless, despite problems with unduly rigid performance benchmarks, the foreign affairs contracts (at least those that are publicly available) appear to fall at the opposite end of the spectrum. Indeed, they seem to possess so few benchmarks and output requirements that they contain virtually no meaningful evaluative criteria whatsoever. In such circumstances, enhanced performance benchmarks could be a useful contractual tool.

Mandating Contractor Self-evaluation

Contracts could also mandate contractor self-evaluations as a means of enhancing accountability. Presented with an internal self-evaluation, an outside monitor, whether governmental or third-party, can often scrutinize the contractor's performance more quickly and efficiently. Of course, self-evaluation gives the contractor discretion to massage the data and indeed can be subject to outright manipulation and abuse.[104] But nonetheless, it can be a useful starting point for outside monitors, who can at least at the outset make a quicker assessment as to whether the contractor has met the contract goals. In addition, self-evaluation can encourage more effective internal policing by the contractor.

Due to these potential benefits, self-evaluation has emerged as a frequent tool in the domestic context. In the world of private prisons, for example, contractors regularly are subjected to self-evaluation requirements. In Texas, prison contractors must "establish performance measures for rehabilitative programs and develop a system to assess achievement and outcomes."[105] Likewise, in the field of health care a health maintenance organization must, if it is to receive accreditation, conduct continuous "quality improvement," in an ongoing internal self-evaluation process.[106] Contracts that require accreditation thus effectively mandate such self-evaluation.

In the foreign affairs context, private foreign aid providers operating under agreements with USAID regularly perform self-evaluation, but foreign aid contracts with other agencies seem to be devoid of provisions that would demand such a practice. Again taking the publicly available Iraq contracts as an example, none requires the private contractor to file self-evaluation reports, develop internal assessment practices, or otherwise engage in self-evaluation.[107] And while self-evaluation on its own is unlikely to significantly improve contract compliance, it can be useful in combination with some or all of the other contractual provisions discussed in this chapter.

Requiring That Contractors Receive Accreditation from Independent Organizations

Another contract-based tool for promoting public law values is accreditation. Independent organizations, often consisting of experts or professionals in the field, can evaluate and rate private contractors. Government authorities can then require that contractors receive certain ratings. Or governmental entities or international institutions, such as the United Nations, could develop accreditation regimes themselves.

Again, the domestic context offers a particularly rich set of examples that could provide useful lessons in the foreign affairs setting. For example, in the field of publicly funded, privately provided health care, JCAHO accredits hospitals receiving Medicare and Medicaid funding. Indeed, such accreditation is required by statute as well as by contract.[108] State laws or contractual terms also often specify that health maintenance organizations must receive accreditation by the National Committee for Quality Assurance (NCQA), an independent nonprofit organization, before receiving public funding.[109] Until recently, NCQA certification was primarily voluntary, offering health maintenance organizations an advantage when competing for lucrative health care delivery contracts. When states became managed care purchasers, however, they adopted NCQA as a benchmark of quality.[110] Indeed, the 2010 federal health care reform statute specifically requires that health care providers receive NCQA approval in order to participate in certain aspects of the plan.[111]

Similarly, many states mandate that the American Correctional Association (ACA) must accredit private prison operators before they receive lucrative state contracts.[112] An organization of correctional professionals that has existed for more than a century, the ACA accredits prisons and provides training for prison personnel while also setting standards that apply to virtually every aspect of prison operation.[113] Not only has ACA accreditation become a standard contract requirement,[114] federal courts have used ACA standards to interpret constitutional and statutory provisions.[115] Even private investors look to accreditation as an indication of quality.[116] Thus, the accreditation requirement creates significant compliance incentives.

Privatized education regimes such as those implementing charter schools have also considered accreditation by independent organizations to be a means of ensuring quality.[117] And although some critics charge that educational accreditation can be ineffective if accreditation focuses on facilities and administrative processes instead of educational quality,[118] that is a problem of the particular accreditation metrics and not the basic idea that accreditation can be used to promote public law values.[119]

In many domestic contexts, therefore, these independent, private accrediting entities are effectively setting the standards that give meaning to public law values. In that regard, the relative insularity of the standard-setting and accreditation process may undermine the ability of broader groups, including consumers and the public at large, to participate in the process.[120] There is also the concern that private accreditors in some cases might be too close to the contractors, and therefore too lenient.[121] Yet, even critics agree that the standards are often much better than those that would be developed by agency bureaucrats, and despite the imperfections, accreditation has served as an important check on the contracting process, as well as a way to get information to the general public.[122]

In contrast, accreditation is glaringly absent in the foreign affairs context.[123] Human rights organizations, governments, and the United Nations have begun to encourage corporations, particularly those in the extraction industries, to comply with voluntary labor, environmental, and human rights standards.[124] A consortium of NGOs that deliver humanitarian relief have initiated the SPHERE project, which is an effort to set standards for the provision of humanitarian aid, including specific guidelines for field operations, training, and self-evaluation.[125] And an industry-founded association of private security companies, the International Peace Operations Association (IPOA), has begun to construct a comprehensive code of conduct that includes human rights standards.[126] Nevertheless, neither the United Nations, nor domestic governments, nor outside groups concerned with potential abuses by foreign affairs contractors have so far undertaken serious efforts either to harness these nascent accreditation initiatives or to promote other accreditation projects.

This failure is particularly striking in the Iraq context. Not one of the available contracts for aid or military services requires that the entities receiving the contracts be vetted or accredited by independent organizations. For example, unlike domestic prison contracts, which routinely require accreditation by ACA and compliance with a comprehensive set of standards, the contracts with CACI to provide interrogators at Abu Ghraib contain only the most basic guidelines and make no mention of human rights compliance or accreditation requirements.[127] The contract between the U.S. government and DynCorp to provide law enforcement advisers to train Iraqi police similarly contains no provision mandating that DynCorp be accredited.[128] Likewise, although contracts could require that humanitarian aid organizations agree to the SPHERE guidelines in order to receive contracts, government authorities have not imposed such a requirement.[129]

Of course, accreditation alone, particularly if the accreditation standards and monitoring regimes are developed by the industry itself, may not be sufficient. For example, in the domestic context scholars have questioned whether accreditation has had a positive impact on prison abuse.[130] Nevertheless, accreditation remains an important potential mechanism for responding to foreign policy privatization. First, I think we should not be so quick to assume that industry accreditation is necessarily ineffective. For example, when IPOA initiated a review to determine whether Blackwater had complied with the IPOA Code of Conduct, Blackwater withdrew from the industry group altogether, suggesting that the accreditation review was not entirely toothless. And IPOA has been active in lobbying for greater contractual regulation within the executive branch, if only because such regulation would allow more compliant firms to separate themselves from what they see as rogue outfits, thereby gaining a competitive advantage. More importantly, we can distinguish between *industry* accreditation—which is the current framework in the private prison setting—and *independent* accreditation, which is the dominant approach in the health care setting. The health care accreditation regime has by most accounts had far greater (though admittedly not perfect) success.

Thus, it is crucial that independent human rights and other organizations focus on accreditation and develop regimes to rate and monitor foreign affairs contractors. Indeed, human rights organizations have been only sporadically engaged in the privatization debate. Although there have been some isolated reports and statements, such as a report by Human Rights First on private security contractors (cited in Chapter 3), these organizations have done insufficient reporting on contractor abuses, and there has been virtually no effort to develop an accreditation regime.

Yet, such accreditation would seem to be particularly important in the foreign affairs area, where, as discussed previously, security concerns and special considerations often eliminate competition in the contracting process, resulting in contracts that are structured without the usual market controls. More NGOs could, like the SPHERE project's efforts in humanitarian aid, begin to rate military contractors independently, regardless of whether the government contracts require such accreditation. These ratings might then become an industry standard that civil society groups could persuade the government to use as a contracting factor. This is the path NCQA accreditation took in the domestic health care context. And even if agency officials negotiating contracts choose not to impose accreditation requirements, the ratings could serve as a point of pressure in Congress and the public at large. Thus, NGOs should spend at least as much energy developing accreditation regimes as they do pursuing transnational litigation under various formal international law instruments. International organizations could also seek to create accreditation regimes. Such accreditation would likely be influential over time, even if states at first formally refused to implement accreditation requirements into their contracts.

Enhancing Enforcement

Finally, Congress or the relevant agencies could improve contract enforcement. Currently, even in the domestic setting, generally only governmental officials and contractors may enforce contract violations, though Congress has provided for limited private enforcement against those who have defrauded the government. Measures that would enhance enforcement might include greater opportunities for third-party enforcement actions in domestic courts, expanded whistleblower protections for contractor employees, and privatized grievance procedures.

Contracts could, for example, include third-party beneficiary suit provisions, empowering contract beneficiaries or other interested parties to sue for breach of contract. In the domestic context commentators regularly call for an expansion of third-party beneficiary suit provisions[131] (which courts generally refuse to imply unless clearly specified in the contract),[132] but such provisions remain rare. In the foreign affairs arena third-party beneficiary suit provisions are virtually nonexistent, and none of the Iraq contracts contains such a provision.

Contracts could also enhance whistleblower protections in order to strengthen enforcement. U.S. government officials currently receive whistleblower protection for reporting abuses in the negotiation or management of contracts, but employees of private companies are not protected under the general Whistleblower Protection Act.[133] In specific statutes, however, Congress has at times extended whistleblower protection to private employees, and the False Claims Act does protect from retaliation private sector employees working for a government contractor who provide information concerning the unlawful performance of the contract.[134] The act also provides for qui tam actions through which an individual can come forward and file suit on behalf of the federal government.[135] Such actions allow the whistleblower to potentially recover money if he or she is successful in exposing contractor wrongdoing. Significantly, however, the False Claims Act only applies to fiscal fraud and abuse by contractors; it does not protect employee whistleblowers who might report human rights or other abuses committed by contractors. Thus, the False Claims Act's whistleblower protections (and possibly its qui tam provisions as well) should be expanded in the foreign affairs context either by statute or as a default contractual provision. Such a change, combined with the availability of third-party beneficiary suits, would go a long way toward making sure that any contract-based efforts to provide accountability will have back-end enforcement to encourage compliance. Short of that, contractors could at least be required to provide their own private grievance mechanisms, which would afford some opportunity for those affected by a contract to complain about its design or implementation. I discuss all three of these possibilities—third-party beneficiary provisions, reforms to protect contractor whistleblowers, and the use of private grievance mechanisms—further in Chapter 5.

The Custer Battles Contracts

The Custer Battles contracts provide a stark picture of the sorry state of the U.S. government's contract management and oversight system in Iraq (at least in the early years of the occupation). In addition to the currency contract discussed at the beginning of this chapter, a second Custer Battles contract—to provide security at Baghdad International Airport—illustrates why the reforms suggested above are so urgently needed. Failures are painfully apparent throughout the process, from the slipshod way in which the airport contract was awarded, to the vagueness of the contractual terms, to the lack of monitoring, to the difficulties in pursuing enforcement. Indeed, authorities in Iraq had difficulty detecting—let alone preventing—the abuse. Looking back, Franklin Willis, whose responsibilities included overseeing contracts (his formal title was deputy senior adviser for Iraq's Ministry of Transportation and Communications and senior aviation official), describes a setting in which "our civilian CPA members were being pulled and tugged in all directions and no one had time to supervise a 'small' $16 million contract."[136]

The problems began with the contracting process itself. Just before Willis arrived in Iraq in July 2003, officials had awarded the airport contract to Custer Battles in great haste. It was not one of the many noncompetitive contracts handed out in this period, but because the competition among firms was so brief and limited, it might as well have been. The Request for Proposals (RFP) was issued in June, and companies had only "three or four" days to submit proposals. Because Custer Battles was the only company that said it could provide a security team by July 15, as the RFP requested, the firm received the contract. To be sure, there was an urgent need for security and logistic support. Yet, in Willis's view "it is not clear . . . whether Custer Battles existed prior to this RFP, or had any experience providing security services anywhere." CPA officials paid Custer Battles $2 million out of its basement vault at the end of June, and another $2 million at the end of July, despite the fact that the contract was never given specific terms beyond the company's own proposal.

Moreover, the entire basis for the contract—the need to provide security at the airport—was no longer relevant by the time of the second payment because officials had by that time rescinded their decision to open the airport to civilian traffic.[137]

Ultimately, two contract monitors concluded that the contract should either be made more specific or terminated altogether. But every attempt to do so was thwarted by Custer Battles, and the monitors were hopscotching around the globe to oversee an unmanageable number of contracts. The CPA struggled to maintain staff members for more than a few months in particular postings. And no one really had the time to focus on this particular agreement. Willis attempted to convince CPA officials to dedicate a staff position to it, and identified a qualified air force civil engineer for the position. But despite air force support, Willis reports, "the CPA front office killed the request." According to Willis, the U.S. government "would have saved $4 million or more" if the CPA had agreed to this request. In the end, Willis reflects, "we simply didn't have enough people to do our job" and suggests that the five hundred or so at CPA headquarters should have been five thousand. For those who were there, "long hours and crises-to-crises management simply wore us down." Indeed, according to Willis, Custer Battles operated on the assumption that "they could outlast any civilian CPA employee who sought to supervise them."[138]

Because of the vague terms, Custer Battles employees appear to have had virtually free reign to "interpret[] their obligations solely by themselves and continue[] collecting on the $16 million." Moreover, by operating the security checkpoint, they controlled civilian access and "used their power to leverage other business interests." On one inspection, for example, Willis observed "beds for more than 150 Filipinos crammed into a few offices in the airport's Terminal D," which had been diverted for Custer Battles catering services and a dog kennel for another of the firm's businesses.[139]

Enforcement proved difficult as well. Because the claim involved fraud and abuse, several whistleblowers were able to file a qui tam suit against the company under the False Claims Act. After the trial, a jury returned a verdict against Custer Battles, but the Court of Appeals ultimately dismissed this claim (even while permitting claims based on the currency contract to stand), in part because the vagueness of the contractual terms left an insufficient basis for deciding that Custer Battles had not adequately performed.[140] And to be fair, much of the blame for the alleged cost overruns can be attributed to the CPA, which created an environment devoid of oversight. Moreover, the aim here is not to demonize Custer Battles or any other particular firms. Rather, the key aim is that post hoc enforcement, while perhaps spurring future reforms, is not a substitute for a better contract regime that includes improved contract terms, monitoring, and oversight.

The contracts that are the very engine of privatization provide an important locus for accountability and constraint. Drawing on the far more extensive domestic administrative law literature on the subject, this chapter has identified a variety of provisions that could be incorporated into such contracts. These provisions seek to encourage compliance with (and enforcement of) human rights and humanitarian law, ensure transparency and democratic accountability, and promote norms against corruption, waste, and fraud. Taken together, they provide a menu of options for regulators, activists, policy makers, and scholars who are concerned about the potential for abuse in our current contracting processes.

Of course, governments may be hesitant to insist on some of these contractual provisions. For example, officials may fear that such requirements could unduly increase the costs of privatization both to the contractor and to the government entity overseeing the contract.[141] Or, more cynically, resistance might stem from the fact that governments actually benefit from a more opaque process with less public oversight. In any event, one seeming difficulty with relying on contractual provisions is that the increased oversight will be included in contracts only as a "matter of legislative or executive grace," and therefore can be rescinded or limited at any time.[142]

Yet, such objections do not render a contractual approach unrealistic. To begin with, concerns about the cost of additional contractual requirements may well be overstated. As the Custer Battles example makes clear, in many cases better oversight could actually save the government far more money than it costs. And as to concerns that added contractual provisions will cause contractors to walk away or prohibitively raise their rates, the short answer is that far more empirical work must be done to assess whether such dire predictions are accurate. After all, it seems quite unlikely that contractors bidding for these extraordinarily lucrative contracts with governments such as that of the United States will pull out of the process just because of some added contract requirements. To the contrary, the government should, by all rights, have tremendous leverage in the contracting process because there are unlikely to be competing customers similarly able to offer billions of dollars in contract awards. Indeed, while government contractors in the past have often raised concerns about increased compliance costs as a way of objecting to enhanced contractual oversight,[143] at least one commentator has challenged such claims, noting the absence of compelling evidence that increased oversight has actually resulted in a significant number of firms refusing to do business with the government.[144]

In addition, while some governmental officials surely would prefer a more opaque process, governments are not monolithic entities, and proposals such as the ones outlined in this chapter may be taken up and championed by members of the bureaucracy, even without the imprimatur of higher level executive branch officials or the legislature. Moreover, it is incorrect to think that more robust contractual monitoring can only come about through official executive branch or legislative action. First of all, some of the proposals for monitoring of contracts and accreditation or rating of contractors could be undertaken by NGOs or other groups without any official action whatsoever. For example, the International Committee of the Red Cross has joined with the government of Switzerland to craft standards for governments that hire contractors to perform military and security tasks.[145] Such an initiative could be paired with an accreditation scheme to evaluate those bidding for the contracts themselves. And while such evaluations might not initially have the power of the state behind them, the example of NCQA indicates that, over time, governments can be convinced to adopt a previously unofficial rating system as their own. Second, even if governments never adopted the standards, simply the process of evaluating and accrediting contractors would provide a rich source of public information about privatization that could be used to bring popular political (or economic) pressure to bear on noncompliant contractors. Such public reporting might also allow citizen watchdog groups (or even competing contractors) to monitor the effectiveness of particular contracts, publicize deficiencies, and lobby government officials for change.[146] Third, advocacy at the international level could result in treaties or other international regimes that actually require governments to include oversight provisions in certain categories of contracts, thus creating increasing pressure for change. In any event, as the domestic examples demonstrate, governments and agencies can, at least at times, be mobilized to require meaningful contractual oversight. And, as noted previously, some security contractors actually favor reforms along the lines suggested.

In the end, whatever the drawbacks of a contractual approach, they are certainly no greater than the weaknesses of the existing formal transnational or international court systems. Indeed, the use of contractual provisions has the benefit of opening up the possibility of legal enforcement regardless of whether or not there is state action and to provide the foundation for legal action in domestic, as well as international, forums. Such contractual mechanisms might also pave the way for statutes and treaties. Thus, scholars, activists, and advocates should spend at least as much time studying and lobbying for contract-based compliance regimes as they do seeking further openings for international or transnational litigation.

5

PUBLIC PARTICIPATION / PRIVATE CONTRACT

DynCorp International is one of three major companies that have provided security for U.S. State Department diplomats in Iraq. But in addition, the firm has quietly built a military logistics support and foreign aid empire that ranges from the coca crops of Colombia to the opium fields of Afghanistan, from the police forces of Haiti and Bosnia to those of Afghanistan and Iraq. In 2008 the firm posted an annual revenue of $2.14 billion and employed fifteen thousand workers worldwide.[1] In Iraq and Afghanistan, DynCorp has held critical contracts to train the Iraqi and Afghani police, among other responsibilities.[2] Yet, though DynCorp has earned praise in some quarters for its efforts,[3] numerous problems have persisted as the firm has undertaken to fulfill its obligations under these agreements.

Significant overbilling and waste have been rampant. A 2007 report by the Special Inspector General for Iraq Reconstruction (SIGIR) concluded that the State Department paid $43 million to DynCorp to build a residential camp for police training personnel outside Baghdad's Adnan Palace grounds, even though the camp was not used. Further, the SIGIR found that $4.2 million of the money was improperly spent on twenty VIP trailers and an Olympic-size pool, all ordered by the Iraqi Ministry of the Interior but never authorized by the United States. The report also criticized the firm for failing to keep proper track of equipment, including weapons.[4]

Other investigations have suggested that the contractors failed to train the Iraqi and Afghani recruits effectively. For example, a joint report released in December 2006 by the State Department and Pentagon Inspectors General concluded that the American-trained police force in Afghanistan was largely incapable of carrying out routine law enforcement work, and that the managers of the program could not say how many officers were actually on duty or where thousands of trucks and other equipment issued to police units had gone. Indeed, most police units had less than 50 percent of their authorized equipment on hand as of June 2006, and no effective field training program had been established.[5]

Experts also criticized the DynCorp effort, charging that the firm failed to vet its own trainers with sufficient rigor. For example, a report published by the U.S. Institute of Peace (USIP) in April 2004 expressed concern that the contractor trainers, drawn from a range of local police forces nationwide, come "from unique regional law enforcement subcultures that often do not prepare them for the unique challenges in stability operations." Thus, despite the nine-day training course, the authors of the USIP report questioned whether such preparation was sufficient. The report emphasized that the police trainers often carried weapons and that there had also been "serious incidents of misconduct" with virtually no legal accountability other than repatriating the offending police trainer. For these reasons, the report recommended the establishment of a professionalized U.S. force, ready to deploy to conflict zones, and suggested that the use of contractors should be confined to "ad hoc" circumstances.[6]

Similarly, a Rand report, while not calling for an end to contracting, emphasized that there "was wide variation in the quality of DynCorp police trainers." The report noted that while "some had significant international police training experience and were competent in dealing with police in a tribal society in the middle of an insurgency," many others "had little experience or competence." The report further criticized the DynCorp program for failing to ensure that the Afghani recruits, after participating in classroom training sessions, received in-field mentoring.[7] *Ali Ahmad Jalali, who served as the interior minister of Afghanistan from 2002 to 2005, said that the expertise of some DynCorp advisers was mixed: "They were good on patrols in Oklahoma City, Houston or Miami . . . [b]ut not in a country where you faced rebuilding the police force."*[8]

These problems have arisen in a context in which there has been little public participation or transparency in the contracting process. Indeed, not only have members of the general public had difficulty in obtaining information about the DynCorp contracts, government officials charged with overseeing the contracts could not even locate copies of the contract documents themselves![9] *In addition, the DynCorp contracts demonstrate how contracting out functions like police training can fragment authority and raise questions about cronyism and corruption, further undermining broader public participation.*

As this example illustrates, foreign affairs contracting raises serious concerns about public participation and transparency (which for simplicity's sake I will often refer to collectively as public participation). Significantly, public participation is simultaneously a value in and of itself—reflecting the view that people affected by an activity should have some input into how that activity is carried out—and a mechanism for either accountability or constraint.[10] For example, if various populations are able to participate in the formulation and critique of future plans of action, such participation may well impact the actions ultimately undertaken. Just as contractual arrangements may be structured to protect and promote public law values, so too public participation may be harnessed to restrain governments from abuses and help to protect other public values, such as human dignity and anticorruption.[11]

This chapter explores the relationship between foreign affairs privatization and public participation. Initially, I survey the administrative law and political science literature and—drawing on examples primarily from Iraq and Afghanistan—I argue that outsourcing has made public participation more difficult by fragmenting authority and responsibility, reducing transparency, and creating the risk of cronyism. I also consider the even greater lack of participation by affected populations abroad.

Next, I outline a number of possible responses, including not only potential governmental initiatives to increase transparency but also ways we might use the private law instruments of contract and trust to create more opportunities for public participation. Of course, governments may outsource foreign affairs precisely to avoid oversight; therefore, proposals to increase public participation are likely to meet with resistance. Nevertheless, public participation initiatives can at times be at least marginally successful, and I therefore discuss the ways in which the World Bank's International Finance Corporation inserted public participation requirements into its financing agreements for a pipeline in Chad. Such initiatives could become more common, particularly if nongovernmental organizations (NGOs), international organizations, and concerned members of domestic bureaucracies focus on exerting pressure for their enactment. Finally I revisit the example of the DynCorp contracts to build the local police forces in Iraq and Afghanistan. I explore how such contracts (and their oversight regime) could better incorporate the same sorts of public participation requirements as in the World Bank scheme. This discussion suggests that although outsourcing poses serious risks from the standpoint of public participation, it does also present openings for fostering participation in the international realm.

Delegation, "Double Delegation," and Privatization

Public participation has long been a central preoccupation of administrative law, a context in which government-run administrative agencies exercise important policy-making responsibility without a direct democratic check by legislatures.[12] Indeed, the so-called delegation problem in administrative law arises specifically from the concern that legislatures may weaken public participation when they confer authority on administrative agencies.[13] Accordingly, much of domestic administrative law is concerned with increasing public awareness, participation, and oversight through statutes and doctrines such as the Freedom of Information Act (FOIA),[14] the Federal Advisory Committee Act,[15] inspector-general oversight,[16] whistleblower protection statutes,[17] civil service conflict-of-interest rules,[18] notice and comment rule making,[19] judicial review of agency decision making under the Administrative Procedure Act,[20] and even the First Amendment.[21] Significantly, the administrative law view of public participation is not simply about making sure a voting polity ratifies all governmental decisions.[22] Rather, it is concerned with ensuring that there is some sort of dialogue, even if informal, between the government and the governed to act as a check on power and guard against the possibility of capture by interest groups.[23] In this scheme, transparency is both an end in itself and a central element of political participation and accountability because transparency helps to maintain a feedback loop between government actors and those affected by government policy, despite the fact that agency officials do not themselves stand for election.[24]

In the international and transnational sphere, political scientists and others have worried about state delegations to multilateral organizations such as the World Trade Organization, the World Bank, and the United Nations because such delegations of authority are seen as even less amenable to public participation than are domestic delegations, where power is at least somewhat constrained by democratic processes. Their responses take various forms. Robert Dahl, for example, has suggested that public participation values are inevitably undermined by delegations to international organizations and therefore such delegations are only justified if the need for interdependence and cooperation outweighs the loss of participation.[25] Others, such as Richard Falk and Andrew Strauss, refuse to accept this loss of public participation and argue for forms of global democracy.[26] However, Ruth Grant and Robert Keohane respond that such a proposal is unworkable because there is "no large and representative global public, even in the relatively weak sense of a global 'imagined community.'" They therefore take a different tack and argue that international institutions are not necessarily as nonresponsive to democratic checks as Dahl or Falk and Strauss assume. To make this argument, Grant and Keohane seek to disaggregate accountability into two types—participation and delegation—and they suggest that power wielders such as international organizations may act pursuant to forms of delegatory accountability even if they are not checked by more direct forms of participation.[27] According to this view, international organizations can function as trustees of the polities that entrust them to act on their behalf. Along similar lines, Benedict Kingsbury, Nico Krisch, and Richard Stewart argue that increased global interdependence has spawned a global administrative space; accordingly, an administrative law framework attuned to the global sphere might offer means of taming and controlling this new form of power. Such global administrative law seeks to reinscribe standards of transparency, public participation, accountability, and constraint.[28]

All of these concerns about authority being delegated to domestic or international administrative agencies, organizations, or bureaucrats are potentially heightened when we turn to privatization, which is in effect a "double delegation."[29] In the domestic setting, administrative law scholars have long worried that privatization of various governmental functions such as prisons, health care, education, and welfare can further erode public participation.[30] For example, sunshine laws, whistleblower protections, notice and comment rule making, judicial review, and First Amendment protections tend not to apply to the acts of private contractors or their decision-making processes.[31] Some scholars have also expressed broader concerns that political debate might be skewed if private entities control large swaths of formerly bureaucratic sectors such as prison management because such entities might come to wield a disproportionate amount of political clout, thereby overwhelming any views that might be expressed by representatives of the public at large.[32]

Turning to foreign affairs functions, outsourcing likewise potentially increases concerns about transparency, public participation, accountability, and constraint. Even with regard to those populations *within* a country projecting its power overseas, foreign affairs outsourcing appears to threaten public participation values and processes. More specifically, outsourcing amplifies three of the core concerns experts have long voiced about the expansion of the administrative state. First, oversight and public participation are more difficult when the size and number of agencies have grown, thereby fragmenting authority and reducing accountability. Second, relevant oversight information may be inaccessible or unusable. Third, agencies may be subject to capture by interest groups and corporations they are purportedly supposed to regulate. Outsourcing significantly worsens each of these problems, arguably straining our existing legal framework past its breaking point. Finally, with respect to populations *outside* the country projecting its power, all of these problems are potentially even greater. I address each of these concerns in turn.

Too Many Agencies, Too Little Responsibility

When agencies proliferate, and their staffs increase in number, oversight may become more difficult. With multiple actors responsible for various aspects of an activity, the work of the government becomes more opaque and less transparent. Public participation suffers because it is difficult to determine which agency is really responsible when multiple agencies address a particular problem. Accordingly, individuals and groups will have a far more difficult time either influencing the agencies directly—through notice and comment procedures, for example—or indirectly through their congressional representatives, who themselves may have a harder time keeping track of what a large number of different agencies are doing. The various agencies may also have difficulties pursuing a given policy agenda when multiple organizations with different cultures and interpretations of that agenda work at cross-purposes.

If each of the multiple agencies in turn uses multiple contractors to perform its work, the number of pieces in the governance picture increases exponentially. Instead of a two-, three-, or four-piece puzzle, we find instead something like a twenty-thousand-piece jigsaw puzzle that would take years to assemble. Under such conditions, even members of Congress and civil society groups—let alone individual U.S. citizens—have a hard time keeping track of the kind of work that contractors are doing.

A striking example of these difficulties has been the failure of many agencies up to the present day even to keep count of the number of contractors in Iraq and Afghanistan. Indeed, since the beginning of the Iraqi conflict none of the agencies that have hired such contractors could give Congress an accurate account of the total number of contractors hired or deployed. A provision of the 2008 Defense Authorization Act[33] mandated that the Department of Defense (DOD) take charge of counting contractors, but as recently as 2009, many years into the Iraqi operation, the government still had no adequate system even to track how many of its own private contractors are in the country.[34] In addition, when a firm working under an agreement with an agency such as the DOD hires a contractor itself, the agency does not consistently include those subcontractors in its tally.[35]

One of the most telling examples of the agencies' failure to keep track of contractors involves the case of Andrew J. Moonen. Moonen had served in the Army's 82d Airborne Division from April 2002 to April 2005, after which time he went to work for Blackwater USA under its contract to protect State Department diplomats.[36] On Christmas Eve, 2006, he allegedly shot and killed an Iraqi security guard.[37] According to a report compiled by the U.S. House of Representatives Oversight and Government Reform Committee, Moonen was off duty when he got drunk and passed through a gate near Prime Minister Nuri Kamal al-Maliki's compound in the Green Zone.[38] When bodyguards of Iraqi vice president Adil Abdul Mahdi confronted him, Moonen "fired his Glock 9-millimeter pistol, hitting one of the guards, Raheem Kahlif, three times." Khalif later died in an American military hospital. Meanwhile, Moonen fled to a guard post staffed by employees of another private security firm, Triple Canopy. He told them he had been "in a gunfight with Iraqis who were chasing him and shooting at him," though the guards did not hear any shots. The next day, he told Army investigators that he had fired in self-defense after the Iraqi bodyguard shot at him. Blackwater flew him out of the country on December 26, and subsequently fired him.[39] Less than two months later, a DOD contractor, Combat Support Associates, hired him to work in Kuwait, where he spent seven months from February to August 2007. A company spokesman said it was unaware of the December incident when it hired him. Meanwhile, the Army, also apparently unaware of the incident, actually tried to call Moonen back into service.[40]

Even if the agencies were to accurately count the number of contractors, keeping abreast of their activities presents yet greater challenges. As discussed in the previous chapter, the woefully understaffed contract management personnel have struggled to oversee contractors in the field, with one contract officer sometimes supervising hundreds of contracts. Few such contract officers want to work in the danger zones of Iraq and Afghanistan, and those who do so rarely stay for very long. The high turnover and lack of expertise that result makes oversight even more difficult.

Consequently, as noted in Chapter 4, agencies have often outsourced parts of the oversight role itself. For example, it is a security contractor, Aegis, that for a number of years had the responsibility to coordinate military contractor activities and monitor incidents in which contractors used force in Iraq.[41] Yet, a 2005 report by the SIGIR found that Aegis failed to vet Iraqi employees or demonstrate that its operators were qualified to use the weapons they were issued. The report concluded that "there is no assurance that Aegis is providing the best possible safety and security for government and reconstruction contractor personnel and facilities as required by the contract."[42] Despite this report, Aegis beat out six other private security companies in September 2007 to renew and expand its contract for an additional two years, at $475 million.[43]

Not surprisingly, a regime in which contractors monitor contractors has fallen prey to serious problems. This is in part because the contractors themselves underreport the number of serious incidents.[44] Ironically, some of this underreporting may be precisely because the oversight centers were for a period of time managed by Aegis, a potential competitor. Indeed, Andy Melville, the head of operations in Iraq for Erinys, a British security firm, told *Frontline* in 2005: "What we do is classified. We don't wish other security companies to know what our clients are, where we're operating, and a very valid concern that we have is that it could give them a competitive and a commercial advantage over us."[45]

Beyond simply the problems of underreporting, an additional concern is that the entire reporting system is not designed to address accountability for injuries to civilians. In a 2008 study of declassified incident reports, Human Rights First determined that a majority of the cases reported during the period of study involved situations in which the contractors perceived threats to themselves, rather than situations involving their own conduct toward others. Indeed, for a number of years there was not even a specific category in the report template for cases in which local civilians were injured. As a result, the reports were not "particularly useful for monitoring, reviewing, or investigating contractor use of force."[46]

A Lack of Transparency

Sunshine laws help make government activities more transparent, and thereby increase public participation. The foundational sunshine law is the federal FOIA, which gives individuals and organizations the right to request government information. Enacted in 1966 and expanded in the aftermath of the Watergate scandal, the statute presumes that each request deserves to be honored; accordingly, the burden is on the government, not the public, to explain why information may not be released.[47] Moreover, the right of access is enforceable in federal court.

To be sure, there are significant exceptions to disclosure for matters affecting national security. For example, FOIA exempts matters that are "specifically authorized . . . by an Executive order to be kept secret in the interest of national defense or foreign policy" and are "properly classified" as such. In addition, the CIA, the National Security Agency (NSA), and a few other agencies are allowed to exempt their working files from the search and review requirements of FOIA.[48] Yet despite these exceptions, the statute has paved the way for the release of numerous documents that have shed light on government security practices. Indeed, during the administration of George W. Bush numerous groups used FOIA requests to discover information about the treatment of detainees and stimulate public discourse on the issue.[49]

Whistleblower laws also promote transparency by protecting government employees from being fired when they go public with information about government misconduct. As noted in Chapter 4, the primary federal statute that protects employees at most federal agencies is the Whistleblower Protection Act, which shields government employees from retaliation when they disclose a broad range of information about governmental misconduct or abuse.[50] Significantly, the type of information covered by the statute includes not only "the violation of any law, rule, or regulation" but also any information that demonstrates "gross mismanagement, a gross waste of funds, an abuse of authority, or a substantial and specific danger to public health or safety." Moreover, there need not be a formal violation of law or even actual mismanagement. All that is required is that the whistleblower reasonably *believe* that the information points toward such misconduct. The only limitation is that the information the employee seeks to disclose cannot otherwise be subject to enforced secrecy by statute or executive order. Even so, employees may disclose wrongdoing based on such information to agency inspectors general.[51] And although employees at intelligence agencies such as the Defense Intelligence Agency, the CIA, the NSA, and the FBI are exempt, employees of other agencies who come forward are protected from retaliation, including firing and demotion. Indeed, they may bring claims in administrative tribunals, and ultimately in court, if they believe they have suffered retaliation.[52]

Other statutes also serve to increase governmental transparency. For example, as noted previously, the False Claims Act enables government employees, as well as contractor employees, to file qui tam lawsuits against individuals or companies that have defrauded the government.

Complaints remain under seal while the government investigates, and the government has an option to join in the litigation. Contractors found to have violated the False Claims Act are liable for triple the amount of damages incurred by the government, and the whistleblower also gets a share.[53]

In the foreign affairs area, federal employees have helped expose a range of governmental misconduct. One noted case involved Bunnatine Greenhouse, the former chief contracting officer of the U.S. Army Corps of Engineers. A Louisiana native, Greenhouse battled poverty and racism to become a successful teacher and then, after entering government service, rose to the top ranks of the procurement bureaucracy.[54] On June 27, 2005, she appeared before a congressional panel to criticize contracting practices in Iraq. Specifically, she charged that the Corps had violated its rules when it secretly awarded a five-year, potentially $7 billion contract for oil field repairs to Kellogg, Brown and Root (KBR), a Halliburton subsidiary. She noted that the Corps had hired the same company months earlier to draw up the plan for the job. She also claimed that officials had waived competitive bidding in granting an extension on KBR's contract to import oil from Kuwait, and that the company had charged too much for the oil. She described one of the contracts as "the most blatant and improper contract abuse I have witnessed during the course of my professional career."[55]

As it turns out, Greenhouse's experience is not exactly a triumphant story for whistleblower protections. Shortly after her congressional testimony, in August 2005, Army Corps authorities demoted Greenhouse in what her lawyer called an "obvious reprisal" for her revelations about the Halliburton contracts. On the other hand, her former bosses claim she lost her position because of poor work habits, and internal agency documents show that while she received high performance ratings for the first three years she held the job, other employees' opinions of her plummeted after the boss who hired her retired in 2000. Now stripped of her position in the Senior Executive Service, she works in a small cubicle where she has little responsibility. Still, it is clear that whistleblower protections did at least have some impact. Greenhouse did not lose her job completely, and her six-figure income has been cut by only $2,000 per year.[56] In addition, the FBI has launched an investigation[57] based in part on Greenhouse's claims, and some Pentagon reports[58] confirm her allegations. Thus, while whistleblower protections could obviously be strengthened, they do serve to bring at least some acts of potential misconduct to light.

Having briefly identified three statutory provisions that increase the transparency of governmental actors, we are in a better position to compare this regime to the one in place regarding the activities of contractors, as opposed to governmental officials. Here we find that the work of contractors performing foreign affairs functions for the U.S. government is far more opaque, and employees of contract firms have far fewer protections if they decide to come forward with information about abuse. The result is that citizens are far more likely to hear about, and be aware of, the acts of governmental entities abroad than they will be about similar acts performed by private contractors. Indeed, even the public research entity that provides information to Congress, the Congressional Research Service, reports that "the lack of public information on the terms of the contracts, including their costs and the standards governing hiring and performance, make evaluating their efficiency difficult."[59]

Weaknesses in the sunshine laws, as they apply to contractors, are part of the problem. While FOIA does give individuals the right to request information about the activities of foreign affairs contractors, its reach over the contractors is more limited than its reach over government actors. First, FOIA confers a right to view only government materials and not private business documents. Thus, in any case involving a contractor, there is a threshold question as to whether the documents even qualify as government documents. Second, in addition to any national security restrictions on government materials related to contractor activities, the statute grants an additional exception for "confidential business information." Thus, any government documents that might involve "trade secrets and commercial or financial information obtained from a person and privileged or confidential" are exempt.[60] As a result, any contract terms that could qualify as "confidential business" matters would not be open to public scrutiny.

Accordingly, although citizens and organizations have used FOIA to obtain information about foreign affairs contractors,[61] the information available is more limited than is information about agency conduct. Indeed, even members of Congress have complained about the difficulty of obtaining information about contractors. Representative Jan Schakowsky of Illinois, for example, has said that she was repeatedly thwarted in efforts to review State Department audit reports of DynCorp contracts because the department was bent on protecting DynCorp's commercial secrets. According to a DynCorp spokesperson, releasing government audit reports would make public cost-per-employee figures that could help competitors undercut DynCorp in future bids. Yet, as Schachowsky notes, the result is that "there seems to be no real interest in overseeing or reporting or holding accountable any of these contractors. And we're talking about billions of dollars of taxpayer money."[62]

Whistleblower statutes also provide weaker protections for contract employees than they do for government employees. For example, although federal law does prohibit reprisals against contractor employees who speak up about misconduct, the information disclosed must "relate[] to a substantial violation of law related to a contract."[63] Federal employees, by contrast, are protected when they speak up about violations of rules as well as laws, and even when they complain about gross misconduct that does not rise to the level of lawbreaking.[64] In addition, federal employees may disclose the information in question to the general public,[65] while contractor employees are protected only if they limit their disclosures to members of Congress, authorized agency officials, or the Department of Justice.[66] Finally, contractors have weaker options for enforcing their rights. If they believe they have suffered retaliation, they may complain to the inspector general of the contracting agency, but it is up to the agency head to decide whether to pursue a remedy against the contractors.[67] Federal employees, by contrast, may complain before administrative tribunals and seek judicial review of those decisions.[68] And although contractor employees may bring suits under the False Claims Act, just as federal employees may, these suits are limited to cases of fraud and do not include other types of misconduct.[69]

In order to see how whistleblower laws fail to shield contractor employees from retaliation, we can look to a striking case that arose out of the conflict in the Balkans. In 2002 two employees of DynCorp Aerospace UK Ltd., a British subsidiary of DynCorp International, blew the whistle on the sex-trafficking ring mentioned in the opening of this book.[70] The company had a contract with the U.S. State Department to provide police training in the Balkans.[71] Ringleaders had lured many of the hundreds of women working in Bosnia's sex industry from Eastern European countries such as Romania and Ukraine to Bosnia with promises of jobs as waitresses. They then delivered the women to brothel owners, who would confiscate their passports.[72] A Human Rights Watch researcher who traveled to Bosnia reported that "Bosnia was absolutely littered with brothels" staffed by women who had been sold as chattel for $600 to $700, "with all the rights of ownership attaching."[73] The two DynCorp whistleblowers, Katherine Bolkovac and Ben Johnston, alleged that other DynCorp employees had forged documents for the trafficked women, aided their illegal transport through border checkpoints, paid for sex with girls as young as fifteen, and tipped off sex club owners about police raids. Bolkovac also alleged that one DynCorp employee purchased a woman for $1,000.[74] And Johnston claimed that buying prostitutes, many of whom were underage, had become so common among DynCorp employees that he had to report the problem to the Army's Criminal Investigative Command.[75] In a subsequent deposition, Johnston reported on a conversation in which a fellow employee told him: "You can have [a woman] for 100 marks a night or buy them for two to three thousand marks . . . and they can be your 'hoes.'"[76] In April 2002, he told Congress that "DynCorp employees were living off post and owning these children and these women and girls as slaves."[77]

Yet, even as subsequent investigation substantiated these claims,[78] DynCorp fired Bolkovac and Johnston. Bolkovac, who was British, initiated proceedings in a British tribunal to challenge her firing under the British Public Interest Disclosure Act of 1998.[79] While DynCorp alleged that Bolkovac was fired for allegedly falsifying a time sheet and not for whistleblowing, the tribunal found in her favor, concluding that she had "acted reasonably" and that "there is no doubt whatever" that she was fired for whistleblowing.[80] In contrast, Johnston, a U.S. citizen, could only make a complaint to an inspector general because he was a contractor and not a governmental employee. In addition, he could not bring a suit under the False Claims Act, because that statute only addresses fraud cases.[81] Accordingly, Johnston was forced to try a creative legal argument, filing suit in Texas court under the Racketeer Influenced and Corrupt Organizations Act, alleging DynCorp employees and supervisors had engaged in various illegal activities for profit, including sex trafficking, and that the company had fired him for reporting these activities.[82] This case eventually settled.[83] Still, while Bolkovac was vindicated before a British tribunal and Johnston received a settlement, both employees arguably fared worse than Bunnatine Greenhouse, who was at least able to retain a position with comparable pay.

Other contractor whistleblowers have also fared poorly. David Vance, a Navy veteran, was working as a security contractor for the Iraqi-owned Shield Group Security company when he observed what he believed to be illegal arms sales—deals for land mines, guns, and rocket launchers sold for cash without receipts. He reported this information to the FBI. He said of his company: "It was a Wal-Mart for guns. . . . It was all illegal and everyone knew it." Shortly after he reported the information, he found himself stuck as an inmate in Camp Cropper, an American military prison outside Baghdad, classified as a security detainee. Like Ben Johnston, he found that his claims did not quite fit within the False Claims Act, and he had no viable claim to be reinstated in his job. So, after spending ninety-seven days in the prison, he could only file a lawsuit alleging illegal imprisonment and abusive interrogation tactics.[84]

These cases seem to be only the tip of the iceberg. KBR employee Julie McBride testified in Congress that as a "morale, welfare, and recreation coordinator" at Camp Fallujah, she saw KBR exaggerate costs by double- and triple-counting the number of soldiers who used the recreational facilities. She also alleged that company employees took supplies meant for a Super Bowl party for U.S. troops and used them instead for themselves. Yet, after she voiced her concerns, she reports, "Halliburton placed me under guard and kept me in seclusion . . . until I was flown out of the country."[85] Likewise, Gloria Longest, a former DynCorp employee, says she was fired when she came forward with allegations that the company routinely overbilled the government for expenses not permitted by the contract, including maid service and swimming pool care. She has alleged that the improper payments totaled "millions of dollars," and she has since filed suit under the False Claims Act.[86] Significantly, the U.S. Department of Justice has yet to join in any of these contractor whistleblower lawsuits. Accordingly, it is clear that even the flawed federal transparency provisions applicable to governmental activities are superior to the regime in place regarding contractors.

Cronyism, Corruption, and "Capture"

Experts have long worried that administrative agencies, particularly those whose main purpose is to regulate industry, are susceptible to improper influence. Outright corruption, when agency officials trade favorable policies for money and other perks, is a possibility. But so too is agency "capture." Because of collective action problems—it is more difficult for individual citizens to band together to articulate their interests than it is for industry and trade groups—agencies might fall prey to manipulations by the very industries they seek to regulate. Although industry representatives may not bribe agency employees outright, their ability to pour resources into advocacy efforts, and to foster personal ties and relationships, brings the risk of special treatment that may not benefit the public at large.

A broad array of federal laws and rules seeks to address this concern. In addition to criminal statutes that prohibit corruption,[87] other statutes and rules protect against conflicts of interest, and seek to limit the "revolving door" whereby federal employees work for the private sector after a stint in government and then return to government.[88] For example, these rules set time limits on the period after government service before a former government employee may work as a lobbyist.[89]

Outsourcing potentially increases the opportunities for favoritism and perks at the expense of the broader public interest. Accordingly, government contracting statutes and rules seek to foster bidding and competition in order to minimize both impropriety and the appearance of impropriety. For example, a former agency contracting official who leaves government to work for private industry must wait at least one year before being awarded a contract.[90] Yet these rules are plainly insufficient, as certain high-level officials are exempt,[91] and competitive bidding requirements are routinely waived for national security reasons.[92]

The contracting activity in Iraq and Afghanistan raises numerous conflict-of-interest concerns. Perhaps most notably, the administration of George W. Bush awarded billions of dollars of Iraqi reconstruction contracts to Halliburton, a company where Vice President Richard Cheney had previously served as chief executive officer and from which Cheney was continuing to receive "deferred compensation" payments of up to $1 million per year. Aides to the vice president emphasized that the payments were insured and therefore would be made regardless of how the company performed and that the vice president was not involved in the bidding process.[93] Still, critics charged that the ongoing financial relationship created at least an appearance of impropriety.[94] And many noted that during Cheney's tenure at Halliburton after a previous stint in government, the firm doubled its U.S. government contract work, as well as its political contributions (mainly to Republicans).[95]

Other members of the Bush administration also had close ties to the contractor industry. For example, when Donald Rumsfeld took office as secretary of defense in the Bush administration, he named executives from military contractor firms to head each of the three services: James Roche, the secretary of the air force was a former vice president of Northrop Grumman; Gordon England, the secretary of the Navy, was a former executive at General Dynamics, and Thomas P. White, the secretary of the Army, came from Enron.[96] Indeed, a study by the not-for-profit World Policy Institute found that the Bush administration, in its first year and a half, named to top policy-making positions no fewer than thirty-two people who were former executives, paid consultants, or major shareholders of top military contractors.[97] According to William Hartung, the author of the study, this pattern exceeded the number of industry-related appointees in either the Clinton administration or the administration of the first President Bush.[98]

Given the potential for conflicts of interest among key decision makers, it is perhaps not surprising that many of the companies that won contracts in Iraq and Afghanistan boasted top brass or former members of Special Forces teams as corporate board members or senior executives.[99] In addition, a 2007 Government Accountability Office (GAO) report concluded that in 2006 fifty-two major defense contractors employed 86,181 of the 1,857,004 former military and civilian personnel who had left DOD service since 2001. That number included 2,345 former DOD officials who were hired between 2004 and 2006 by one or more contractors. Although these employees may have complied with the law, the report concludes that "defense contractors may employ a substantial number of former DOD officials on assignments related to their former DOD agencies or their direct responsibilities."[100]

Of course, the existence of this revolving door does not necessarily spell corruption. Indeed, Steven Kelman of Harvard's John F. Kennedy School of Government has argued that, due to the low pay in government jobs, the prospect of a future career in industry is an important incentive for public service. "Given the lower salaries in government for senior people," Kelman has observed, "if you prevented them from having careers after they left government in the area where they worked, it would be harder to recruit and retain civil servants." Furthermore, he maintains that a stint in government can instill public values that then infuse the private sector when an individual shifts positions.[101]

Still, critics such as former senator Robert Byrd of West Virginia argued that such ties are "too chummy." Byrd proposed tightening the ethics laws in 2005 to require a two-year waiting period before a government contracting official could join a military contractor, or, if the official wanted to start work immediately, he or she would have to work in an affiliate or division unrelated to his or her government work. Senator Byrd's proposal would also have extended the rule to cover high-level officials. Byrd's effort stalled,[102] though it may be revived during the Obama administration.

Beyond simply revolving door problems, a 2004 report prepared by the Democratic minority staff of the House Government Oversight Committee found conflicts of interest among contractors hired to supervise infrastructure construction in Iraq. Specifically, as noted previously, the CPA not only outsourced many of the major projects to rebuild Iraq's infrastructure but also outsourced the task of *monitoring* the companies doing the rebuilding. Thus, by March of 2004, the CPA had awarded ten contracts worth an estimated $18.4 billion to companies to develop oil fields, rebuild the electricity sector, improve the water distribution system, and do other projects. At the same time, the CPA awarded contracts to seven companies to monitor these projects. The report, which examined two monitoring companies, Parsons and CHT Hill, found that "neither . . . is an independent watchdog" and that "each oversight contractor has significant conflicts of interest." For example, Parsons had close ties to Fluor, a company charged with public works and water projects. Indeed,

Parsons and Fluor were partners in a $2.6 billion joint venture to develop oil fields in Kazakhstan, and yet Parsons was charged with overseeing the work of Fluor. Similarly, CHTM Hill had "ongoing domestic contractual relationships with three of the firms" it was responsible for overseeing.[103]

Foreign Publics

So far we have looked at the ways in which the use of contractors may hamper the ability of interested parties within the United States to access information and participate in discussion and oversight concerning the scope of U.S. contractor activities abroad. However, the problem is even greater if we turn our focus to the populations in the host nations who are *directly affected* by contractors wielding the power granted to them by foreign states or international organizations. The foreign states sending the contractors, of course, are unlikely to open their democratic processes to these populations in the host countries.[104] If the affected people happen to live in a functioning democracy, such populations may be able to invoke their own domestic democratic processes to pressure their government to take diplomatic action. But even in those cases, influence is likely to be limited. And in states that are not democratic, or are barely democratic, the channels of participation are even fewer. Thus, for example, if the United States hires a contractor to build and service a camp for internally displaced persons (IDPs) in Sudan, and the firm's employees rape and intimidate IDPs in the camp, those IDPs have little recourse to democratic channels, whether in Sudan or in the United States. To be sure, Sudanese nationals might bring the case to the attention of international NGOs, which might publicize the abuse, lobby the U.S. Congress, or urge the contracting agency to terminate the contract or demand the firing of the employee in question. But such avenues will succeed only rarely.

These problems are not, of course, unique to contractor activities abroad. After all, the possibilities of public participation are likely to be almost as limited when foreign countries or international organizations intervene directly, *without* outsourcing. Thus, at least for affected populations abroad, the baseline of accountability is already reduced in the international context, making the turn to privatization perhaps less of a change from the status quo than we might first assume. Indeed, as the next section discusses, there may actually be some ways to build into the privatization agreements some transparency and public participation arrangements that would not be available when governments intervene directly.

Strengthening Public Participation in a World of Private Contracts

As discussed previously, public participation can function as a mechanism of accountability and constraint, and it is therefore not only a value in and of itself but also a way of safeguarding other values, such as human dignity and anticorruption. When considering activities abroad, however, the idea of public participation is complicated by the fact that there are always at least two different publics whose participation might be desirable: the community sending contractors abroad and the affected community in the host country. So then the question becomes: With regard to either or both of these communities, how might one build more public participation into the foreign affairs privatization process? And, assuming such mechanisms are possible, how might they be implemented despite inevitable governmental resistance to any oversight at all, particularly with regard to imperial projects abroad?

Public Participation in the United States

Turning first to the sending community, we might return to the conception of accountability through delegation. Here the idea is that the sending community delegates authority to a private contractor and could therefore always withdraw that authority, at least in theory. The success of a delegatory model, however, requires some degree of transparency and opportunity for public feedback in order to impose the requisite disciplinary check. Not surprisingly, then, much of the political science and global administrative law literature is focused on structural transparency and preserving opportunities for the lines of authority assumed by the delegatory model to operate effectively.

So, how do we better build in possibilities for public participation in an era of foreign affairs privatization? To begin with, we need to streamline contract management and unify oversight responsibilities so as to help eliminate the web of complex agency relationships that have muddled authority and thereby reduced the opportunities for public participation. To this end, something like the proposed Office of Rule of Law Operations,[105] might be a good idea, at least for contractors such as police trainers whose work relates to rule-of-law programs. Whether such an office is in the State Department, the DOD, or another agency, the key is that the policy direction and management supervision of all police training work should have one core home, with on-the-ground interagency teams working together to ensure that related agencies know what is going on.

Furthermore, whichever agency retains control, Congress should require regular reporting on the work of contractors. Such reports should go beyond intermittent fiscal reporting on how money is spent and include substantive evaluation of each contractor's work, its effectiveness, and any related problems, such as abuse of force by contract employees. Currently, agency inspectors can provide such reporting, but it is scattershot. While such reports require resources, they would likely improve the effectiveness of program management, and would channel information to Congress and the public at large. The State Department already provides an annual report detailing the human rights abuses of countries around the world[106] and another on the efficacy of other governments' attempts to prevent human trafficking.[107] Surely the department can also prepare a document evaluating the work of its own contractors.

Congress should also expand the reach of FOIA and other transparency rules, and improve protections for whistleblowers. Steps have already been taken in this direction. Sections 842 and 845 of the 2008 Defense Authorization Act enhance the reporting requirements of agency inspectors general and the SIGIR. When there is no competitive bidding for a contract, section 843 of the statute also requires disclosure of documents supporting the decision not to allow bidding. But the statute could go further, by simply mandating release of all contract terms except those that interfere with national security or companies' trade secrets. Such a provision would enable terms to be open for public comment and debate, rather than subject to the delays that FOIA requests inevitably encounter. Moreover, government officials should construe the national security and trade secrets exceptions narrowly, in order to foster maximum transparency. The 2008 Defense Authorization Act also broadens protections for

DOD contract employee whistleblowers, expanding the type of information that may be disclosed and giving employees a right to jury trial in federal court.[108] Yet the statute could go further still, covering contract workers employed under agreements with other agencies and allowing disclosure to the public at large, not just a specified list of governmental employees.

Finally, with respect to the appearance of cronyism and corruption, Congress could further limit the revolving door for government contracting officials and senior management and board members at contracting firms. Current statutes and agency rules create a confusing web of obligations with gaping loopholes. Most notably, the one-year cooling-off period for federal contracting employees is too short, it does not apply to employees with broad policy-making authority, and a covered employee may still leave government service to work for a firm to which that employee awarded a contract, as long as the employee works for a division of the company unrelated to the division that won the contract award.[109] Furthermore, while agencies used to keep statistics on employees who passed through the revolving door, they no longer do so. New legislation enhances transparency by requiring senior government contracting officials seeking employment with a contractor to first obtain an ethics opinion.[110] Yet the statute could provide an even longer cooling-off period, ensure that policy-making employees are covered, and eliminate the exception enabling employees to work for a division of a company different from the division to which they awarded a contract. Furthermore, the statute should require the agencies to report on the overall turnover to private business.

Public Participation Abroad

The reforms described in the previous section would help increase transparency and public participation in the community projecting its power abroad. But what of the community *affected* by contractor activities abroad? Here the "accountability through delegation" model will be less helpful because in most cases it will be difficult to say that the affected community in any way delegated authority to those carrying out the activity. For example, refugees do not delegate authority to build refugee camps. Accordingly, we are forced to consider alternative mechanisms to foster more direct public participation. But what sorts of participation are possible? Clearly, we cannot limit our vision to actual voting, because it will be rare for an affected population to have any direct voting authority over foreign affairs activities. Thus, we must focus more broadly on all forms of input by parties affected by governmental policies or practices, either before or after the fact, including any possible feedback mechanisms between affected populations and those who carry out the policies. Such feedback mechanisms obviously include direct voting, but can also involve consultation, representation by elected officials, and a wide variety of transparency initiatives that can help foster participation, representation, and interinstitutional (and NGO) oversight and monitoring. Finally, although, as noted previously, Grant and Keohane only consider a trusteeship model with regard to accountability exercised by the power-wielding polity,[111] it is worth considering whether we might profitably deem those affected by a privatization contract to be beneficiaries of a trust relationship as well. After all, a trust is a three-way interaction, which makes it a potentially useful way of including affected populations in the calculus.

Employing this sort of broad framework for conceptualizing public participation, we might find that foreign affairs outsourcing, rather than necessarily weakening possibilities for public participation, may actually *create* such opportunities. And while such participation is not a panacea, in some circumstances it could at least function as a marginally effective mechanism of accountability or constraint. For example, when governments or international organizations enter into contracts with private organizations, the contracts can require forms of public participation, which might include involvement in both the design of foreign affairs projects and their evaluation, as well as mechanisms by which affected populations can lodge complaints.[112] More broadly, we might come to envision international privatized activity as similar to the formation of a trust relationship, where the affected populations are considered the beneficiaries of the privatization arrangement, with at least some limited enforcement rights. It is true that the creation of such trust relationships might be seen as a paternalistic throwback to the colonial and postcolonial era.[113] Moreover, formal international law instruments mandating this sort of three-way relationship are unlikely to be adopted. Nevertheless, it is not inconceivable that individual contracts could include third-party beneficiary provisions and participation requirements. These contractual terms could effectively enshrine a trustee-beneficiary relationship, at least in some circumstances. And though the idea that a state such as the United States might have *any* public participation obligation to noncitizens overseas is a controversial one,[114] it is difficult to deny that providing opportunities for participation and feedback in some circumstances is at least an appropriate goal.

CONTRACTUAL MECHANISMS The agreements between governments and military contractors, foreign aid providers, and other for-profit and nonprofit groups can themselves promote public participation and accountability. In Chapter 4, we saw that such agreements can be structured to enhance a broader set of public law values, including norms of human dignity and the rational, noncorrupt provision of services. Here, we turn to two additional types of contractual provision that are of particular relevance with regard to fostering forms of public participation. Again drawing on the rich domestic privatization literature and using the publicly available Iraq contracts as a cautionary counterexample, I suggest, first, that at least some government contracts could explicitly include affected populations in their design, and second, that such contracts could strengthen public participation by providing opportunities for feedback (through a privatized adjudication regime or some other means) if a particular program goes awry.

Allowing for Beneficiary Participation or Broader Public Involvement in Contract Design Contracts could permit beneficiaries or the broader public to help shape contract terms and evaluate performance. In the domestic context, commentators have suggested that such beneficiary participation or involvement by the broader public could greatly enhance the extent to which contractors fulfill public law values.[115] Indeed, as Fred Aman has argued, precisely because privatization contracts are difficult to terminate and sometimes become "immutable," it is "important that the participation of the public and the public's representatives be maximized as early in the process as possible." He thus advocates allowing the broader public to play a role in the design of the contracts themselves.[116]

Some state and local governments have begun to adopt such suggestions. For example, Wisconsin's contracts with managed care organizations to provide health care to Medicare and Medicaid recipients include provisions for participation by community groups.[117] Other states have gone even further and now require broad public involvement in virtually all privatization decisions. In Montana, for example, any privatization decision must be made subject to a plan available to the public and open to public comment.[118] Other states have similar provisions.[119] And while it may make less sense to allow involvement of those noncitizens affected by military contractors overseas, due to obvious security concerns, beneficiary involvement or broader public participation in the design and evaluation of foreign aid contracts might be particularly useful.

The Iraq contracts are notably devoid of such provisions. Of the approximately sixty contracts publicly available as of 2005,[120] only three appear to contain any provisions that might be read as requiring beneficiary consultation or participation. For example, the agreement between the Army Corps of Engineers and Tetra Tech to provide munitions support and removal includes a provision requiring "public involvement." Specifically, the contractor undertakes to "assist in responsiveness summaries, public meetings, restoration advisory boards, community restoration planning, administrative record establishment and maintenance, and other stakeholder forums that facilitate public involvement."[121] A contract between the Army Corps of Engineers and Zapata Engineering to remove hazards in Iraq (and Afghanistan) to ensure that lands and waters can be used safely contains a virtually identical provision.[122] And an agreement between the former CPA and Washington Group International to improve power systems within Iraq provides for "public participation in public outreach activities."[123] Such provisions could be standard terms; yet in the Iraq context, contracts with such features seem to be in the overwhelming minority.

Despite the absence of such provisions in the Iraq contracts, governments, including the government of the United States, have to some degree incorporated forms of public participation in the design of long-term development aid. USAID, for example, has long allowed local beneficiaries and NGOs to help design development aid agreements, usually on an informal basis and most frequently when such agreements are negotiated through field offices. Agencies other than USAID, however, are less likely to engage in such consultation. The deficiencies in the Iraq setting may thus partly stem from the fact that USAID remained largely on the sidelines in the initial years, with most contracts being awarded through the DOD. Emergency humanitarian aid and postconflict reconstruction assistance are also less likely to incorporate such an approach, though the U.N. High Commission on Refugees has begun to explore the possibility of refugee and internally displaced person evaluation of refugee camp services and other humanitarian aid.[124]

The time is thus ripe to explore ways of involving in the contracting process itself those affected by foreign affairs agreements. To be sure, the type and nature of consultation can vary considerably. The decisions subject to participation can range from the initial decision by the relevant government agency *whether* to outsource a particular project, to the question of *which company or NGO* to use to deliver the services at issue, and once a private entity has been chosen, to decisions by that entity about *how* to provide the services in question. At the same time, the nature of the participation could include, at one end of the spectrum, mere consultation or notification of proposed actions, to taking views of affected populations that could factor into decisions, to giving particular populations a veto power or even voting rights on certain projects. Moreover, consultation and participation of this nature, outside state democratic channels, raises concerns about the relevant population to be consulted. Do conversations with local civil society leaders count as participation? If so, how can claims of selectivity be avoided? Are local town meetings a better approach? In postconflict settings where no viable state exists, such concerns are perhaps the most pressing. In authoritarian societies, such consultation may be forbidden or made impossible by the lack of a vibrant civil society. In any event, all of these issues require greater study and analysis. Nonetheless, explicit contractual terms would go a long way toward facilitating consultation with beneficiary populations, thereby effectuating through contract a broader form of public participation.

Encouraging the Creation of Private Adjudication and Grievance Mechanisms Contracts could also provide for complaint mechanisms that affected beneficiaries can invoke. As noted in Chapter 4, such contracts, at their most robust, could include third-party beneficiary suit provisions, empowering contract beneficiaries or other interested parties to sue in domestic courts for breach of contract. Alternatively, and perhaps more realistically, they could at least give beneficiaries the opportunity for privatized administrative hearings.

In the domestic context, many private aid providers are required to offer individual complaint mechanisms for affected beneficiaries.[125] Although these contractors are not state actors and would therefore generally be immune from constitutional review, such contractual provisions allow for notice and opportunity to be heard, thereby incorporating elements of constitutional due process. These private grievance systems are perhaps most evident in private prison contracts, which typically require such mechanisms.[126] But they appear in other contexts as well, such as health care. For example, the Medicare statute requires that health maintenance organizations receiving federal funding to cover their treatment of Medicare beneficiaries must "provide meaningful procedures for hearing and resolving grievances between the organization . . . and members enrolled."[127]

Foreign affairs contracts could provide for this same sort of privatized quasi-administrative process. While such avenues of relief would not likely be subject to judicial review, a privatized hearing process of some kind, established by the private contractor, would allow for some measure of due process and an opportunity for those adversely affected by the activities under the contract to give voice to their claims.

International organizations have been experimenting with such procedures. For example, the office of the U.N. High Commissioner for Refugees has entered into partnerships with hundreds of NGOs around the world for various services, including refugee protection, community services, field security, child protection, engineering, and telecommunications in emergency relief situations.[128] These contracts generally include provisions for feedback and participation by affected groups.

Similarly, the World Bank permits aid beneficiaries to bring grievances before special tribunals.[129] Civil society groups had long urged the World Bank, the largest multilateral development agency in the world, to respond more directly to local communities affected by Bank projects, rather than negotiating primarily with governmental officials in countries receiving aid.[130] They called on the Bank to establish an independent complaint mechanism to enable groups and individuals to protest Bank projects when those projects are alleged to violate Bank social and environmental policies.[131] In response to an intensive lobbying campaign that included hearings before donor government legislatures, the Bank adopted an Independent Inspection Panel in the summer of 1993.[132]

The panel mechanism has developed into a more or less independent reviewing forum that can be invoked by NGOs and other nongovernmental actors.[133] The panel, which consists of five independent experts appointed for five-year terms,[134] formally has only limited power. It needs Bank authorization to investigate a case, and its findings and recommendations are not binding because the board of the Bank retains discretion to determine whether to act on those recommendations.[135] On the other hand, the panel's report, the recommendations, and the board's ultimate decision are publicly available. Accordingly, pressure can be brought to bear on the Bank's management and board to follow the panel's recommendations.[136] Through 2004, individuals or their representatives had lodged nearly fifty complaints before the panel, the majority of which assert that the Bank violated its own policies requiring it to assess environmental harms, protect indigenous people, and prevent involuntary resettlement.[137] The panel had recommended investigation in fifteen of the cases it received, and the executive directors approved ten of these recommendations.[138]

The World Bank Group has also created a separate office of the Compliance Advisor Ombudsman (CAO) to handle complaints about two of its subsidiary entities—the International Finance Corporation (IFC) and the Multilateral Investment Guarantee Agency (MIGA)—that do not fall within the jurisdiction of the Independent Inspection Panel.[139] A somewhat more flexible, settlement-oriented mechanism than the panel, the CAO assists in dispute resolution, conducts independent audits to assess whether the IFC and MIGA are adhering to environmental and social policies in particular cases, and recommends practices to ensure that the IFC and MIGA will follow these policies in the future.[140] As of January 2006, the CAO had accepted twenty-five complaints and proceeded to the audit stage for six of those complaints.[141] Greater use of such measures, whether by international organizations, national governments, or by private contractors themselves, would greatly enhance public participation of those affected by the contracts.[142]

THE IDEA OF A TRUST RELATIONSHIP In Chapter 4, we saw that government contracts could be modified to include specific third-party beneficiary rights that could be actionable in domestic courts. Private grievance procedures similarly provide some opportunity for affected parties to be heard. Intriguingly, once contracts are written to provide such rights to third parties, they start to become very similar to trust agreements.[143] Indeed, the law of trust in its default forms already contains many of the features that contracts can be modified to incorporate through extensive negotiation and revision, including not only enforcement rights for beneficiaries but also fiduciary obligations on trustees.[144] Therefore, framing governments' and international organizations' agreements with private contractors as trust arrangements may reduce transaction costs and offer other distinct advantages as well. Indeed, although, as noted previously, Grant and Keohane discuss trust principles with regard to the potential oversight wielded by delegating governments,[145] such a model is perhaps more naturally applied to affected populations. This is because the trust is always a three-way relationship, making the trustee responsible not only to the delegating settlor but to the third-party beneficiary as well.

The trust is, of course, no newcomer to public international law. As part of the legacy of colonialism, states have long treated certain territories as trusteeships, and the international legal order has incorporated this framework. The League of Nations mandate system[146] and the U.N. trusteeship system[147] both provided for the administration of non-self-governing territories, primarily former colonies, by "developed" states acting on their behalf.[148] In each context, the international organization exercised supervisory control, through the Permanent Mandates Commission in the case of the League, and the General Assembly assisted by the Trusteeship Council in the case of the United Nations.[149] A central distinction between the two was the United Nations' explicit mandate to promote the "progressive development towards self-government or independence as may be appropriate to the particular circumstances of each territory and its peoples and the freely expressed wishes of the people concerned."[150]

Although the Trusteeship Council effectively suspended its activities when Palau gained its independence in 1994,[151] a number of scholars and policy makers have advocated a revival of the form for certain failed states and postconflict territories.[152] Steven Ratner, for example, argued not long after the end of the Cold War that the United Nations should assume trusteelike functions in postconflict territories.[153] More recently, Richard Caplan has contended that various forms of U.N. transitional administrations in territories such as Kosovo and East Timor might be construed in trust terms.[154] Rosa Brooks has suggested that, in view of the failure of many states, the international community might experiment with different forms of governance such as trusteeships rather than holding out quick elections and statehood as the end goal of conflicts and repressive regimes.[155] And Noah Feldman has argued that the United States should conceive of its role in the Iraqi occupation as a trustee.[156] Despite the important contributions that such scholars have made, each is haunted by the colonial underpinnings of trusteeship, as critics have charged that such proposals are tainted by imperialism.

While this project is inevitably similarly encumbered by the postcolonial baggage of the trusteeship form, I am attempting to escape at least some of its weight by focusing on the idea of the foreign government or international organization not as the *trustee* but rather as the *settlor.* It is my contention that the privatized relationship, which puts distance between the governmental actors and the beneficiaries in a relationship that is mediated by private entities, may, as a result, be more free of the colonial legacy and therefore be more attractive as a vehicle of public participation. Thus, while the law of the various postcolonial trusteeships is relevant to this project, I am focusing here on the way in which the law of the private trust might be used to adapt privatized foreign affairs relationships to give them public-regarding features that can, among other things, enhance public participation. Specifically, through the three-way relationship that is the framework of trust and the fiduciary obligations imposed on trustees, the trust as a form has significant potential to promote public involvement and accountability. It is to these features that I now turn.

The Three-Way Settlor-Trustee-Beneficiary Relationship One of the distinctive features of the trust is that it establishes, in its default form, a three-way relationship between a settlor, a trustee, and a beneficiary or groups of beneficiaries.[157] The settlor confers an interest on the beneficiaries, but they hold only a "beneficial" interest. The trustee owns the legal title and has a corresponding obligation to manage the interest. The trustee has a wide degree of discretion in discharging his or her responsibilities but must comply with the settlor's intent, as well as certain fiduciary duties designed to protect beneficiaries. Beneficiaries can, in certain limited circumstances, enforce their interests against a trustee whose decisions they do not like, but courts have applied fairly deferential standards. Historically arising as a mode of managing interests in land, trusts are now regularly used to manage multiple types of assets. They are touted for their flexibility, but because they separate ownership and management, they entail a certain amount of agency cost.[158]

Structuring foreign affairs privatization agreements as trusts, rather than as contracts, holds certain advantages stemming from the inherent three-way nature of the relationship built into the trust as a form. If the government funding a contract were conceived as the settlor, and the private organization fulfilling that contract were conceived as the trustee, with those affected deemed beneficiaries, the obligations of the trustee to the beneficiary would be encoded into the relationship itself. And beneficiaries have certain rights inherent in the relationship, rights they can enforce against the trustee. Thus, if the contract between the State Department and DynCorp to train police officers in Iraq were framed as a trust agreement, the Iraqi police trainees, or perhaps Iraqi citizens more broadly, could be seen as beneficiaries who would have some limited rights as against DynCorp for gross failures in the management of the program. Those rights would secure a measure of public participation for beneficiaries, with the trustee serving as a kind of representative of beneficiary interests.

To be sure, as John Langbein argues, contracts can be structured through third-party beneficiary provisions to establish essentially the same type of relationship. Indeed, some of the contractual mechanisms discussed in Chapter 4 would in fact create something similar to a trust. However, even if a trust is best understood as a three-way contract, the form still has advantages because, as a default, it eliminates the transaction costs required to add the terms into the contract.[159]

Moreover, the trust form arguably does even more than merely provide a template of a certain type of contract. The idea of trust conveys a sense of responsibility to its beneficiaries. To be sure, that responsibility is not always carried out. But even in the absence of strong enforcement mechanisms (which may well be the case in the transnational context), the idea of trust or trusteeship may *itself* structure the relationship in ways that exert an effect. At a minimum, the beneficiaries of the arrangement are automatically included in the agreement's terms. To use the Iraq contracts as an example, the virtual absence of provisions referring to Iraqi beneficiaries is striking. While such terms could be included, contract by contract, framing the agreements as trust relationships would automatically signal that those interests are, in addition to the settlor-government's interest, an essential part of the deal.

The Fiduciary Obligations of the Trustee The model of the trust is also appealing in the foreign affairs privatization context because of the framework of fiduciary obligations that the law of trust imposes on the trustee. Such a framework binds the trustee, but it also confers a good deal of discretion. Thus, beneficiaries can enforce their rights in extreme cases, but courts give a good deal of latitude to the trustee. This sort of delicate balance may be more difficult (and costly) to strike on a contract-by-contract basis. Moreover, the flexibility of trust is less likely to squelch the discretion that can enable contractors to innovate and thereby realize cost savings.[160]

At the same time that the fiduciary obligation permits a good deal of discretion to the trustee, it does exert a more robust constraint than the corresponding fiduciary obligations on corporate managers, which are notably weak.[161] For example, although the duty of care for corporations has—through the business judgment rule—been interpreted as a rule of considerable deference, it retains much more bite in the trust context. Indeed, courts have developed quite specific subrules to govern the conduct of trustees, including rules that require the trustee to keep and control trust property, enforce claims, diversify assets, minimize costs, furnish information to the beneficiaries, and so on.[162]

If applied in the foreign affairs privatization context, to be sure, many of these rules would not be sufficient to ensure public law values in general, or public participation in particular, because the rules primarily concern issues such as asset management. Even here, however, the rules about managing resources might serve as a useful constraint on corruption and waste. And disclosure rules promote transparency, which is an important element of the public participation feedback loop.

Moreover, because most foreign aid extends beyond the management of assets and includes, importantly, the provision of services, additional clarifying rules would be needed. The spendthrift trust, in which the trustee typically engages in decisions about wide-ranging aspects of the beneficiary's life, might offer a useful analogy. But an even more relevant set of rules might be borrowed from the fiduciary obligations of professionals such as doctors and lawyers. Indeed, David Luban has argued that a lawyer's role in a democracy is akin to that of a trustee for society at large, and as such that trusteeship promotes public participation values.[163] Of course, the development of such principles and rules to guide and shape all varieties of foreign affairs contractors is crucial. For this reason, the independent accrediting organizations discussed in Chapter 4, such as SPHERE and IPOA, are important because they seek to develop codes of conduct that may be incorporated, regardless of whether the model of contract or trust is used.

Case Studies in Public Participation

The Chad Oil Pipeline Project

The World Bank–financed oil pipeline project in Chad is an example of publicly funded private aid delivered to a nondemocratic regime. It demonstrates how aid-giving public agencies such as the World Bank can, through agreements with private actors such as corporations, influence those actors to seek public participation at the local level. Development entities' engagement with a local population might run along a continuum from (1) complete disengagement; to (2) mere notification to the affected population; to (3) an informal process of gathering feedback that could influence the design of the project or the extent of compensation to affected groups; to (4) allowing the affected population to exercise veto rights; to (5) allowing affected individuals to bring grievances through a formal grievance procedure; to (6) conferring full voting rights on affected groups. In this case, the degree of engagement probably fell between (2) and (3), although some formal grievance procedures do exist within the World Bank (even if such procedures are not provided by the oil companies themselves).

The World Bank required that the oil companies, as a condition of its low-interest loans, pursue grassroots popular consultations on many aspects of the project. Moreover, even before these loan agreements were actually signed, the mere knowledge of the Bank's requirements prompted the companies to seek local input. Thus, Exxon, the leading oil company in the consortium, engaged in extensive consultations with local groups during the research phase of the project, from 1993 to 1996.[164] Although the Bank had not, at that point, formally entered into the loan agreements, the prospect of Bank involvement shaped Exxon's approach. Bank guidelines on consultation with beneficiaries, as well as environmental and resettlement policies, "were gradually converted into internal documents to be used by Exxon's employees, subcontractors, and consultants." An Exxon spokesperson said at the time that "understanding the social map of the area where you are is very important."[165]

During this period, Exxon's subsidiary in Chad, known as Esso Tchad, sent sociologists, ethnologists, and various experts and consultants to the region. For example, according to Exxon, an American sociologist conducted 129 Human Environment survey village meetings, with more than five thousand participants, in the oil region. One Exxon document states, "The project has conducted one of the most extensive consultation efforts ever undertaken in Africa for an industrial development project. Few similar . . . projects in Europe or North America have held so many village-level public consultation meetings over such a wide area."[166] To be sure, as World Bank officials noted, the meetings during this period were more informational than consultative. Moreover, the meetings typically took place under military escort—even though the rebels in the southern region made it clear that they did not oppose the pipeline or seek to intimidate those who did—thereby limiting the possibilities for fully free exchange.[167]

Nevertheless, Exxon and the other consortium companies went beyond merely notifying local groups of the development project and actually began to incorporate feedback from those meetings into the design of the project. For example, in 1998, the oil companies sponsored a week-long conference with local NGOs to discuss the project. These NGOs raised concerns about both the amount of money the companies would provide in compensation for damage to natural resources (such as mango trees) and the fact that the proposed route of the pipeline passed through environmentally fragile areas. Within a year, the oil companies had agreed to increase the compensation amount and divert the route of the pipeline.

Despite these gains, NGOs remained concerned about the project's impact, and filed a complaint with the World Bank's Independent Inspection Panel shortly after the loans were first approved.[168] While the complaint generated a fairly hard-hitting report by the panel—and may have resulted in some greater attention being paid to environmental, health, and other concerns—most outsiders view the impact of the report as minimal.

The Chad case also illustrates the difficulty of achieving public participation or consultation with civil society groups outside formal governmental processes, and in particular the difficulties of such consultations in a nondemocratic society. As one World Bank staff member observed: "How do you define civil society? We try to listen and consult with all the people who have something to say. But this kind of interaction with civil society was somewhat new for us. Traditionally, we are used to dealing with governments: they are our clients. Civil society is by definition informal, not well defined. Finding responsible partners is not easy."[169] Moreover, in a repressive society, free and open debate is difficult. In such an environment, consultations in the presence of military personnel, as was the case here, have a chilling effect. The lead author of the inspection panel complaint, a member of Parliament, was thrown into jail and tortured after filing the complaint, demonstrating the high stakes involved for those who opposed the government position on the pipeline.

In the end, the construction of the pipeline continues to engender significant controversy, most notably due to concerns about corruption, the environmental impact of the project, adequate compensation of indigenous populations forced to relocate, increased spread of HIV/AIDS and other diseases due to the construction and operation of the pipeline, the ability of the government to spend oil revenues on poverty-reduction programs rather than weapons, and the risk of human rights abuses by a government keen to squelch opposition to the project. In the face of these significant problems, it would be hard to label the project a success. Nonetheless, the World Bank involvement did spur the oil companies to seek feedback from affected communities to a greater extent than they might otherwise have done—at least in comparison to similar extractive projects in Sudan and Nigeria in which the Bank did not subsidize the oil companies. In addition, it is important to note that the companies incorporated the feedback they received into the design of the project, at least to a limited degree. Finally, the Chad experience may provide evidence of a "representation-reinforcing" effect. Constituencies in democracies (such as the United States, France, and the Netherlands) voiced concerns about their own governments' support for the project through the Bank. Indeed, in the United States, members of Congress with strong Christian ties raised questions about the impact of the pipeline on religious persecution of the largely Christian population in the south of Chad and demanded Bank accountability. Such concerns arguably played a role in the Bank's increased focus on local consultation and its encouragement of the oil companies to engage in such consultation. Thus, the case provides an example of how agreements between public agencies and private organizations can become a site for various forms of at least somewhat effective public participation.

The DynCorp Police Training Operations Revisited

We now return to the example that opened this chapter, the contracts between the U.S. government and DynCorp International to conduct police training operations in Iraq and Afghanistan. Here the question is: Might there be ways in which we could build into the contractual arrangements greater transparency and more opportunities for public participation (both in the United States and in the affected country)? Let us see.

In order to understand the scope of the problem to be addressed, we need to recognize the range of DynCorp's operations and the difficulties DynCorp's contracts have faced. Founded in 1946 as two companies, Land-Air Inc. and California Eastern Airways, the firm has its roots in aviation equipment maintenance and freight service to Asia and the Middle East. By the mid-1990s, DynCorp began to take on what would become a major specialty for the firm: the recruitment and training of peacekeepers and police. The firm won a critical contract in 1994 to train, deploy, and support U.S. civilian police to serve as U.N. peacekeepers in Haiti. Then, during the conflict in the Balkans, the firm supplied peacekeepers in Bosnia Herzegovina and elsewhere. During the conflicts in Iraq and Afghanistan, DynCorp's police training work surged yet again, as the firm won lucrative contracts to train both police forces.[170] In Africa, DynCorp employees work for the U.S. State Department reforming Liberia's defense and security institutions, providing logistical support for the peacekeeping efforts in Somalia and Darfur, building infrastructure for the government of Southern Sudan, and providing advisers to institutions like the African Union and the Economic Community of West African States.[171] The firm has also reportedly secured a State Department contract to train Lebanon's Internal Security Forces.[172] According to DynCorp's Web site, the company has "deployed more than 6,000 law enforcement professionals for peacekeeping and police training duties to Kosovo, East Timor, Sudan, Liberia, Afghanistan, Iraq, with the Palestinian Authority in the West Bank, and other places trying to recover from armed conflict."[173]

DynCorp's police work shows no signs of flagging. In the fall of 2008, for example, the State Department issued a new task order for the firm, worth $317.4 million for a period of eighteen months, to provide police advisers to assist the State Department and the Combined Security Transition Command in Afghanistan to meet the U.S. goals of increasing Afghanistan's overall capability to provide police presence, improve public security, and support the rule of law. The firm also continued to expand its work in Haiti and Liberia, with new task orders worth an estimated $7 million. The new work in Haiti includes a mandate to train up to 444 Haitian national police, to procure basic nonlethal equipment, including vehicles and communications equipment, and to refurbish the main police station in Cité Soleil.[174] In Liberia the new contract includes a plan to train and equip up to five hundred Liberian National Police members who will establish an emergency response unit with the U.N. police and the U.N. Mission in Liberia. The project also involves constructing and renovating police buildings.[175]

In addition to its police work, the firm has been heavily involved in narcotics eradication and anti-drug-trafficking initiatives. In the 1990s the firm was a key player in Colombia, where the company supported Plan Colombia, a government initiative spearheaded by General Barry McCaffrey, the director of drug policy under President Bill Clinton and now a DynCorp board member, to fight the left-leaning guerrilla movement that was taking over much of the country's cocaine and opium trade and using the profits to expand their civil war. Under the contract, DynCorp sent employees to the region to dust crops and intercept drug smugglers, using Vietnam-era Huey combat helicopters with "mini-gun" systems that can spray out three thousand rounds of ammunition in one minute. In one incident, three DynCorp employees were killed in crop-eradication missions, and several employees were taken hostage. During the subsequent search-and-rescue operation, four American employees of DynCorp participated in a helicopter firefight against one of the most prominent Colombian guerrilla groups.[176] Concerned that these Dyn-Corp employees were straying beyond the terms of their mission, members of Congress held a series of hearings in which they accused the government of using DynCorp to carry out combat-related missions even though existing legislation prohibited the use of U.S. troops in the country.[177] To address the issue, Congress enacted legislation in 2000 limiting to four hundred the number of DynCorp contractors who could be present in Colombia at any one time.[178] More recently the firm has expanded its drug eradication efforts from Colombia to Afghanistan, and expanded from its police training work to a broad array of military logistics operations.[179] Thus, DynCorp's reach is truly vast.

Let us now turn to a closer examination of DynCorp's police training contracts in Afghanistan and Iraq. By doing so, we can easily see the risks such contracting poses to public participation. For the police training contracts, DynCorp recruits the typical trainer from local police forces around the United States. The recruit is then required to complete a nine-day Police Assessment Selection Process, conducted by DynCorp. As part of the process, the recruit undergoes psychological and medical tests, takes refresher courses in police skills and firearms, and receives briefings on human rights, foreign living, and the country of assignment. At the end of the course, the recruit learns whether he or she has been selected. Once deployed, the trainer is generally issued a weapon and can be authorized to shoot to kill in certain circumstances. The job can pay up to $118,000 per year in Afghanistan and $134,000 per year in Iraq, with a significant bonus at the end of the term.[180]

Once under way, the DynCorp training contracts have run into difficulties, including waste, overbilling, and training challenges. Some of these problems were undoubtedly due to the fragmentation of contract oversight responsibility discussed in Chapter 4. In this case, the State Department's Bureau of International Narcotics and Law Enforcement Affairs (INL) assumed initial control over the police training mission, and awarded the contract to DynCorp. The bureau directed the contract through its embassy office in Kabul. But due to concerns about mismanagement in the embassy, an interagency working group reorganized responsibility for the program, assigning "overall direction" of the police training programs to the military's Combined Security Transition Command–Afghanistan (CTSC-A).[181] Meanwhile, responsibility for "policy guidance" remained with the embassy's Chief of Mission in Afghanistan. The State Department's INL Bureau in Washington retained contract management authority and provided the CTSC-A with an embedded senior staff officer.[182]

Not surprisingly, this confusing web of responsibilities resulted in a host of contract management and oversight problems. Indeed, even as the military assumed operational control of the police training program, the CSTC-A "did not have anyone on its staff with technical knowledge of the Department of State's police training contract." Moreover, there was "still confusion at CSTC-A and in the embassy's INL office over what [was] contained in the Department of State contract and its numerous modifications." Even more shockingly, when the inspector general's assessment team requested a copy of the contract, no one could produce it, nor could anyone locate copies of the various contract modifications the State Department had made over the years during which it had been enforced.[183] In these circumstances, it is perhaps not a surprise that, one year later, the SIGIR concluded that the firm had charged the government for millions of dollars in projects about which the contract management staff were completely unaware.[184]

The tangled web of managerial relationships also created a lack of transparency and openness about DynCorp's work. As noted above, the terms of DynCorp's various agreements were not always even accessible to those supposedly monitoring the contracts. Some organizations—such as the Center for Public Integrity—and media outlets—such as the *Los Angeles Times*—used FOIA to request additional materials. Yet FOIA's restrictions, discussed above, meant that some terms remained undisclosed, because they related to business information. At the same time, the fact that multiple agencies were contracting with the firm enhanced the confusion, making it more difficult for Congress, interest groups, or the public at large to gain information.

The contracts also illustrate the risks of cronyism and capture—or at least the appearance of impropriety—that outsourcing poses, because many of DynCorp's senior management or board members had previously served within the Clinton or Bush administrations. For example, as noted above, General McCaffrey, the director of drug policy under President Clinton and a key architect of Plan Colombia, joined the firm's board of directors shortly after he left the administration. Similarly, Marc Grossman, a Bush administration undersecretary of state who helped implement the Colombian counternarcotics program, also joined DynCorp's board after leaving government service.[185] Of course, the mere fact that such a revolving door exists does not mean that firms will implement poor policies or that government agencies unjustifiably award contracts. Yet the thick web of relationships in this case illustrates how, given the small number of firms that could perform the types of tasks DynCorp has undertaken, the appearance of cronyism might arise.

Outside the United States, public participation by affected individuals is also weak. DynCorp does not appear to have a systematic, formalized structure for consulting with interest groups or individuals in Iraq. To be sure, the firm appears to have engaged in some ad hoc consultations with local actors. For example, in Afghanistan Interior Minister Ali Ahmed Jalali appears to have helped to vet some of the police trainers.[186] And in Iraq local officials contributed somewhat to the firm's decision making. Yet, in such circumstances ad hoc contacts without a clear formal mechanism for public participation might simply create problems of local cronyism (or the appearance of impropriety), the kind of influence that can beget luxury trailers and a VIP swimming pool.

Thus, the various possible approaches discussed previously might actually be useful with regard to DynCorp. Of course, one response might be to try to prohibit the outsourcing of police training missions altogether. As previously noted, the U.S. Institute of Peace report has, in fact, advocated this approach, proposing instead that the State Department establish an Office of Rule of Law Operations (ORLO), which "would have the permanent authority to recruit, deploy and manage constabulary units and individual police, judges, attorneys, court staff, and corrections officers in peace and stability operations."[187] Thus, this office would itself maintain a ready roster of police trainers and manage them directly in the field.

Yet, as discussed in earlier chapters, the contracting approach is already so entrenched that it will be difficult to dislodge, at least for the foreseeable future. DynCorp's contracts alone number in the dozens and are worth millions of dollars over many years. Thus, at a minimum the government will need to manage these contracts better while they run their course. And, of course, economic and other pressures might well delay any possible phase out. Thus, a more realistic approach would be to improve the public participation and transparency requirements of the contracts, even if one hopes ultimately to eliminate such contracts altogether.

How might such transparency and public participation initiatives be implemented? To begin, we need to streamline lines of authority and unify oversight responsibilities to help eliminate the web of complex relationships that currently exist. To this end, as noted previously, an office such as the proposed ORLO might be a good idea, but not necessarily to bring all of the police training operations back in house. Rather, whether it is in the State Department, the DOD, or another agency, the key is that the policy direction and management supervision of the police training work should have one core home, with on-the-ground interagency teams working together to ensure that related agencies know what is going on. Furthermore, whichever agency retains control, Congress should require regular reporting on the work of contractors. And expanding the scope of FOIA and increasing whistleblower protections for contractor employees will be necessary. New rules to require written justifications for circumventing the competitive bidding process may also help. Finally, Congress could further limit the revolving door for government contracting officials and senior management and board members at contracting firms, in order to try to diminish the pulls of cronyism.

As to the DynCorp contracts themselves, they could be reformed to include requirements that affected populations be involved in the design of the police training programs. Such involvement could take the form of broad consultative meetings with local officials and civil society groups, open "town hall"–style meetings, and the like. And while critics might point out that such consultation events are impractical when discussing military security contracts, there is no reason people in Iraq and Afghanistan cannot be consulted about the broad policies and frameworks to be pursued for reconstituting their domestic police forces.

In addition, the contracts could require DynCorp to establish private grievance mechanisms as part of their police restructuring and training efforts. Again, there is no reason such mechanisms cannot be created; certainly all domestic U.S. police forces have some sort of grievance or adjudication process for handling civilian complaints and whistleblower claims. And although these private dispute resolution mechanisms may not have much practical enforcement from the local court system (which is often in disarray in reconstruction settings), these forms of public involvement will be better than nothing and may contribute to local acceptance of the new police units.

Finally, the DynCorp contracts could be restructured as trusts that allow Iraqi or Afghan citizens to make third-party beneficiary claims under the contracts within the United States. Such provisions are likely to be the most controversial of the ones I propose. Yet, permitting such suits would go a long way toward making sure there is accountability for our government-contracted efforts abroad, and at least some transparency with regard to both U.S. and indigenous populations.

In short, a range of mechanisms is available to increase public participation in the design and implementation of private contractual agreements. Indeed, such mechanisms may even be more robust than when governments act directly abroad because participation requirements can be imposed, via contract. In any event, importing public participation norms into a world of private contracts is an underexplored avenue for imposing accountability and constraint.

6

UNIFORMED MILITARY LAWYERS, ORGANIZATIONAL STRUCTURE AND CULTURE, AND THE IMPACT OF PRIVATIZATION

It is Baghdad, circa 2005 or 2006. The U.S. military has turned over the operation of some of the checkpoints to the Iraqi Army, and at one such checkpoint, a contractor kills an Iraqi Army lieutenant. The contractor maintains that the shooting did not violate the rules on the use of force applicable to contractors, but nevertheless refuses to talk to military investigators. Instead, he asks: "What authority do you [the military] have to require me to provide a sworn statement?" Moreover, the contractor refuses to turn over a videotape of the incident.

The military investigators have to agree that it is not at all clear that they do in fact have any authority to investigate. And while the judge advocate pursuing the matter does not in the end reach a final conclusion as to whether this was a "valid shoot," the lawyer is troubled by the incident because it took place at a "fixed" checkpoint. The lawyer emphasizes that if the contractors "had had any sense, they would have known that," and the likelihood of an incident could have been minimized.

In the end, the military pays compensation to the family of the Iraqi lieutenant, who was a "well-respected individual." According to the lawyer, this is a big stretch as a legal matter because the compensation program was established for instances in which U.S. troops injure local civilians; it does not appear to include coverage of violence committed by contractors. Yet, because the contractor company could not be convinced to make a payment to the family, the judge advocate concluded that compensation was the *"right answer because U.S. personnel were involved in the shooting,"* even if it was *"wrong as far as the rules go."*[1]

So far, we have looked at whether legal and regulatory changes— either to criminal law, contract regimes, or democratic accountability mechanisms—might help protect core public values in an era of military privatization. This chapter explores a different approach, one grounded in the idea that organizational structure and culture have a real impact on compliance with public law values. Indeed, scholars of organizational theory have argued that organizations, through their structure, can have even more impact on members than external controls do. Thus, we consider the potential impact of privatization on the structure and culture of the U.S. military and other military and security operations abroad. In particular, we shall see that key actors within the U.S. military have tried, especially since the Vietnam War, to inculcate public values such as those embodied in the law of armed conflict and human rights law into military decision-making structures in order to shape a more law-abiding culture. These efforts have had some significant success. The use of military contractors may pose a threat to this military culture, both because the intermingling of contractors and uniformed troops on the battlefield may weaken public values within the military, and because contractors operating outside the military chain of command may themselves develop different organizational structures as well as a set of values that come to predominate in conflict and postconflict situations as contractors as-sume ever-greater responsibilities there. Thus, if we are to address how to maintain public law values in an era of privatization, we must take orga-nizational structure seriously and consider the ways it might be shaped.

Scholars have, in the domestic context, attempted to isolate structural features of institutions that might make them more or less likely to fos-ter a rule-abiding culture. As such, we might fruitfully begin to apply the insights of organizational theory to the study of international law compliance. This chapter therefore uses the framework of organizational theory to guide a qualitative study of international law compliance in what is perhaps the most fraught arena possible: the wartime battlefield. Through a series of interviews with U.S. military lawyers—many in the

Army's Judge Advocate General's (JAG) Corps but a few who were judge advocates in other services—I describe and analyze the mechanisms by which these lawyers, embedded with troops in combat and consulting regularly with commanders, have internalized and seek to operationalize the core values inscribed in the international law of armed conflict, in particular the imposition of limits on the use of force. To be sure, the lawyers are not always successful, and it would be simplistic to assume that their accounts prove that the U.S. military always obeys international law. But their stories support the idea that the presence of lawyers on the battlefield can—at least sometimes—produce military decisions that are more likely to comply with international legal norms.[2]

Just as importantly, their experiences suggest that military lawyers are most likely to function effectively and encourage legal compliance if certain organizational features are present. In particular the lawyers (1) must be integrated with other, operational employees; (2) must have a strong understanding of, and sense of commitment to, the rules and values being enforced; (3) must be operating within their own separate hierarchy; and (4) must be able to invoke a system that confers benefits or imposes penalties on employees based on compliance. These findings track the organizational theory literature about what makes compliance officers within firms effective. Accordingly, the experience of these military lawyers provides a useful case study for testing this broader theoretical literature and suggests links between organizational structure and legal compliance.

I shall begin with a brief introduction to some basic insights gleaned from the literature on organizational theory regarding effective compliance agents, as well as a look at the organizational changes initiated by the U.S. military after the Vietnam War that were intended to foster a rule of law culture within the military. I then present the results of my study of military lawyers operating in Iraq, focusing on the role that organizational structure and culture has played in the effectiveness of these attorneys and contrasting the military's regime with the organizational structure and culture of the private security firms. What emerges from this analysis is a far more nuanced understanding of how compliance with international legal rules actually operates on the ground. From this perspective, we can begin to see that fostering greater compliance may sometimes be less a matter of writing new treaty provisions or increasing the activity of international courts and more a matter of subtly influencing organizational structures and cultural norms. Moreover, only by studying organizational features can we hope to address a world where states are no longer the only relevant agents of international law compliance.

Organizational Theory and Military Culture

Organizational theory has not generally formed part of the study of international law compliance. Yet, as I attempt to show, this literature, particularly if further developed to focus on organizations and institutions applying international law norms, holds tremendous promise and could meaningfully reshape compliance debates. Of particular importance to our analysis here is how compliance agents within an organization—such as lawyers—can most effectively help ensure compliance with central rules and values of the firm as well as various public norms. Accordingly, I first summarize the contributions of organizational theory concerning the elements that make for effective compliance agents. Then, I turn to the U.S. military and describe efforts to create a rule-of-law culture within the armed services. In particular, I suggest that key actors within the U.S. military have tried, especially since the Vietnam War, to inculcate public values such as those embodied in the law of armed conflict and human rights law into military decision-making structures in order to shape a more law-abiding culture. These reforms have created structures that the organizational theory literature predicts would likely have some positive impact on compliance.

The Importance of Organizational Structure and Culture

Organizational theorists have long recognized that group norms and internal organizational structures can further (or hinder) an organization's goals, as well as the goals of individuals within organizations.[3] These theorists are a diverse bunch, and they span multiple disciplines, from law[4] to economics[5] to sociology[6] to political science[7] to anthropology.[8] Moreover, they study a wide range of organizations, from corporations[9] to private associations[10] to public bureaucracies.[11] Thus, it is difficult to generalize about this literature, and a detailed survey is beyond the scope of this chapter. Instead, I focus on some of the core structural features within organizations that the literature has identified as important in helping to ensure a culture of compliance with external norms, such as legal rules.

As Edward Rubin has argued, organizational theorists can perhaps be divided into four camps: those who view organizations as a nexus of contracts, those who understand organizations as complex decision-making hierarchies, those who see organizations as influenced by broader societal forces or institutions, and those who describe organizations as complex systems or organisms.[12] For our purposes, these theories are important because, despite their differences, each would predict that the structure of an organization and its culture will have distinct impacts on the organization's efficacy and the likelihood that actors in the organization will conform to external norms of behavior.

The first group, which includes economists such as Harold Demsetz, Michael Jensen, and William Meckling,[13] views organizations as simply a nexus of contracts or agreements between rational, autonomous actors. In this view organizations are simply the sum of the contracts that constitute them, and little more. Accordingly, this theory suggests that the terms of the contracts themselves would be the most important way to influence employee behavior. We have already discussed how the terms in the private security contracts could usefully be reformed in order to affect compliance. Further, as we shall see in this chapter, the formal, contractually established job duties of lawyers within an organization can also impact the culture of compliance that the organization develops.

Even more significant for purposes of this study is the second group—"decision theorists" such as Herbert Simon, James March, and Richard Scott,[14] as well as economists such as Douglass North and Oliver Williamson[15]—which views the organization as a decision-making hierarchy. According to this approach, the organization is much more than the sum of its parts: just as important is the formal governance structure of the organization, as well as the informal norms of behavior that cannot be captured in a contract. Moreover, this group acknowledges that individuals may not always make rational decisions, and identifies many ways in which the structure of a group or organization impedes individuals from making such decisions, contributing to "bounded" rationality.

From the perspective of decision theory, systems of "control, management, supervision, [and] administration, in formal organizations" are critical.[16] Accordingly, leaders within the organization can define and seek to fulfill the organization's purposes by giving incentives and setting penalties for the organization's members. In addition, the location of a decision within the organization's hierarchy will affect its impact on the organization's members. Employees may respond more readily to senior managers than to isolated corporate counsel; indeed, Sally Simpson has found that the idea of violating the law might have a positive appeal as an indication of aggressive business practice.[17] Nevertheless, as Rubin has noted, an internal compliance program that increases the size and authority of corporate counsel "will tend to increase the salience of the criminal law for operational employees," and their "uncertainty about the consequences of their actions may convince them that it is better to follow the instructions of the compliance personnel."[18]

Other structural factors are also important. For example, Serge Taylor, in a study of environmental regulation, found that the ability of compliance personnel to monitor lower-level personnel and then report back to higher-level personnel within the firm increased compliance.[19] And, as Rubin explains, "in the absence of a compliance program, an employee who decides to engage in legally risky behavior, like instituting a cheaper production process that creates more waste, may have nagging doubts about the wisdom of doing so, but will suppress some of those doubts in reporting to his superior, who will, in turn suppress some of the doubts that were expressed to her in reporting to her superior. Compliance staff may short circuit some of these bureaucratic levels by reporting the employee's doubts directly to top management."[20] Accordingly, the existence of a compliance unit, combined with the ability of compliance employees to report misconduct up a chain of command separate from the operational employee management chain, may enhance compliance.

In addition to the formal organizational structures, informal features and culture can help promote (or undermine) compliance. As Scott notes, citing the classic organizational theorist Chester Barnard, "informal organizations are necessary to the operation of formal organizations as a means of communication, of cohesion, and of protecting the integrity of the individual." Moreover, Scott highlights the needs for inducements of a "'personal, non-materialistic character,' including the 'opportunities for distinction, prestige, personal power, and the attainment of dominating position . . . and ideal benefactions [such as] pride of workmanship, sense of adequacy, altruistic service for family or others, loyalty to organization in patriotism, etc., aesthetic and religious feeling.'" Thus, "shared values and meanings, internalized by participants, [can] constitute a strong system of control—much more powerful than one based exclusively on material rewards or on force."[21] Anthropologist Mary Douglas likewise has maintained that one cannot make "good organizational theory without a systematic approach to culture." Thus, for example, the common culture generates conceptions of esteem, a powerful idea that in turn motivates the organization's members: "Individuals negotiate with one another over what kinds of esteem their organization will provide (a gold watch at the end of a lifetime of service, a place at High Table, a medal, an obituary notice, a memorial plaque) and the sources of disesteem they will not tolerate (South African investments, dirty washroom, no parking, insult from employers)." The critical point, here, is that culture matters, that it varies across organizations, and that "what the individual is going to want is not entirely his own idea, but consists largely of a set of desires that the social environment inspires in him."[22]

As we shall see, the U.S. military has adopted several organizational practices that, according to decision theory, should enhance commitment to the rule of law. With respect to formal structures, judge advocates have a strong role both in training troops and commanders and in advising commanders in the field, which increases the salience of the law for operational employees. In addition, their ability to mete out criminal and administrative sanctions within the military justice system gives them strong authority. And judge advocates can report abuse through a separate chain of command, as in many of the successful compliance units that theorists have described. Finally, with respect to informal norms and culture, judge advocates construct narratives of commitment to rule-of-law values that contribute to their loyalty to those values.

More recently, a third group of scholars has turned its attention to how organizations respond to external forces, rather than just internal factors. Like the decision theorists who examine the informal norms within organizations, this group is also preoccupied with organizational culture. Yet economists and sociologists who define themselves as "institutionalists" take special interest in the ways the broader environment shapes that internal culture.[23] As a consequence, they might see an organization as adopting a set of values or practices not merely because of their promotion internally but also because of outside influence.

Thus, scholars of corporations have considered whether elements of national culture have influenced individual and group behavior within particular firms.[24] In the realm of education within the United States, the sociologist John Meyer has examined whether norms within professional associations might influence their members' practices more than the organizations in which they work.[25] Meyer and others also observe the existence of "global scripts," which result when many institutions in many settings start to speak about their organization in similar terms by virtue of a prevailing influential narrative.[26] International law scholars Derek Jinks and Ryan Goodman have argued that states often follow such scripts in adopting and implementing treaty obligations.[27]

For our purposes, the significance of this body of scholarship lies in the suggestion that organizational culture can actually be affected by external forces, including laws, norms, values, and aspirational targets. Consequently, articulating (and defining) international law norms, for example, may have a real impact on institutions even absent mechanisms of enforcement.[28] This literature also suggests that training regimens can have lasting effects on institutional culture by changing the normative space within the institution.

Finally, a fourth group of scholars—drawing on the work of Talcott Parsons,[29] Niklas Luhmann,[30] and others[31]—has also focused on the impact of external forces on organizations, but through the lens of systems theory. These scholars have argued that organizations such as corporations and bureaucracies are themselves systems as well as entities within larger systems. As such, these organizations seek homeostasis when faced with any particular input, although at least some systems theorists argue that external sanctions can have real impact if the external norms are translated and internalized into the terms of the organization.[32] Accordingly, once again it may be important to have independent compliance agents who can perform this translation function.

Of course, organizations might simply adopt the forms of the external script without imbibing or inculcating the rule. For example, a corporation might adopt compliance or audit requirements simply as a formality without any significant change in internal organizational culture. Moreover, what distinguishes a purely formal shift from one that has a deeper valence can be difficult to distinguish,[33] and the seepage of an institutional change may take years to become truly part of organizational culture. In addition, as scholars in all four of the groups would probably acknowledge, the effectiveness of any of these structures will be constrained by certain limits. There may be a deeply pervasive culture of real compliance with particular norms. Or the culture may be only one of paper compliance. The official culture may be committed to particular norms, while an unofficial culture is much more complex. Or a culture of compliance may be found at the top of an organization and resistance at the bottom, or the reverse.

What is clear, however, is that organizational culture is one of the most significant factors in determining whether actors will behave in preferred ways and pursue jobs in accordance with preferred norms and values. Furthermore, from the organizational theory literature, we can begin to tease out those structural elements that will help ensure that compliance agents within an organization—such as lawyers—are actually effective at inculcating values and affecting the behavior of operational employees. These compliance agents are likely to be most effective, it appears, if: (1) these agents are integrated with other, operational employees; (2) they have a strong understanding of, and sense of commitment to, the rules and values being enforced; (3) they are operating within their own separate hierarchy; and (4) they can invoke a system that confers benefits or imposes penalties on employees based on compliance.[34]

Empirical research confirms the importance of these four organizational structures. For example, it turns out that the more company lawyers mingle with other corporate employees, the more likely all employees will be to begin to internalize the legal rules the lawyers seek to enforce.[35] As a result, the nonlawyer employees become more likely to take those rules into account when they make decisions.[36] At the same time, lawyers who interact with other employees learn to frame the rules better in terms of broader organizational goals, which in turn enhances the likelihood that operational employees will follow them. Research on corporate lawyers also indicates that if lawyers have a strong sense of obligation to report violations—stemming either from fealty to more senior lawyers within the organization or to a broader professional group and its norms and values—they will be more disposed to confront operational employees who are flouting the rules.[37] As to the need for a separate chain of command, the data suggest that accountability agents are more likely to enforce rules and norms if their own promotion, reputation, or advancement is to some degree independent of the operational employees. Finally, and perhaps not surprisingly, if accountability agents can impose some form of sanction or confer a benefit on employees based on rule compliance, their ability to promote compliance increases.[38]

Accordingly, we must consider the degree to which the organizational structures of the military track the four features described above and thus contribute to a culture of compliance with public law values. And if the organizational structure of the uniformed military *does* contribute to a culture of compliance, we will need to take those organizational and institutional factors into account when understanding international law compliance more generally, both within the military and in other settings, public and private.

Organizational Structure and Culture in the U.S. Military

The U.S. military has a long tradition of at least formal respect for the rule of law and the limits that the law of war places on soldiers. As far back as the U.S. Civil War, the U.S. Army published the *Instructions for the Government of Armies of the United States in the Field* of 1863, known as the Lieber Code. The Code set forth rules of conduct for U.S. military personnel that included limits on the use of force against civilians and requirements that detainees be treated humanely. Specifically, the Code states that "military necessity does not admit of cruelty—that is, the infliction of suffering for the sake of suffering or for revenge, nor of maiming or wounding except in fight, nor of torture to extort confessions."[39] Indeed, the Lieber Code helped spawn the branch of international humanitarian law that governs the law of hostilities, commonly known as Hague law.[40] Following the Civil War, the U.S. Armed Forces embraced a culture of respect for law.[41] The United States also played an active role in furthering the evolution of international humanitarian law from the Civil War to the period after World War II, which culminated in the adoption of the four Geneva Conventions and the enactment of the Uniform Code of Military Justice (UCMJ). Throughout this period, the U.S. Armed Forces trained troops in this emerging law of war. Indeed, the U.S. Military Academy began offering courses in the subject as early as 1863. At the same time, lawyers within the military played a significant role in interpreting and applying these developing laws. The Army, for example, has maintained a permanent corps of military lawyers since 1862.[42]

Nevertheless, the aftermath of the Vietnam War marked a turning point in the uniformed military's relationship to the law of war. The existence of such legal norms obviously had not prevented U.S. troops from committing widespread atrocities at My Lai and elsewhere. After My Lai, a high-level Army investigation blamed the military's failure both to train troops adequately in war crimes law and to provide procedures for reporting abuses.[43] In response, the U.S. military strengthened its internal codes of conduct, updating the *U.S. Army Field Manual* so that, in addition to specifying prohibited acts, it emphasized that the main objective of wartime detention operations is "implementation of the Geneva Conventions."[44] At the same time, the Department of Defense (DOD) dramatically stepped up training activities and gave military lawyers a greater role by initiating a "law of war program," run primarily by judge advocates, that was designed to educate troops from all services in the law of war.[45] Military lawyers also gained new responsibilities on the battlefield: they were placed in the field to develop and review operations plans to ensure compliance with the law of war and to refine the specific rules of engagement for the conflict in question.[46] Each commander thus had the benefit of a lawyer's advice in the field, and military lawyers became involved in operational decision making as never before. Such actions helped institutionalize the authority and role of these lawyers in the military bureaucracy. In this way, the military as a whole deepened its commitment to the law of war, and, just as significantly, put in place a group of lawyers with a clear mission to enforce adherence to that law.

As a result of these shifts, judge advocates now play a key role training troops and commanders, both before deployment and between deployments. They also give continuing on-the-ground advice to troops and commanders on a range of legal matters, including appropriate limits on the use of force. And they are deeply engaged in investigating misconduct by troops and imposing punishment, either by assessing administrative penalties or by criminally prosecuting troops in military courts.

The judge advocate training role is extensive. Before deployment, all troops receive training from military lawyers that includes sessions on the legal limits to the use of force. These sessions may be tailored to the specific types of functions the troops will be performing[47] and include training in the specific rules of engagement for the particular operation.[48]

In addition, judge advocates themselves receive extensive training. Beyond legal training at an accredited law school, all judge advocates must attend a course at one of the four judge advocate training schools.[49] Indeed, in the aftermath of Vietnam and in response to experiences in Grenada, the military determined that military lawyers should receive training specifically in "a broad ranges of legal issues associated with the conduct of military operations." The recognition that judge advocates need to advise troops and commanders on the ground while deployed resulted in the development of "operational law," which is a "compendium of domestic, foreign, and international law applicable to U.S. forces engaged in combat or operations other than war."[50] After seven years of service, judge advocates are required to return to the school for another period of extensive training. The school is staffed by experienced officers, who generally serve for terms of two years.[51] The schools also produce legal handbooks, annually updated by the professors, which judge advocates carry with them into the field. In the case of the Army JAG School, the International and Operational Law Department prepares the *Operational Law Handbook*, a comprehensive treatise that lays out and analyzes key legal rules.[52] The judge advocates also help draft rules of engagement prior to the operation.[53]

Training continues during deployment and includes "training exercises" that incorporate specific, realistic scenarios designed to teach the limits on the use of force in actual circumstances the troops are likely to face. Thus, Frederic Borch relates that during Operation Uphold Democracy in Haiti, soldiers "were confronted with a vignette in which a speeding vehicle crashed through a traffic check point barrier." A judge advocate "evaluated the soldiers' response and discussed alternative responses available within the limits set by the rules of engagement."[54] Judge advocates likewise held these types of on-the-ground training sessions in Iraq.[55] As one senior military lawyer noted, the decisions made as to whether a particular use of force complies with the law of armed conflict or the rules of engagement are "highly situational" and require complex judgment honed by practical experience.[56]

How successful have these reforms been in building an organizational culture among the judge advocates that emphasizes respect for international human rights and humanitarian law? Such a question is probably impossible to answer definitively and almost certainly varies from person to person and context to context. Nevertheless, especially in light of abuses at Abu Ghraib, Guantánamo, and other detention sites, neither the presence of military lawyers in theater nor the various organizational reforms described above have been wholly successful at stopping unlawful behavior.

Yet, the period of abuse under the administration of George W. Bush may actually be an illustration not of the failure of the judge advocate system but of its success, at least at the margins. Indeed, we may see the notorious incidents of abuse as precisely what occurs when the judge advocate culture is deliberately *undermined*. In the months preceding the abuses at Abu Ghraib, Bush administration officials took a series of steps that weakened long-standing commitments within the military to the norms and values of the law of war, and in particular norms regarding the treatment of detainees. Specifically, administration authorities circulated statements and memoranda suggesting that the law of war might not apply to certain categories of detainees; issued multiple, confusing directives to troops on the ground regarding permissible interrogation techniques; allowed civilian intelligence personnel, Special Forces, uniformed troops, and private contractors to comingle without clear lines of authority or divisions of responsibility; and greatly expanded the role of private contractors. Together, these practices helped set the stage for the abuses that took place.[57]

Just as importantly, the commitment of many within the military to the values of international law, and the organizational structures that the military had constructed over many decades to maintain those commitments, proved surprisingly difficult to dislodge. For it was, primarily, the *civilian* political employees who sought to change long-standing military practices. Uniformed military personnel and military lawyers, by contrast, in many cases took the lead in criticizing the administration and sought to tame the effect of administration policies, while reaffirming (and perhaps even reinstitutionalizing) the military's respect for international law. As David Luban has pointed out, "Their primary roles as criminal litigators and military advisors converge to make JAGs staunch and faithful rule of law devotees, possibly to an extent greater than many civilian lawyers."[58]

In fact, although senior administration officials seeking to narrow the reach of international law in the fight against terrorism often deliberately excluded uniformed military lawyers from the conversation, those lawyers, active and retired, worked both in public and behind the scenes to try to thwart or moderate administration policies. For example, during the debate that followed the president's initial order establishing the use of military commissions to try terrorism suspects, uniformed military lawyers were notably vocal. A team of administration political appointees from the White House, the Office of Legal Counsel, and Vice President Dick Cheney's office worked largely in secret to prepare the order, and excluded military lawyers (as well as lawyers from the State Department) from the process.[59] Immediately after the release of the order, however, uniformed military lawyers strongly criticized the plan, specifically the denial of important procedural protections to defendants, including the plan's failure to provide for a right to choose a lawyer or a requirement that death sentences can only be imposed by unanimous vote.[60] These lawyers also expressed concern that the lack of protections in the proposed military commissions would undermine perceptions of the fairness of military justice more broadly, even though the UCMJ includes strong protections for the rights of the accused.[61]

Partly in response to such criticisms, the Bush administration developed regulations that softened some of the most disputed provisions and required, for example, unanimity before the death penalty could be imposed, a presumption of innocence, proof beyond a reasonable doubt, and a military appeals process.[62] Yet, as the commissions began their work, the uniformed military lawyers appointed to defend the accused continued to challenge the process, particularly because of the lack of judicial review in civilian courts.[63] And after the Supreme Court struck down the use of commissions as originally constituted, military lawyers again asserted themselves as vocal opponents of the administration's efforts to resurrect the panels. Uniformed lawyers objected, above all, to the new commissions' rules that would allow the admission of evidence defendants had not seen.[64]

Uniformed military lawyers also repeatedly criticized the broad policy guidance and field directives regarding interrogation practices. Indeed, these lawyers strenuously resisted the recommendations in the memoranda of the Office of Legal Counsel and a Defense Department working group that largely adopted a very narrow definition of torture and a broad definition of presidential authority. For example, Brigadier General Kevin M. Sandkuhler, a senior Marine lawyer, wrote in a memorandum of February 27, 2003, that the harsh interrogation regime could ultimately have adverse repercussions for American service members. The statement pointedly declares that the Department of Justice "does not represent the services; thus, understandably, concern for service members is not reflected in their opinion." Likewise, Major General Thomas J. Romig, the Army's top-ranking uniformed lawyer, wrote in a memo of March 3, 2003, that the approach recommended by the Justice Department "will open us up to criticism that the U.S. is a law unto itself."[65]

Criticism of the field directives regarding specific interrogation practices was similarly strong. The deputy judge advocate general of the air force, Major General Jack L. Rives, advised that many of "the more extreme interrogation techniques, on their face, amount to violations of domestic criminal law" as well as military law. Rives argued that the use of these techniques "puts the interrogators and the chain of command at risk of criminal accusations abroad" in other countries' domestic courts or in international tribunals.[66] And in September 2003 military lawyers objected to General Ricardo Sanchez's authorization of the controversial interrogation techniques in Iraq discussed previously. The lawyers argued that these techniques were "overly aggressive," presumably because they would run afoul of the UCMJ and international law. Finally, military lawyers pushed for significant revisions to the *U.S. Army Field Manual* on intelligence interrogations.[67] The new *Manual*, released in September 2006, specifies that the Geneva Conventions apply to all detainees and eliminates distinctions between prisoners of war and enemy combatants.[68]

Thus, throughout the period 2002–2006 we see a military legal culture fighting back against efforts by political appointees to weaken or muddy the U.S. commitment to the law of war.

This Bush-era experience does suggest that organizational structure and culture can play a crucial role either in weakening or in giving effect to international law. To the extent that international law failed to constrain troops on the ground from committing abuses, it was at least in part because Bush administration political appointees took steps that effectively undermined a bureaucratic culture that had institutionalized respect for that law. Yet that culture—a military committed to the law of war and the fair treatment of detainees—ultimately proved to be difficult to dislodge.[69] Organizational practices and values remained resilient and served as the impetus for much of the critique of, and resistance to, these changes.

The foregoing seems to indicate that the existence of a cadre of lawyers within the military structure who retain primary allegiance to human rights norms and the law of war can have a real impact, at least in the main. Further, the most effective organizational structure would be one designed to give these lawyers a deeply contextual role, helping design rules of engagement, providing situational training in theater, and advising commanders on a day-to-day basis. Yet, organizational design, when translated into practice, can obviously fall short of its lofty aims. Thus, we next turn to empirical data on the way this organizational structure plays out on the ground.

Judge Advocates on the Battlefield

Uniformed military lawyers—the career judge advocates—are essentially the compliance unit within the military. These lawyers work to ensure that commanders and troops obey the rules of engagement, which are the rules that operationalize the law of armed conflict in a given war or occupation. A core public value undergirding this body of law is the principle that the use of force, even in an armed conflict, is limited. Specifically, troops may not target civilians, and the use of force must be proportional to the risk or danger present. Thus, military lawyers are essential to inculcating this public value into military culture.

Interviews with more than twenty uniformed military lawyers who served primarily in Iraq and Afghanistan indicate that the current military structure includes all four elements of a successful compliance unit that were discussed above. Judge advocates comingle with operational employees, the commanders and troops on the battlefield. They help devise the rules of engagement and train troops in those rules, both before they deploy and on the battlefield. At the same time, their ongoing advice to commanders and commanders' staff on the battlefield appears to make the legal rules they seek to enforce more salient throughout the organization. The lawyers report that they frame the rules in a way that describes them as supporting the broader goal of the organization: military effectiveness. These lawyers also profess a strong sense of commitment to the rules and the values that underlie them. And while the judge advocates face some challenges in establishing credibility, a somewhat separate chain of command—which obliges them to report incidents, provides a structure for supplemental guidance in the field, and serves as a basis for promotion that is separate from that of the operational employees—helps bolster the lawyers' independence and objectivity. Furthermore, uniformed lawyers play a key role in ensuring that commanders impose penalties on rule breakers within the military justice system. These include administrative punishments such as loss in pay or rank, as well as more severe criminal penalties.

Of course, the accounts of judge advocates are likely to be self-serving and may therefore overstate the effectiveness of military lawyers. And, as noted above, an organizational structure, even if effective, can certainly be undermined through strategic maneuvering. Nevertheless, while having all of the organizational features in place does not necessarily guarantee norm compliance, there is evidence that the military lawyers do exert a very real impact on military operations, at least some of the time. As a result, we need to study the organizational structures that tend to increase norm compliance, even if that compliance remains imperfect. After all, no norm compliance regime is perfect, and an imperfect regime may still be significant, particularly when compared with even more imperfect alternatives.

Integration of Lawyers and Troops on the Battlefield and the Salience of Legal Rules

As discussed above, since Vietnam the military has vastly expanded the role of judge advocates in the field. Judge advocates now serve alongside commanders on the battlefield, giving advice on a range of issues from troop discipline, to fiscal decision making, to vetting targets, to interpreting rules of engagement. Indeed, during the Iraq War the Army has actually expanded the role of the judge advocates. Accordingly, military lawyers who once served primarily at the higher, division level and above now work with commanders in the field down to the brigade level.

THE LAWYER'S ROLE ON THE BATTLEFIELD: "EVERY DAY WAS A LONG DAY" Judge advocates based in Iraq and Afghanistan describe assuming a wide variety of roles: they might investigate, prosecute, or defend soldiers in criminal matters or matters of military discipline; they might train troops on emerging issues involving the rules of engagement; and they might provide a range of operational legal advice to commanders on everything from fiscal issues, to troop discipline, to targeting. The precise set of legal questions addressed depends in part, of course, on the level of the assignment and the particular service. In the Army, for example, the division level includes multiple lawyers who are likely to specialize in particular areas of law, all reporting to a division judge advocate who supervises the lawyers and provides advice to the division commander. At the brigade level, in contrast, usually only one or two lawyers handle all matters that might arise.

The location and type of military assignment—Baghdad or Kirkuk, a detention facility or a city neighborhood—also affect the types of issues these lawyers face. For example, one lawyer, assigned to a brigade in Baghdad, said that his legal role was linked to the overall role of the brigade: "patrolling the battle space, controlling and pacifying it." Accordingly, the lawyers were there "to bring the rule of law" to the area: "We owned that land."[70] Another, by contrast, advised a commander in charge of a military detention facility.[71] Yet another served as the senior defense counsel for a region of Iraq. Based in Baghdad, this lawyer observed that "every day I was flying out, trying cases, interviewing witnesses, talking to [the Criminal Investigative Division]."[72]

But regardless of the assignment, the judge advocates were clearly putting themselves right in the heart of the conflict. The danger was particularly acute during one of the most violent periods of the Iraq engagement, the Shiite uprising of 2004–2005. As one judge advocate noted, during this moment in the conflict "every day was a long day."[73] In the period from March 2004 through February 2005, there were 1,018 coalition troop fatalities, an average of eighty-five each month.[74]

The ideal relationship between law and operations is one in which lawyers have the ear of the commander and the commander's staff for a range of operational decisions. As one judge advocate who served in Baghdad described it, "All targets are supposed to be cleared through us." And, as he further noted, "It's a big job because you can't shoot at a lot of stuff in Baghdad."[75] Another judge advocate reported that the operational law issues that arose "tended not so much to be targeting issues but rather issues related to troops in contact with civilian populations and the limits on using force in self-defense." This judge advocate further observed that "not all situations are rehearsed; you can't train for everything. That's why it was important that I was on the scene. You involve yourself in the fight."[76]

TRAINING TROOPS AND REVISING THE RULES OF ENGAGEMENT Training is an important part of the operational role. As one judge advocate noted, the training predeployment is "extensive."[77] Another observed that "we spend a lot of time training up our kids. . . . They get [the rules of engagement] beaten into their heads at the start," before they deploy. "Then, they get more training in Kuwait," just before they enter the theater.[78] And when they are on the battlefield, they receive yet more training in the appropriate limits on the use of force. Moreover, at each stage, the training goes beyond a recitation of the rules and involves detailed discussion (and sometimes role-playing) about specific scenarios likely to arise on the particular battlefield in question. As one judge advocate described it, training is not merely in the classroom: "We go through scenarios, we practice, and see what happens."[79]

To be sure, the judge advocates acknowledged that training might not always prevent troops from crossing the line and using excessive force. As one interviewee conceded, "If a soldier's scared, he's going to shoot." This lawyer reasoned that, as a consequence, "it's important not to set too many restrictions [and instead] to train them to realistic scenarios."[80]

The judge advocates also give updated refresher courses to troops in theater, and revise both the training scenarios and the rules of engagement themselves to reflect the conditions on the ground. One judge advocate emphasized the importance of this "revised training in the field."[81] As another judge advocate put it, "We reset the training to build up habits—we give them a refresher in the status quo."[82] And the judge advocates play an active role in revising the training scenarios. According to one of those interviewed, "There were 30,000 soldiers in Baghdad. Every time there was an incident [in which a soldier used force] we'd . . . report it. That way, we'd pick up real-life scenarios that we'd use for training. We'd update it on a monthly basis. There were probably thirty incidents a day."[83] This judge advocate noted further that whenever there was a potential issue of excessive force, they would conduct an investigation. Another judge advocate stated that "we take a look at the circumstances in which people are getting killed," and think about "how we can stop so we don't need to use deadly force but at the same time ensure that our soldiers are not attacked." This judge advocate recounted circumstances in which he thought "we weren't getting it right," so he sent a report tracker to division headquarters to alert "people at a higher level that we have a problem."[84]

Likewise, one judge advocate noted that, when it became clear that troops might be firing their weapons unnecessarily at checkpoints, military officials revised the rules of engagement applicable in that context. As this judge advocate observed, "We were killing drunk Iraqis" who were "driving through the checkpoints."[85] Indeed, according to Lieutenant General Peter Chiarelli, who authorized a systematic review, many escalation of force incidents involving Iraqi civilians were taking place at checkpoints, in situations when a driver would fail to stop.[86] In response to this review, the military changed its "tactics, techniques and procedures . . . to better ensure that civilians were not confused by military orders to stop at checkpoints and that soldiers did not fire without cause."[87] These changes to the rules of engagement based on contextual, on-the-ground information are obviously an essential part of efforts to minimize abuses and mistakes in volatile war settings.

COMINGLING AND CREDIBILITY: "PART OF THE TEAM [AND NOT] A WEENIE LAWYER" Uniformed lawyers describe their integration with officers and troops on the battlefield as essential to their ability to inject legal norms and values into the decision-making process. They emphasize that their position on the battlefield gives them the opportunity to interact at the moment that the decisions are made. Moreover, they were present when the commander and staff laid out the battle plan.

In that connection, the judge advocates have a strong sense that they should get to know as many on the staff as possible: "[You] need to get out. . . . [You] can't sit in your office all day. You've got to be out shaking hands, getting to know people; . . . it's a huge task."[88] Relatedly, judge advocates stressed the need to vet legal concerns with the commander and the commander's staff at an early stage, before a formal meeting takes place. As one judge advocate put it, "If I raised a serious legal concern for the first time at a meeting with the commander and staff, I'd get my head handed to me." This judge advocate emphasized that "it's important to try to find legal alternatives [at the planning stage]."[89]

According to the judge advocates, the integration of lawyers and troops also enhances the lawyers' credibility, because it demonstrates that they are participating in a common mission; although they are lawyers, they are soldiers first and foremost. As one judge advocate noted, "When you're a JAG at the brigade level, you have to assume a soldier role, not just a lawyer role. You don't earn trust unless you do the soldier part." This judge advocate recalled that "we used to look at the lawyers like the doctors," who played no combat role. But now, "the lawyers sit in the room" when combat decisions are made: "When there's a military decision-making process in place, the lawyer should be there. If you are involved, everyone can see the value added. The staff and the commander see you as part of the team rather than a weenie lawyer."[90] And just as important as developing rapport with the commander is building rela-tionships with staff officers, because "it's a cell of staff officers who work on [each] issue." Accordingly, "[you have to] inject yourself . . . so they know you're not there just to [sit behind a desk] but to add value. . . . [You have to] inject yourself socially so you can be there professionally."[91]

Many judge advocates noted that combat experience before becoming a lawyer helped them to build trust with the commanders and their staffs once they assumed the role of lawyer. For example, one judge advocate, a Marine, argued that "it's easier in the Marines" than in the other services because "every Marine, whether serving in the infantry, in supply, or as a lawyer . . . everyone goes to the same officer candidate school and has the same basic training: how to be an [infantry platoon commander]." There is "a common culture, a common crucible of experience." As a result, "yes, there is commander skepticism. But less than in the Army."[92] Another judge advocate emphasized that his prior experience as an armor officer before joining the JAG Corps had helped: "I'm comfortable with a [combat role]. I had a common background I could share."[93]

Similarly, a judge advocate who had previously trained to become an officer in the armed forces said that because he had attended the Naval Academy and then West Point before he became a lawyer, he had "instant credibility." "People remembered me," he said. "[In addition, by] doing [physical training], combatives, going to the range, and wrestling with the non-coms and staff . . . I stayed in shape. . . . I showed them that I didn't mind bloodying my nose. . . . It was clear that I was one of them."[94]

Several judge advocates specifically stressed the need to go out in the field with troops and be with them in dangerous situations. As one lawyer explained, "If [there was an issue involving] troops in contact, if [there was a] developing situation, my job was to be there . . . not in the back of the [tactical operations center] listening to the radio, waiting until something happened."[95] Consequently, "I would engage [the enemy] if necessary, [and] I worked closely with fire support, field artillery. . . . I became tied in. . . . Even if you're not needed, you're there."[96]

It is precisely this kind of comingling of accountability agents and operational employees that organizational theory credits with increasing the effectiveness of these agents. Thus, instead of being walled off from the rest of the organization, judge advocates speak with commanders and their staffs about the rules of engagement every day in the thick of battle, which increases general awareness of the importance of these rules, and together they engage in discussions about how best to interpret them. As one judge advocate recounts, "My brigade commander was brilliant, and he expected alternative views. . . . If an IED [improvised explosive device] went off, and we were going to respond, he wanted to know, 'Is it a good shoot or a bad shoot?' . . . [And if] I had concerns, he listened to me."[97] This kind of integral involvement of lawyers in core decisions gives greater depth and meaning to the legal rules.

To be sure, the judge advocates face challenges in building credibility and rapport in the field. As one noted, "Some people see lawyers as difficult. . . . [So, they engage in] tough guy banter and make lawyer jokes. They see lawyers as making [the military] less effective."[98] Another acknowledged that, in the field, commanders and staff really include judge advocates in the decision-making process only "50 percent of the time."[99] In addition, there is the problem of "forum shopping: [a commander or staff officer might] request an opinion from three different JAGs."[100]

For these reasons, one judge advocate, a professor at the Army's Judge Advocate School, reported that the school actually teaches "building rapport." Accordingly, the professors emphasize in the classroom that "all law is in an operational environment." Each judge advocate should therefore seek to "build a relationship with everyone in [the commander's] staff. Hopefully, they come to you. Hopefully they do it before they take action. Hopefully you've vetted [their plans]: you can say something like, 'All three causes of action look legal,' [but the third is riskier from a legal perspective.]"[101] Putting such advice into action, one judge advocate described his approach in similar terms: "If there were three options on the table, and all were legal, I might say something like, 'This option is close to the line, this one is safe, and this one is in the middle. As long as the option is legal, I'm there to ensure you accomplish the mission.'"[102]

As a result, the judge advocates carefully translate their legal advice into operational terms, making it clear to commanders that the lawyers' job is not to say no but rather is to help their commanders achieve the objectives of the mission. As one judge advocate put it, "You can't be Dr. No." Even if a particular course of action posed legal problems, "our job was to give an alternative course of action that would accomplish the goal without the legal concerns."[103] As another judge advocate put it, "[I] wanted to help my commander get to yes."[104] Similarly, a third reported that his job was "finding a way to yes. . . . Your first response shouldn't be no." Instead, "you should think, 'How can I help my commander accomplish the objective?'" If there's a legal problem, "then you say, 'O.K. you want to do x, but why do you want to do x? Maybe it's better to try something else.'"[105]

Many judge advocates also observed that the personal relationship between a judge advocate and a commander is crucial and that the best way to build credibility is to give good advice. According to one judge advocate, "Each commander is very different, so the job is very personality driven. You could be successful with one commander, but not another."[106] In that vein, another lawyer emphasized that every relationship "has to be built from scratch. You start with little things and build up to bigger things." Furthermore, when you are "deployed, it can be harder to do" than when you are in the garrison.[107] In one judge advocate's view, "Your credibility depends on how much the commander respects [your] individual competence." Consequently, "it's hard. If you give one bad opinion, [the commander] may be less likely to come to you. You take the risk that [the commander might go] to another unit, or above you to the corps/division level."[108] In contrast, if the commander "follows your advice" and has good results and gets "credibility," that will build his trust and respect.[109]

A Strong Sense of Commitment to the Legal Rules and Underlying Values

The judge advocates expressed a strong sense of commitment to the legal rules applicable in theater and the underlying values they reflect. Indeed, they seemed to see their role as the guardians of ethics within the military, and all those interviewed tended to describe their role in similar terms. Thus, one judge advocate said that uniformed lawyers have an "ethical duty" to protect the applicable rules and laws, including the rule regarding the use of force.[110] Another related that the "JAG[s] in the Army push to inject ethics" into the conduct of a military conflict. "When [your] job is to fight and kill, you try to do it with some sense of integrity; . . . you want the Army to be able to say that."[111] A third judge advocate described his role as standing for "integrity and to be the commander's conscience . . . not like an inspector general but rather an internal conscience."[112] Yet another said, "We're the organization's ethics counsel."[113]

This ethical role is viewed as having both an internal and external component, encouraging integrity within the military as well as advancing the military's mission in the eyes of the broader public in the United States and elsewhere in the world. One judge advocate expressed that idea as follows: "The linchpin that holds us together at the end of the day is that the rule of law has to exist where citizens believe in equal protection, fairness, equity, justice. [We] make sure it exists within the military, and through leverage within our own organization to other countries we're trying to help, from demonstration."[114]

With respect to the internal culture, another judge advocate noted that "sometimes JAGs get jaded. . . . [They see] all the crap . . . that there are criminals, child molesters, and child pornographers in the military" just like everywhere else. This lawyer stressed the importance of the judge advocate's role in impressing upon the military itself, as well as the broader public, that the services are "not controlled by criminals." For example, when a general testifies in Congress "we want to be able to say we do everything right . . . [and take] the moral high ground."[115] Another judge advocate added that "we can only fight the global war on terror by holding onto our core values [and by] establishing the rule of law."[116]

Judge advocates also emphasized that uniformed lawyers make every effort to remain independent and objective. One pointed out that "you want to set your commander up for success." And to do that "you [need to give] objective advice on Army policies and the law." Moreover, this judge advocate noted, you have to remember that your "client is the U.S. Army," not a particular commander. Accordingly, it is crucial not to let the thick of war cloud one's judgment: "You need to [say the same] thing in the theater as in the garrison."[117]

A Separate Hierarchy

Judge advocates describe another feature that enhances their effectiveness in the field, the ability to seek what they call "top cover" from other judge advocates assigned to more senior officers in the chain of command. This path of alternate authority—somewhat separate from the commander to whom the judge advocate is assigned—serves as a backup in cases where a commander may be reluctant to listen to the assigned judge advocate. Thus, a judge advocate working with a brigade commander might seek the advice of a judge advocate at a higher level in the chain of command, such as the staff judge advocate assigned to the division commander (to whom the brigade commander reports). As one judge advocate noted, "[You might seek] top cover if you want higher-level support. It's common if your commander doesn't seek your advice, or if you advise your commander that the course of action he wants to take is a violation of law. It's relatively common for a judge advocate at the brigade level, for example, to seek advice from the lawyer at the division or corps level and ask, 'Could you look at this and see if I'm right?'" This judge advocate emphasized, however, that the practice "could be abused if the judge advocate routinely seeks such opinions."[118]

Numerous other judge advocates described using the practice of top cover. One of them explained that "we do have a system: . . . your commander's commander has a lawyer." This judge advocate found that it is sometimes helpful "to talk to lawyers at higher headquarters."[119] The more senior lawyer can provide further ammunition in arguments with the commander or, through the senior lawyer's commander, influence the lower-level commander. As one judge advocate recounted, "If I disagreed with my commander, I could go to the division staff judge advocate, who was a friend." He believed that "talking to the division staff judge advocate" was most useful if "you had a horrible relationship with your commander or you disagreed." And he acknowledged that "the staff judge advocate might say that you're wrong," but "if you're right, the staff judge advocate could talk to the brigade commander."[120]

The judge advocates reported that the practice is relatively common, though it poses some challenges of its own. According to one judge advocate, "Top cover happens often. It's not looked down upon. You may need more seasoned advice. For example, if you have time and you're faced with a difficult targeting decision, you may want to run it by a more senior lawyer. . . . Or if you're having a problem with your commander, you might want to ask a more senior lawyer to speak to your commander and say, 'I need you to intervene, and tell him my role.'"[121] Another judge advocate related that he "would often send stuff up to the corps level and get a quick turnaround." Furthermore, he said that he "had no problem going to corps if needed," and "they were very good about sending down advice."[122] Yet several judge advocates warned against seeking such advice on basic questions.[123] While "you can talk to the lawyer" up the chain without seeking permission to do so, going up the chain of command works best if "you get permission from your commander first." But, this judge advocate continued, "If he says no, [it's a sign that] something is wrong. . . . Your conscience should say, 'Wait, the train is off the track.'"[124]

In addition to using the top cover, some judge advocates report using the "CNN factor" to persuade commanders to follow their advice, meaning that a certain action "would look bad on CNN."[125] As noted previously, the possibility of congressional testimony is also a motivating factor: "When the generals are called to testify in Congress, you want them to be able to say, 'We do everything right.' You want them to be able to take the moral high ground."[126]

When it comes to incidents involving the use of force, judge advocates described a strong sense of obligation to report such incidents to higher authorities: "What does a JAG do if there are organizational issues at the brigade? You have to go outside the brigade, even if there are career repercussions. Your client is the Army, and you have an ethical obligation to the Army. There's no attorney-client privilege with the commander; . . . it's a very important concept." This judge advocate also observed that "it's important to err on the side of caution and report incidents [up the chain of command]." Moreover, "you have to have little career ambition. . . . [Even if it hurts our professional advancement], we have to police ourselves."[127] Another lawyer recalled that "any time a soldier fired, we'd report it up through the division" And that in "any incident where the force might be excessive, we investigated." If, for example, "there was a shooting at a checkpoint, we'd do a [report]."[128]

The ability to report incidents to higher authorities appears to give judge advocates extra leverage in trying to persuade commanders to follow a particular course of conduct. For example, one judge advocate described how his ability to report independently helped him convince a reluctant commander to report an incident of potential abuse. He noted that "you can go through the divisional chain, if you need to. . . . Sometimes you can win an argument [with the commander] if you say you have to report; . . . you may burn a bridge, but it's necessary." According to this judge advocate, though it was "understandable" that the commander preferred not to record the incident, "I told him I had to report it up to the division, and he understood."[129]

Significantly, senior uniformed lawyers, and not just the commander for whom the judge advocate is working, file performance reviews and make promotion decisions regarding individual judge advocates. The judge advocates indicated that the commanders to whom they are assigned do provide performance evaluations, but the more senior supervising judge advocate in the field also contributes an important evaluation. As one judge advocate noted, "I worked directly for G3 [my commander], but my rating chain of command was through the SJ [senior judge advocate]."[130] This structure helps insulate the judge advocates and gives them a greater sense of independence.

The Ability to Impose Administrative and Criminal Sanctions

In protecting the public values that are embedded in military rules, judge advocates wield a strong stick: they can investigate soldiers who violate those rules, and, in appropriate cases, recommend that those soldiers be brought before courts in the justice system internal to the military, where they may be tried and punished. In fact, the ability of uniformed military lawyers to refer miscreants to this system is one of the most significant differences between judge advocates and corporate counsel or other organizational accountability agents, who lack the ability to invoke a criminal justice system internal to their organization. Corporations and bureaucracies do not have their own criminal courts. And corporate counsel typically do not have the authority to recommend that employees be penalized within the organization for rule infractions—and in most cases may not even disclose such infractions to civilian criminal authorities. The closest analogy is to corporations or bureaucracies with an internal dispute resolution mechanism that can impose noncriminal penalties on employees who break the rules.

The judge advocates' ability to recommend punishment through the internal military justice system extends not merely to criminal acts but also to acts in violation of military rules that, while not ordinarily rising to the level of a crime, would undermine military discipline.[131] Accordingly, in any given case a judge advocate can recommend that a commander initiate either a general court-martial procedure, which allows for the full range of penalties including jail time, or a more abbreviated Article 15 proceeding, which permits only weaker administrative penalties.[132] The penalties that can be imposed pursuant to the latter proceedings can consist of reductions in pay or rank, or dishonorable discharge.[133] The judge advocates are therefore central enforcers of military discipline.

Enforcement begins at the investigation stage. In cases in which troops allegedly have misused force, the judge advocate will work together with the criminal investigative unit. Judge advocates, at least in the Army, must report any incident in which a soldier fires a weapon. The judge advocates reported that they often learned of cases from civilians, who would complain to the battalion in charge of the area when they or family members were injured in an incident involving the military. The judge advocate would then make an assessment based on the quality of the evidence as to whether to proceed: "We would move ahead when the claim sounded legitimate; . . . it depends on the source, on the evidence."[134] If the facts so warranted, judge advocates could initiate a process that would compensate the victims financially.

The judge advocates could also recommend that commanders initiate proceedings against troops who might be implicated in such an incident, or indeed any incident that would constitute a crime under military law or a violation of military discipline. As one judge advocate observed, "If a Marine violated the rules, he'd be court-martialed and punished." This judge advocate cited the example of a Marine who was implicated in an act of extortion. The judge advocate noted that the Marine was sent back to the United States to Camp Lejeune and punished. Troops who flouted military rules—such as those banning drinking and drugs—could also be subject to court-martial.[135] To be sure, judge advocates can also sometimes seek to reduce penalties as well. One judge advocate described urging a commander to opt for an Article 15 process to discipline a soldier who had misbehaved, rather than use the general court-martial process and its stiffer penalties. This judge advocate said that, in an Article 15 proceeding, "you can take rank and pay. It saves face with troops. It takes a fair approach . . . [and] allows them to rehabilitate, which is important, especially if the person is a good soldier."[136]

In sum, judge advocates are present in the field at all stages of the law: they seek to shape behavior in advance by advising commanders, staff, and troops. And when violations occur, they can initiate punishment.

Effectiveness of Judge Advocates—Saying No

Of course, it cannot be said for certain how effective these various organizational features—the comingling of lawyers and troops, a separate chain of command, the ability to invoke criminal and administrative penalties, and so on—are in actually protecting public law values on the ground. And as noted previously the perceptions of the judge advocates are bound to be somewhat self-serving. Nevertheless, the interviews do shed some light on this question. For example, one measure of whether judge advocates help protect public values (such as the rules limiting the use of force) is whether they are actually able to guide commanders away—at least on occasion—from behavior that would undermine those values. And while judge advocates take care not to describe their role as saying no to commanders, many were able to name instances in which they were able to persuade commanders not to follow a particular course for legal reasons. The judge advocates interviewed were by no means pollyannas about their role. On the contrary, they were acutely aware that the system breaks down, and that loyalty to a particular commander or unit sometimes trumps the lawyer's commitment to broader public values. Yet they see themselves as having an impact.

Despite the natural bias of military lawyers on this question, it does seem clear that, at least some of the time, having a strong, independent lawyer present matters. As one judge advocate reported, "[On occasion] I said, 'Sir, this is a bad idea, you should do this differently.' I saw my role as helping my brigade commander keep out of jail and helping to keep troops out of jail."[137] With regard to steering a commander away from a particular course with legal problems, one lawyer noted that "with fiscal issues, it's easy. You just can't buy certain things with unit money. But even then, there may be some other way to accomplish the goal." Especially in the wake of Abu Ghraib, he added, "Interrogation is also easy; . . . no commander wants to [go to jail]."[138] Indeed, in most circumstances in which a legal issue arises, "it's a plan that's just not well thought out, so . . . you try to work around the problem." As an example, a different lawyer told of advising his commander to take a more restricted response after an IED went off at the base. Likewise, when a commander wanted to respond in a certain way to a hand grenade attack, the judge advocate "did not say no, [but] I said [the response] was not legal."[139]

Admittedly, the judge advocates described difficulties that might arise in steering commanders away from legally questionable actions. Several brought up the case of Haditha, an incident from 2005 in which Marines allegedly fired without provocation on Iraqi civilians as revenge after their compatriot was killed by a roadside bomb.[140] These lawyers remarked on the fact that the battalion unit's lawyer, Captain Randy W. Stone, did not report the misconduct. The system "didn't work at Haditha" one interviewee noted, because the "judge advocate didn't encourage the commanding officer to investigate."[141] The Marines ultimately court-martialed Captain Stone, as well as three other officers, including the commander, Lieutenant Colonel Jeffrey R. Chessani, of the Third Battalion, First Marines.[142] Although the charges against the lawyer (as well as two of the other three officers) were ultimately thrown out,[143] many of the judge advocates interviewed criticized him for going astray. One said that "the JAG got charged for a cover-up because he didn't tell—he went native." That is, "his loyalty to the command trumped his ethical duty, and because he was in combat with them, it was very difficult." But, this judge advocate concluded, "he needed to report the [problems]. That's what JAGs are needed for: you have to have an unquestionable level of integrity . . . [and] it needs to trump the loyalty to the command."[144] Another judge advocate pointed to one of the problems at Haditha as lack of "sunshine" because the lawyer failed to report the misconduct up the chain of command.[145] And, as discussed above, many of the judge advocates underlined the importance of saying no in some cases, but suggested that framing the legal advice as part of helping commanders do their job better and with more credibility was generally a more effective approach.

Soldiers who use excessive force also face disciplinary action. A recent report on detainee abuse cases concluded that one-third of the uniformed military personnel implicated in abuse were recommended for court-martial or other disciplinary proceedings, and most of those received criminal or administrative penalties, evidence that the military lawyers were at least somewhat effective as compliance agents. While the report criticizes the military for not punishing more soldiers, and for failing to punish high-ranking officers, the percentage of troops punished is much higher than it is for, say, military contractors, whose firms (as we shall see) typically do not place compliance agents on the ground to advise and police contractors in theater. Indeed, of twenty contractors implicated in the cases documented in the report, only one faced criminal punishment.[146]

Uniformed military lawyers have also exerted influence to protect public values threatened by acts of other officials in the executive branch. As discussed previously, they were a powerful force behind revising the

Bush administration's detainee treatment rules to prohibit torture, and they strongly criticized the limited due process protections for terrorism suspects brought before military commissions.[147] Indeed, numerous judge advocates have resigned rather than take part in proceedings before military commissions. For example, two Air Force prosecutors, Major John Carr (a captain at the time) and Major Robert Preston, requested that they be reassigned rather than participate in the proceedings, having charged that fellow prosecutors were ignoring torture allegations, failing to protect exculpatory evidence, and withholding information from superiors.[148] More recently, Lieutenant Colonel Darrel Vandeveld, a U.S. military prosecutor at Guantánamo, quit because his office suppressed evidence that could have cleared a client.[149] These actions, as well as the interviews recounted here, suggest that, at the very least, having an independent corps of judge advocates embedded with troops has some constraining effect by injecting public values into volatile wartime contexts.

Organizational Structure and Culture, and the Problem of Private Military Contractors

By contrast, the interviews reveal that contractors largely fall outside this organizational accountability framework. While they may receive some training in the rules regarding the use of force, that training does not typically include updated advice on the battlefield about how the rules apply in specific scenarios likely to arise on that battlefield. Contractors also do not receive ongoing situational advice from military lawyers or even from private lawyers employed by the firm itself. Indeed, although the contract firms do employ lawyers, these lawyers do not generally spend time on the battlefield and do not have the same opportunity to invoke the advice and backing of more senior uniformed lawyers in the command hierarchy. Finally, the accountability system that has applied to troops has not, at least until recently, been extended to contractors. Thus, the interviews suggest that many crucial, though subtle, mechanisms of compliance with public values are significantly weakened in the privatization process.

Judge advocates described a somewhat uneasy relationship between contractors and troops. Not surprisingly, impressions differed depending on the type of work performed. For example, logistics contractors posed the least concern. As one judge advocate remarked, bases were "like the cantina in *Star Wars*," with contractors of every nationality, "Filipinos, Turks, Ugandans" performing a range of activities, "from cutting hair to serving food in the mess halls, to translating for troops, to selling [provisions] in the commissaries."[150] Yet, as another observed, "Most of the contractors are well behaved. . . . They're there because they're making money for menial work."[151] Nevertheless, even in this relatively benign context, the lawyers worried that the lack of adequate disciplinary controls over contractors undermined soldiers' conduct and morale. For example, the judge advocates noted that if contractors drank or used drugs and troops joined in and got caught, the service members would be punished because these actions violated military discipline, while the contractors would not be subject to the same rules.[152] Furthermore, when logistics contractors did sometimes commit crimes, the failure of the system to provide adequate accountability for them was galling.[153]

Far worse, according to the military lawyers, was the intermingling of security contractors and troops. Interestingly, these lawyers were not initially very aware of the security contractors. But by the end of 2004, contractors were far more visible and were providing both stationary security on bases—guarding mess halls and other facilities—and mobile and static security for CPA and State Department personnel, as well as Iraqi government officials, contract employees, and NGOs. One judge advocate who served in Iraq in 2004 noted that "you would see a lot of Blackwater guys if you went down to the Green Zone," though he noted that "it was hard to distinguish between Blackwater and special forces."[154] Another judge advocate who served in Iraq beginning in December 2004 through the end of 2005 disagreed, observing not only that there were "quite a few" security contractors in Baghdad but also that "it was very clear who they were, in their black SUVs carrying weapons." As this judge advocate noted, "They had weapons and were ready to engage a threat [that might arise]. They had flak jackets." This judge advocate also encountered some security contractors accompanying logistics contractors who came to the base to get paid. "It was my assumption that they were security contractors—they were dressed like they were."[155] By 2007 the security contractors were even more visible. For example, a judge advocate who served in Iraq at that time observed many security guards providing both mobile and static security. As he notes, "At the entrance/ exit of the base, there was lots of testosterone, adrenaline, everyone has guns, it's not a good mix."[156]

To be sure, the judge advocates generally acknowledged the risks that the security contractors were taking. As one judge advocate emphasized, "It was a dangerous job—they were outside the wire every day, transporting Iraqi politicians or delegates or congressmen of the US."[157] Nevertheless, although they respected the willingness of these contractors to put themselves in danger, the judge advocates interviewed perceived security contractors to be more willing to shoot than troops, and therefore they worried about the impact of these contractors on the overall missions in Iraq and Afghanistan. As one judge advocate put it, "I have the impression that generally security contractors are a bunch of cowboys doing what they want, not following the rules, shooting people up," though he noted that when he left Iraq in February 2004, he "didn't necessarily have that impression at the time."[158] Another judge advocate described the security contractors as like "Hessians," and noted that, in particular, the "Blackwater guys were odd because they were like a paramilitary unit, comparable to mercenaries."[159] As another observed, "It was the Wild West. . . . Some of the contractors were carrying sawed-off shotguns. . . . There was really no guidance. . . . They would make it up as they would go along."[160]

Judge advocates who served in areas frequented by contractors reported numerous incidents. One judge advocate who served in Baghdad in 2005–2006 said that there were problems with security contractors using force "on a weekly basis if not more." Specifically, there were "shootings at checkpoints" and other incidents that suggested a "reckless disregard for Iraqi civilians." This judge advocate also observed that the contractors' use of force was very different from troops' because "their mission was different, and they didn't hesitate to shoot."[161]

Another judge advocate who served in Baghdad in 2007 referred to the infamous Nisour Square shootings involving Blackwater and observed that "that stuff happened frequently." As this judge advocate noted, "I saw Blackwater use warning shots to clear traffic. That's not something our troops do. People get hurt, property gets damaged, people get killed." In this judge advocate's view, "contractors don't care, and they don't stop and ask questions." As a result, "my soldiers are stuck with the consequences." Indeed, "once or twice a week, there would be an incident involving the use of force by a contractor, or a contractor killed someone. . . . Were the rules regarding the use of force violated? Yes." This judge advocate also gave another example in which a Blackwater helicopter flying around to protect diplomats started shooting ducks in a lagoon. As this judge advocate said, "You know what you're supposed to do with a weapon, and that's not it."[162]

Judge advocates also expressed frustration with the security contractors because, when they used force, the military felt the repercussions. As one lawyer reported, the Iraqi civilians "were very angry, and they came to us." Commanders wouldn't know when the contractors were coming through an area. According to another lawyer, "If an incident occurred in our area," it was to the contractor's "advantage to fly under the radar." But it was "our job to respond, to take the flak from families." The "military has to clean it up, conduct an investigation." And it can be "frustrating" because "we're responding to the insurgency, taking out patrols, and sweeps," and our "combat operations get shifted. That's a serious issue."[163]

Beyond simply the number of questionable incidents, the judge advocates generally reported that the training for the private security contractors was not as extensive as for troops. As one judge advocate recounted, "We were told they received training in their own rules on the use of force. We were told that they received certification from their supervisors, and there was a form." But, as this judge advocate observed, "there was no looking behind the forms." Under federal law, contractor employees must be certified as having no prior convictions for domestic violence, but judge advocates report that the certification process was "completely ineffective" because "while violence against women is a serious offense," it is not the best indicator of whether someone will use a weapon properly in Iraq. And as for whether third-country nationals had a criminal record or had even been convicted of war crimes, "no one was looking behind the veil on this."[164]

To the extent that contractors had prior careers in the Special Forces, it is significant that "special forces units have drastically different rules" regarding the use of force. In addition, prior training might be out of date, and security contractors do not seem to be receiving the kind of in-theater retraining that judge advocates provide to troops. As discussed previously, this retraining offers realistic scenarios that reflect the ways in which the judge advocates have refined the rules based on the conditions on the ground.[165] As one judge advocate noted, "It's really important to reset the training in context and to build up habits." The contractors, however, were outside the military training framework.[166] Indeed, another judge advocate who served in Iraq in 2005–2006 reported that some of the security contractors themselves, once in theater, wanted more training in the rules regarding the use of force. He noted that "a contractor came to us" to ask for such training. Moreover, because incidents regarding the use of force by contractors were such a problem, "we set up meetings with the [Contract Officer Representative], and briefly the issue was routed through the [Staff Judge Advocate]." But, in the end, the conclusion was that "we couldn't do the training because it was outside of military jurisdiction."[167]

Finally, judge advocates expressed frustration with inequities regarding the accountability of troops, as compared to contractors, painting a picture of a system in which soldiers who commit serious crimes or who violate military rules face punishment, while contractors face little or no sanction. Soldiers, of course, are subject to the military justice system for disciplinary violations or serious crimes. Contractors, by contrast, are not bound by the same disciplinary rules. Moreover, though contractors are nominally subject to civilian criminal punishment back in the United States, those laws remain unenforced.[168] Thus, in practice the most serious punishment an individual contractor might face is being fired and sent home. One judge advocate put the disparity in accountability in stark terms: "If a Marine violated the rules, he'd be court-martialed and punished. There was an established process. The worst that would happen to a civilian contractor who was just as culpable would be that he'd be sent back home to California." This judge advocate further emphasized that the "unfairness of the process" was palpable. While "service members were being held accountable for things across the board," contractors "were getting away with murder if you believed reports."[169]

Another judge advocate suggested that the lack of accountability fueled further abuses: "If a contractor misbehaved, he knew he could cover it up."[170] According to another lawyer, "Blackwater gave the impression, 'we're going to do what we want and we don't have to follow the rules. We're not in America.'" Such an attitude "was bad for us because the soldiers saw it. I would talk to company commanders, with 6–9 years military experience, supervising young soldiers putting boots on the ground, on the receiving end of insurgents. They could see the Blackwater guy drinking, on steroids, not following rules. It fostered discipline problems." This judge advocate further observed, "My brigade commander in the green zone was worried about the issue. Soldiers are held to a different standard. Soldiers couldn't travel, but contractors could."[171] As another commented, "Contractors can do anything—drink alcohol," and so on, but if "young soldiers go to the same place, do the same thing, the young soldiers will get punished, and the contractors won't."[172] One judge advocate gave as an example a case in which a Marine translator and a contractor were accused of extorting money. The "Marine involved went through the court martial process, was sent to Camp Lejeune, and was disciplined through the normal chain." For the contractor, by contrast, no disciplinary process existed. According to the judge advocate, "We restricted him to his quarters on the commander's general authority." A subsequent report was sent to the Department of Justice, but nothing further happened. As this judge advocate noted, "Ultimately we dropped it all. . . . We weren't going to force it. . . . We weren't going to keep calling." In the end, "we just debarred him from the base and eventually theater-wide."[173]

The judge advocates report that the existence of contractors also undermined troop morale because contractor pay was often better. As one lawyer observed, "Young soldiers want to go work for contractors because they get paid a lot more. . . . They see contractors sporting cowboy boots and jeans, growing a beard, and buying a Harley afterwards."[174] Another judge advocate reported that "quite a few of the soldiers just say, 'Why not go work for them?'"[175] Indeed, judge advocates observed that the pay disparities between troops and contractors have created retention and recruitment problems for the military. As one judge advocate commented about the use of contract interrogators: "A need for interrogation arose, and there weren't enough military interrogators, so we reached out and hired contractors." As a result, "there was a domino effect. It paid well.

So people would sign up to do military training, they would do three years in the military and then go work as contractors, where you can make 2, 3, 4 times as much as [a low-level soldier]." As a consequence, "this created a challenge for recruiting/retaining military interrogators."[176]

A number of judge advocates reported that individuals who had left the military because of discipline problems sometimes were later hired by private firms. As one judge advocate observed, "There were plenty of stories that a guy working as a contractor got court-martialed when he was a platoon member, and now he's back making $100 grand [per year]," as compared to uniformed military specialists who earn only $20,000.[177] As another judge advocate noted, "I used to hear that some of the contractor guys, security contractors and others, had been kicked out of uniform, not for serious disciplinary issues, but rather because they got administratively separated. Now they were making $80,000 riding desk at [the Coalition Provisional Authority]."[178] Yet another judge advocate reported, "There are stories that circulate among the JAGs, that a soldier who's been kicked out of the Army with a bad conduct discharge can turn around, and earn twice as much working for a contractor."[179] While, as the judge advocates acknowledge, these stories may be apocryphal, they reflect the unease that the judge advocates feel about the ability of contractors to flout military rules without suffering employment consequences.

Reforming the Organizational Structure and Culture of Private Contractors

The picture painted above relies on the stories of uniformed judge advocates and is therefore incomplete. Yet, a smaller group of interviews with contractors, combined with accounts in government and media reports, strongly suggests that the contract firms do in fact lack the kind of well-developed internal organizational features that the military has constructed through the judge advocate system. Therefore, reform efforts are urgently needed. On the one hand, we might seek to bring the contractors more within the organizational structure and culture of the military itself, by expanding the judge advocate's authority over them. On the other hand, we might seek reform of the firms' internal structures—either through voluntary measures or through regulation—combined with efforts to establish broader industry-wide standards.

Organizational Structure and Contractors

If, as discussed above, organizational structure and culture matter, then the next question is to determine what organizational structures are in place, either within contractor firms or industry-wide, to prevent and police abuses. Here the evidence is mixed, but tends to support the judge advocates' view that the contract firms do far less to prevent and police abuse than the military does.

First, it appears that few of the security contract firms have accountability agents or ombudspersons who are charged with monitoring abuses and who are actually integrated in the field with operational employees, as the judge advocates are. While the firms typically rely on their general counsel for legal advice, the lawyers in these offices appear to remain primarily at headquarters rather than deploying in the field. Moreover, reporting processes are not clear. For example, in the case involving the Triple Canopy employee who allegedly shot unprovoked at two Iraqi cars, subsequent litigation raises questions about the firm's internal reporting and investigation methods. Two employees who eventually spoke up about the incident were fired, and they ultimately filed suit against the company, alleging wrongful termination. A jury decided in favor of the company, but the jury forewoman asserted: "Although we find for [Triple Canopy], we strongly feel that its poor conduct, lack of standard reporting procedures, bad investigation methods, and unfair double standards amongst employees should not be condoned. . . . [W]e do not agree with Triple Canopy's treatment of the plaintiffs."[180] Although company representatives assert that they fired the employees and would have launched an investigation had the employees reported the incident promptly,[181] the jury statement suggests that the employees did not at the time have a clear internal accountability agent or ombudsperson to whom they could report or a clear set of guidelines to follow.

Second, the employees of such companies seem to lack a strong sense of even what the applicable laws and norms are, let alone have any great commitment to them. For example, Blackwater CEO Erik Prince, in his congressional testimony concerning the Nisour Square shootings, appeared to have at best a murky understanding of the precise legal rules and regulations that governed his employees' use of force and available accountability mechanisms for the misuse of that force. Thus, he asserted that his employees were subject to punishment in military courts under the UCMJ,[182] even though the military had not yet implemented recently enacted legislation extending military jurisdiction to contractors, and even though the UCMJ jurisdiction over State Department—as opposed to DOD—contractors had still not been clearly established.

Employees of other security firms have likewise expressed confusion about the applicable law and appear to have a somewhat cavalier attitude about rule of law norms. For example, one of the two Triple Canopy employees who filed the lawsuit stated that "we never knew if we fell under military law, American law, Iraqi law, or whatever." Furthermore, "we were always told, from the beginning, if for some reason something happened and the Iraqis were trying to prosecute us, they would put you in the back of a car and sneak you out of the country in the middle of the night." Isi Naucukidi, a former Triple Canopy employee also involved in the shootings, said he ultimately left the company voluntarily because "I couldn't stand what was happening. It seemed like every day they were covering something [up]." The firm's attitude, according to Naucukidi, is: "What happens here today, stays here today." Indeed, Naucukidi asserted that after the shooting, both the shift supervisors and other employees laughed as they sped away from the shooting, and one employee told the shift supervisor, "Nice shot."[183]

Third, contract employees seem to receive insufficient training in applicable laws and rules, particularly those that govern the use of force. While such contracts often now require training, government reports and other investigations have suggested in numerous instances that this training has not been adequate. For example, General George Fay's report in the wake of the Abu Ghraib incident concluded that a number of the contract interrogators had "little, if any training on [the] Geneva Conventions," and little interrogation experience.[184] In 2005 the Special Inspector General for Iraq Reconstruction (SIGIR) found that the Aegis security firm—which held a three-year, $293 million contract to provide a range of security and intelligence services to the DOD in Iraq—had not complied with contract requirements, failing to properly vet Iraqi employees or to demonstrate that its operators were qualified to use the weapons they were issued. The SIGIR concluded that "there is no assurance that Aegis is providing the best possible safety and security for government and reconstruction contractor personnel and facilities as required by the contract."[185]

Fourth, the fact that many companies use foreign labor complicates training and accountability efforts, as well as the broader effort to instill public law values. The market for security contractor labor is a truly global one, with firms hiring from dozens of countries around the world and with more than thirty countries represented among the security contractors in Iraq alone.[186] To be sure, contractors maintain that they use well-established practices to train and supervise the third-country nationals (or TCNs, as they are often called). For example, Blackwater's president, Gary Jackson, has asserted that "As far as the third-country nationals that we are required by United States government contract to use, we can't ask them to swear the same oath, but all of Blackwater's deploying professionals, both U.S. and third-country nationals, undergo extensive training in core values, leadership and human rights before they deploy. Each of them is issued a copy of the U.N.'s Universal Declaration of Human Rights in their native language to carry with them and remind them of their commitment to legal, moral and ethical standards."[187] Likewise, another private security firm reports that it "has developed a fairly sophisticated model for managing third-country national security guard forces."[188]

Yet in practice, training and vetting pose serious difficulties. For example, in 2005, the security firm Your Solutions sent 147 Chileans into conflict zones in Iraq. Twenty-eight of the recruits "broke their contracts and returned home early, claiming they received inadequate training and poor equipment."[189] And vetting is perhaps even more difficult. Many of the recruits have experience as police officers or soldiers in their home countries, but in some cases that experience includes a role in the state apparatus of dictatorships or former dictatorships with a history of gross human rights violations. South African security contractors, for example, may have served in the apartheid regime and have engaged in attacks on the black population during that era.[190] Likewise, Blackwater has hired Chilean commandos, many of whom were trained in the military of the dictator Augusto Pinochet, whose regime tortured and disappeared thousands of dissidents.[191] And while some firms rely on U.S. embassy records to determine whether an individual has a past that might disqualify him or her from employment, these records may be incomplete. In addition, tensions among personnel may arise because the noncitizen employees from developing countries earn far less than their counterparts from developed nations such as the United States, Australia, and Great Britain.[192]

Possibilities for Reform

The four obstacles discussed above may in the end render it impossible to build within contractor firms an organizational culture that sufficiently protects core public law values. Nevertheless, following the example of the judge advocate system, we might try to mandate—via contract or regulation—a more direct role for governmental accountability agents. Thus, the judge advocates, and perhaps other accountability agents such as contract monitors, might assume an expanded role in training, interacting with, and disciplining contractors.

Congress has already taken a step in this direction by expanding the jurisdiction of military courts to allow contractors to be tried under the UCMJ.[193] Under the military's guidelines, judge advocates now have the authority to investigate and prosecute cases of contractor misconduct. This authority remains limited, however, as judge advocates cannot bring a case unless central command approves.[194] In addition, the authority appears to apply only to contractors supporting a DOD mission.[195] Military oversight now exists, but it is only a last resort, meant to apply when the civilian justice system does not work.

Perhaps even more significantly, judge advocates now can assume more authority over contractors, even before the commission of an offense. The DOD recently moved in this direction by issuing a rule that would require security contractors to receive training from judge advocates.[196] The State Department has, in the wake of several shootings, gone farther and adopted a rule requiring that agency diplomatic security personnel ride along with all State Department security contractors whose mission requires them to travel (as opposed to monitoring stationary sites).[197] The new State Department rule would thus achieve greater integration of agency accountability agents, which, as we have seen, appears to be one institutional feature that tends to cause increased compliance.

While important, these reforms remain baby steps. For example, even under the State Department's rule, the judge advocates accompanying contractors do not have the authority to impose sanctions, and they do not have a separate hierarchy with clout in the upper echelons of the contractor firm. Thus, a more ambitious approach would be to try to re-create the full panoply of organizational features that the military created post-Vietnam for its own personnel. Such features could be mandated either as terms in the contracts with private firms or through direct regulation. And though it is debatable how best to implement these organizational features outside the uniformed military context,[198] it is clear that this is an area that should be seriously considered in any effort to reform the contracting process.

Rather than seeking more comingling of government accountability agents with contractor employees, another possible reform approach would seek to encourage or compel contractors themselves to institute processes that would help establish the organizational or professional culture necessary to protect public values. Thus, through governmental regulation or independent industry efforts, contract firms might create internal organizational structures to enhance compliance with the public law norms and values we have been discussing. Such efforts would involve firms adopting the kinds of reforms that the military adopted post-Vietnam with regard to its judge advocates. These efforts include requiring contractors to establish compliance units or hire ombudspeople who would accompany operational employees in theater, advise commanders, report through a separate chain of command, and have authority to confer benefits and impose punishments. In short, the idea would be to create within firms themselves a cadre of accountability agents who would be analogous to the judge advocates within the military. More broadly, the industry as a whole—either independently or by means of government regulation—might seek to professionalize the conduct of contractor employees through ethical codes, accreditation schemes, and the like. Interestingly, the International Peace Operations Association, the trade association for military contractors, has actually welcomed at least some of these reforms and attempted to create professional norms.

Thus, although the obstacles are enormous, both the organizational theory literature and the on-the-ground observations of military lawyers suggest that when we think about reforming the private military contractor process, we cannot ignore organizational structure and culture. Indeed, it is likely that these sorts of reforms, if they could be enacted, would run deeper and last longer than any other possible reforms that have been suggested to rein in military contractors. Accordingly, a serious consideration of how organizational culture can be linked to compliance suggests that, instead of focusing exclusively on new treaties or new international judicial rulings seeking to formally extend norms to contractors, we might instead look to how best to alter organizational structure and culture within private security firms.

The On-the-Ground Impact of Organizational Structure

To return to our example from the beginning of this chapter, if the judge advocates had played more of a role in training and supervising private security firms operating in Iraq, the contractor who shot and killed the Iraqi man at the checkpoint might never have done so. As noted previously, the military revised the rules of engagement for troops at fixed checkpoints after seeing problems on the ground. The military lawyers also undertook to train soldiers in how best to deal with various specific scenarios that might occur at these checkpoints. Had contractors been subject to use-of-force strictures based on these revised rules of engagement and had they received training from military lawyers, the contractor who fired his weapon might have more readily recognized other alternative options. Further, if the military lawyer had possessed explicit authority to initiate an investigation of the contractor (authority that is now more clearly established), there would have been less confusion about how the military should respond, how accountable the contractors were, and how to initiate compensation to victims or their families.

Alternatively, if the contractor firm itself had lawyers revising rules regarding the use of force based on military rules of engagement and conducting in-theater, scenario-specific training regarding checkpoints, that might also have given the contractor the strategic tools necessary to refrain from shooting. Moreover, an organizational structure that included the on-site deployment of committed compliance officers and the certain investigation of alleged abuses might well have affected the attitude of contractors as to their responsibilities to conform to rules regarding the use of force and to comply with disciplinary standards. And though having such organizational structures would be unlikely to prevent all potential abuses, they could well change the day-to-day reality at checkpoints and other sites of potential conflict throughout the areas of contractor deployment.

Conclusion

The use of private military contractors is not likely to end anytime soon. Accordingly, if we are to maintain core human rights values in military operations, we must address how best to build organizational structures and internal cultures within these firms that are most likely to inculcate and operationalize these values. And in approaching this difficult task, it will not be enough to reform our formal laws to make them applicable to contractors or expand court jurisdiction to hold contractors accountable. In addition, we need to think about the more inchoate, but perhaps even more salient, ways in which a culture of respect for human rights norms is actually created and maintained in military and security organizations.

This consideration of military lawyers on the battlefield demonstrates some of the mechanisms by which such a culture can be established. Though obviously not perfect, the system created since Vietnam—through which highly trained military lawyers are embedded with troops, advise commanders on the battlefield, answer to their own separate chain of command, and possess the authority to invoke sanctions—has had real impact. Significantly, none of these organizational features currently exists within privatized firms. Thus, reform is urgently needed. But these reforms must go beyond conventional legal frameworks and work toward deeper organizational and institutional change.

7

CONCLUSION

The past two decades have seen a quiet revolution in the way the United States and other countries act abroad. Privatization, long a fixture of the domestic American scene, has gone global. Moreover, simply resisting privatization in the foreign affairs context is probably no longer an option. Indeed, if anything the scope and pace of privatization in the international arena are increasing. To give one example, in late 2009 President Obama announced that he would send additional troops to Afghanistan, bringing the number of U.S. troops there to approximately ninety thousand.[1] Not mentioned in the president's speech was the fact that there are currently far more than ninety thousand U.S. contractors in Afghanistan. The Department of Defense alone counts some 104,101 contract employees, and that does not even count contractors operating based on agreements with other agencies. Accordingly, a ratio that had climbed to one to one in Iraq has now pushed even farther, and it would not be at all surprising to see in the near future a contractor force deployed overseas that is double the size of the uniformed military presence.[2]

Thus, it will not do simply to rail against privatization *in toto* or try to ban outright the use of contract labor in deployments abroad. To be sure, there may be some settings where using contractors poses such a grave risk of abuse that banning contract labor may be appropriate in certain circumstances. For example, the U.S. military currently forbids contractors to participate in direct offensive military action. And it may be that interrogation activities are similarly so rife with the possibility for abuse that outsourcing is inappropriate. But what we really need is a more nuanced response, one that recognizes both the advantages and the disadvantages of the privatization trend and seeks appropriate avenues to constrain abuse, instill public law values, and provide mechanisms of accountability.

Moreover, in looking for mechanisms of constraint and accountability, we must not limit ourselves to classic legal mechanisms. Although it is tempting to respond to reports of abuse by calling for new treaty provisions or new criminal statutes, it will not be sufficient merely to tweak existing international law treaties or doctrines (or even invent new ones) in order to bring private contractors within the ambit of formal international law. After all, even if international or domestic courts could be convinced that private contractors should be held liable for violation of international law norms (which is far from certain), international and transnational public law litigation will never be able to hold accountable more than a handful of people. And even domestic criminal or civil suits are only a partial solution, at best. Accordingly, those who seek to preserve or expand core public law values will also need to look elsewhere to find mechanisms for ensuring accountability in a privatized world. Fortunately, there are many alternative ways of trying to affect behavior, and some may be even more useful in the privatization context than the ordinary legal approaches. Thus, we need a broad-based, multifaceted perspective, one that does not seek to gloss over the significant threats posed by privatization, but one that seeks creative responses rather than simply giving up.

This book is an effort to begin that discussion. As to the threats, the most obvious is the concern that private contractors may be more likely to commit human rights abuses than government actors would. In addition, privatization makes activities abroad even more opaque and therefore less amenable to democratic deliberation and public participation. And this same lack of transparency increases the specter of corruption. Finally, the intermingling of contractors and members of the uniformed military may create confused chains of command and uncertain rules of engagement, and may undermine aspects of military culture that are crucial to maintaining adherence to public law values. Accordingly, there are reasons to be very wary of this new privatized world in which we find ourselves.

And yet, if we start from the premise that we shall not be able to wish privatization away, then simply noting the dangers will not be enough. I therefore seek to begin a dialogue among scholars of international law, administrative law, and organizational theory, and to use insights from each of these areas to recommend mechanisms of accountability and constraint that, while not perfect by any means, could at least help protect important values that might otherwise be undermined completely in this new era. Moreover, some of these avenues of reform, such as rewriting the contracts that drive privatization, are actually more readily available in the outsourcing context than if only governmental actors were involved. Thus, privatization may weaken certain avenues of accountability and constraint, but it also enables others.

The reforms I propose are summarized below.

A Multifaceted Agenda for Reform

Enforcing International Legal Norms

- Governments, international organizations, and NGOs should clarify standards of conduct and develop best practices for contractors.
- Courts and tribunals should clarify that in the case of gross violations of international human rights and humanitarian law, a nexus to state action is either not required or is satisfied in the situation of a government contractor.
- Courts should clarify that gross violations of international human rights and humanitarian law are actionable under the Alien Tort Statute.

Enforcing Domestic Criminal Law

- Congress should eliminate current ambiguities by expanding the Military Extraterritorial Jurisdiction Act to apply to all contractors accused of committing federal crimes, no matter which government agency is the contracting party and no matter where in the world the criminal acts occurred.

- Congress should require the Department of Justice to establish a dedicated office for investigating and prosecuting criminal cases involving contractors abroad. This office should be required to report regularly on the status of contractor investigations and prosecutions.
- Congress should require the FBI to establish "theater investigative units" to deploy in theater to work in partnership with military investigators in cases involving allegations of serious abuses.
- The military should use its new authority to pursue criminal enforcement actions under the Uniform Code of Military Justice against contractors serving with or accompanying an armed force in the field.
- The various governmental agencies employing contractors should do a better job tracking the total number of contractors employed and logging and investigating any serious incidents involving possibly unlawful uses of force.

Enforcing Domestic Civil Law

- Courts should clarify that civil tort suits against contractors do not implicate the political question doctrine.
- Courts and/or Congress should clarify that the Federal Tort Claims Act does not immunize contractors from suit or preempt civil suits unless the contractors are operating within the military chain of command.

Reforming Contracts

- Agencies should explicitly incorporate public law standards into contractual terms, including references to specific legal frameworks and provisions for training. Likewise, agencies should ensure that these terms are included in contractors' agreements with subcontractors.
- The executive branch should make contract monitoring, oversight, and coordination a higher priority. Ideally, the president should establish a high-level interagency working group to ensure increased staffing and training of contract management personnel, greater consistency of standards for contractors working for different agencies, and monitoring of contracts for all kinds of law compliance,

not just financial waste or fraud. In addition, this entity should require contract oversight personnel from different agencies to work together in teams on the ground in the theater of operations.
- Agencies should ensure that contracts include performance benchmarks and self-evaluation requirements.
- Agencies should require contract firms to receive accreditation from independent organizations, and nongovernmental organizations should create accreditation bodies applying uniform standards.
- Agencies should make sure that contracts include third-party beneficiary provisions and should require their contractors to create private grievance mechanisms.
- If agencies do not implement the reforms listed above, Congress should mandate such reforms.
- Congress should expand whistleblower protections and the availability of qui tam actions with regard to contractor employees.

Enhancing Public Participation

- A new federal office of Rule of Law Operations should be created to provide unified policy direction and management supervision of all police and security contractors, and the office should be required to report regularly to Congress on the activities of contractors, including any problematic uses of force.
- Legislation should require automatic release of all contract terms not implicating national security concerns, so that members of Congress and watchdog agencies can scrutinize the agreements and raise objections if necessary.
- Legislation should make it more difficult for government officials awarding and administering contracts to move to jobs with those same contractors.
- Contracts should require that those affected by the performance of a contract be consulted in order to help shape contract terms beforehand and evaluate efficacy afterward, at least as much as possible given security concerns.
- Contracts should be structured as three-way trust relationships where possible, with the government as settlor, the contractor as trustee, and the affected population as beneficiary.

- Agencies employing contractors should issue regular public reports on the extent to which contractors are complying with core public values.

Reforming the Organizational Structure and Culture of Private Security Firms

- Judge Advocates should be given broader authority to train contractors, advise on security-related missions, and oversee contract performance in theater.
- Military commanders should be vested with greater authority to supervise and discipline noncompliant contract personnel.
- Private military and security contractors should be required, through contract or regulation, to create a legal corps that would be embedded with operational troops and have authority to enforce core rule-of-law norms.
- Private military and security contractors should adopt comprehensive codes of conduct and best practices.

None of these mechanisms is perfect, of course. The legal avenues remain regrettably meager, contract compliance and oversight are expensive and often unsuccessful, democratic participation requirements (even limited ones) may be unwieldy or normatively unpalatable, and changing internal organizational structures and culture is a difficult, slow, and uncertain process. And it is possible that attempts to build mechanisms of public accountability into a privatization regime could possibly jeopardize some of the purported efficiency gains that were part of the justification for privatization in the first place.

Yet, for international law scholars who must grapple daily with the limited enforcement power of international legal institutions, privatization actually provides an important opportunity because the moment of contracting is always a moment when oversight is possible. Particularly now, when the general public is becoming increasingly aware of, and alarmed by, the privatization trend, a variety of constituencies may be mobilized to seek creative solutions. For example, governmental decision makers can be made to see that they have a strong interest in avoiding the reputational hit that accompanies incidents of abuse such as those committed at Abu Ghraib. In addition, better mechanisms of constraint and account-ability could save millions of dollars currently lost in waste and corruption, could result in better project designs with greater public input, and could ensure that important elements of military culture are maintained. For their part, activists and NGOs interested in maintaining core public values should spend at least as much time seeking to establish accreditation regimes and lobbying for governmental adoption of them as they currently do calling for an end to military privatization altogether. And of course we must remember that the proper management of privatization will almost certainly require a variety of approaches, and we need not choose one to the exclusion of others.

In short, this is the moment for thinking broadly and creatively about how best to respond to the threats posed by the massive increase in foreign affairs outsourcing described in this book. We are truly in a new era of privatization, and it will not do simply to resist the trend altogether. Instead, we must seek new ways to build in to the engines of privatization alternative mechanisms of accountability and constraint. Only by doing so will we be able to protect core public law values in the brave new world in which we now live.

NOTES

1. Introduction

1. Blackwater has since changed its company name to XE, but for narrative consistency the company will be referred to as Blackwater throughout this book.

2. David Johnston & John M. Broeder, *FBI Says Guards Killed 14 Iraqis Without Cause*, N.Y. Times, Nov. 14, 2007, at A1, *available at* http://www.nytimes.com/2007/11/14/world/middleeast/14blackwater.html?_r=1; James Glanz & Alissa J. Rubin, *From Errand to Fatal Shot to Hail of Fire to 17 Deaths*, N.Y. Times, Oct. 3, 2007, at A1, *available at* http://www.nytimes.com/2007/10/03/world/middleeast/03firefight.html.

3. *Id.*

4. *Blackwater Faulted by U.S. Military: Report*, Reuters, Oct. 5, 2007, *available at* http://www.reuters.com/article/topNews/idUSN0439965120071005?sp=true.

5. Office of the Special Inspector Gen. for Iraq Reconstruction, *Review of DynCorp International, LLC, Contract S-LMAQM-04-C-0030, Task Order 0338, for the Iraqi Police Training Program Support, SIGIR-06-029, DOS-OIG-AUD/IQO-07-20*, at 12 (2007), *available at* http://www.sigir.mil/reports/pdf/audits/06-029.pdf.

6. *See* Barry Yeoman, Op-Ed, *Need an Army? Just Pick Up the Phone*, N.Y. Times, Apr. 2, 2004, at A19.

7. Tom Jackman, *U.S. Contractor Fired on Iraqi Vehicles for Sport, Suit Alleges*, Wash. Post, Nov. 17, 2006, at A20.

8. Steve Fainaru, *Four Hired Guns in an Armored Truck, Bullets Flying, and a Pickup and a Taxi Brought to a Halt. Who Did the Shooting and Why?*, Wash. Post, Apr. 15, 2007, at A1, *available at* http://www.washingtonpost.com/wp-dyn/content/article/2007/04/14/AR2007041401490.html.

9. *See, e.g.*, Anthony R. Jones & George R. Fay, Dep't of the Army, *AR 15-6 Investigation of the Abu Ghraib Detention Facility and 205th Military Intelligence Brigade*

50–51 (2004), *available at* http://fl1.findlaw.com/news.findlaw.com/hdocs/docs/dod/fay82504rpt.pdf [hereinafter *Investigation of the Abu Ghraib Detention Facility*].

10. *See* GAO Report, *Contingency Contracting: DOD, State, and USAID Continue to Face Challenges in Tracking Contractor Personnel and Contracts in Iraq and Afghanistan 9* (Oct. 2009), *available at* http://www.gao.gov/new.items/d101.pdf. Amazingly, it appears that even as recently as 2009, many years into the Iraqi operation, the government had no adequate system even to track how many of its own private contractors are in the country. See id. at 8–15.

11. *See generally* Gregory P. Bailey, Note, *United States v. Passaro: Exercising Extraterritorial Jurisdiction over Non-Defense Department Government Contractors Committing Crimes Overseas under the Special Maritime and Territorial Jurisdiction of the United States*, 58 Cath. U. L. Rev. 1143 (2009).

12. Mark Mazzetti, *U.S. Is Still Using Private Spy Ring, Despite Doubts*, N.Y. Times, May 15, 2010, *available at* http://www.nytimes.com/2010/05/16/world/16contractors.html?hp.

13. Doug Brooks & Jim Shevlin, *Reconsidering Battlefield Contractors*, 6 Geo. J. Int'l Aff. 103, 104 (2005).

14. Cong. Budget Office, U.S. Cong., *Contractors' Support of U.S. Operations in Iraq, Publ'n No. 3053*, at 8, 13 (2008), *available at* http://www.cbo.gov/ftpdocs/96xx/doc9688/08-12-IraqContractors.pdf; Richard J. Hornstein, *Protecting Civilian Logisticians on the Battlefield*, 38 U.S. Army Logistician 14, 15 (2006), *available at* http://www.almc.army.mil/alog/issues/JulAug06/pdf/jul_aug_06.pdf.

15. For example, nearly 80 percent of British Army training and most shore-based Royal Navy training is now undertaken by private military companies, *see* U.K. Foreign and Commonwealth Office, *HC 577 Private Military Companies: Options for Regulation 2001–02*, at 13, *available at* http://www.fco.gov.uk/resources/en/pdf/pdf4/fco_pdf_privatemilitarycompanies, and the Canadian Forces Contractor Augmentation Program provides logistics services to the Canadian military. *See* Can. Dep't of Nat'l Defence, *Backgrounders: Canadian Forces Contractor Augmentation Program, BG-04.010* (2004), *available at* http://www.admpa.forces.gc.ca/news-nouvelles/news-nouvelles-eng.asp?cat=03&id=1409.

16. Juan Carlos Zarate, *The Emergence of a New Dog of War: Private International Security Companies, International Law, and the New World Disorder*, 34 Stan. J. Int'l L. 75, 95 (1998).

17. *See, e.g.*, Chris Tomlinson, *U.S. Hires Contractor to Back Somalis*, Assoc. Press, Mar. 7, 2007 (summarizing military contractor activity in Africa).

18. *See, e.g.*, Doug Brooks & Gaurav Laroia, *Privatized Peacekeeping*, Nat'l Int., Summer 2005.

19. *See, e.g.*, P. W. Singer, Corporate Warriors: The Rise of the Privatized Military Industry 182–86 (2003) [hereinafter Corporate Warriors].

20. *See generally* Mary H. Cooper, *Privatizing the Military*, 14 CQ Res. 565 (2004).

21. Moshe Schwartz, *Department of Defense's Use of Private Security Contractors in Iraq and Afghanistan: Background, Analysis, and Options for Congress* 6 (Cong. Research Svc., 2010), *available at* http://www.fas.org/sgp/crs/natsec/R40835.pdf.

22. *See, e.g.,* Beyond U.N. Subcontracting: Task-Sharing with Regional Security Arrangements and Service-Providing NGOs (Thomas G. Weiss ed., 1998) [hereinafter Beyond U.N. Subcontracting]; Ian Smillie, *At Sea in a Sieve? Trends and Issues in the Relationship Between Northern NGOs and Northern Governments, in* Stakeholders: Government-NGO Partnerships for International Development, at 7 (Ian Smillie & Henny Helmich eds., 1999) [hereinafter *At Sea in a Sieve*]; Michael B. Likosky, Law, Infrastructure and Human Rights (2006).

23. *See* Singer, Corporate Warriors, *supra* note 19, at 144.

24. *See* USAID, *DCHA/PVC-ASHA Portfolio, Fiscal Year 2004,* at B-5 (2005), *available at* http://pdf.usaid.gov/pdf_docs/PNADJ534.pdf.

25. U.S. Agency for Int'l Dev., Bureau for Democracy, Conflict and Humanitarian Assistance, Office of U.S. Foreign Disaster Assistance, *OFDA Annual Report 14* (2008), *available at* www.usaid.gov/our_work/humanitarian_assistance/disaster_assistance/publications/annual_reports/pdf/AR2008.pdf.

26. Smillie, *At Sea in a Sieve, supra* note 22, at 9 (describing foreign aid in France, Sweden, and the E.U.); *see also* Andrew S. Natsios, *NGOs and the U.N. System in Complex Humanitarian Emergencies: Conflict or Cooperation?, in* NGOs, the U.N., and Global Governance, at 73 (Leon Gordenker & Thomas G. Weiss eds., 1996) (noting the relationships of UNICEF and UNHCR with NGOs); Ruth Wedgwood, *Legal Personality and the Role of Non-Governmental Organizations and Non-State Political Entities in the United Nations System, in* Non-State Actors as New Subjects of International Law, at 21, 23 (Rainer Hofmann & Nils Geissler eds., 1999) (describing the use of private contractors by UNHCR).

27. *See, e.g.,* Mark Duffield, *NGO Relief in War Zones: Toward an Analysis of the New Aid Paradigm, in* Beyond U.N. Subcontracting, *supra* note 22, at 139, 146 ("By the mid-1980s, a noticeable change in donor funding policy had occurred, from direct donor assistance to recognised governments in favour of international support for private, non-governmental sectors.").

28. *See* Leon Gordenker & Thomas G. Weiss, *Pluralizing Global Governance: Analytical Approaches and Dimensions, in* NGOs, the U.N., and Global Governance, at 37 (Leon Gordenker & Thomas G. Weiss eds., 1996).

29. For useful histories of private mercenaries in the context of modern private military contractors, *see* Singer, Corporate Warriors, *supra* note 19; Todd S. Millard, *Overcoming Post-Colonial Myopia: A Call To Recognize and Regulate Private Military Companies,* 176 Mil. L. Rev. 1 (2003); *see also* G. T. Griffith, The Mercenaries of the Hellenistic World 4 (Bouma's Boekhuis 1968); Hans Delbrück, History of the Art of War: Within the Framework of Political History 250 (Walter J. Renfroe Jr. trans., 1975); Anthony Mockler, The Mercenaries 43–73 (1969); John Keay, The Honourable Company: A History of the English East India Company (1993); Nicholas Parillo, *The De-Privatization of American Warfare: How the U.S. Government Used,*

Regulated and Ultimately Abandoned Privateering in the Nineteenth Century, 19 Yale J.L. & Human. 1 (2007).

30. See Max Weber, *Politics as a Vocation, in* The Vocation Lectures (David Owen & Tracy B. Strong eds., Rodney Livingstone trans., 2004).

31. Singer, Corporate Warriors, *supra* note 19.

32. Deborah D. Avant, The Market for Force: The Consequences of Privatizing Security 6 (2005); see also Allison Stanger, One Nation Under Contract (2009).

33. Paul R. Verkuil, Outsourcing Sovereignty: Why Privatization of Government Functions Threatens Democracy and What We Can Do About It (2007) [hereinafter Outsourcing Sovereignty].

34. Jeremy Scahill, Blackwater: The Rise of the World's Most Powerful Mercenary Army (2007).

35. David Isenberg, Shadow Force: Private Security Contractors in Iraq (2010). Other journalistic accounts of the private security industry include Robert Young Pelton, Licensed to Kill: Hired Guns in the War on Terror (2007) and Steve Fainaru, Big Boy Rules: America's Mercenaries Fighting in Iraq (2009).

36. From Mercenaries to Market: The Rise and Regulation of Private Military Companies (Simon Chesterman & Chia Lehnardt eds., 2007).

37. Government by Contract: Outsourcing and American Democracy (Jody Freeman & Martha Minow eds., 2009) [hereinafter Government by Contract].

38. James Risen, *Contractors Back from Iraq Suffer Trauma from Battle,* N.Y. Times, July 5, 2007, at A1, *available at* http://www.nytimes.com/2007/07/05/us/05contractors.html.

39. *See* Convention Relative to the Protection of Civilian Persons in Time of War, Aug. 12, 1949, 6 U.S.T. 3516, 75 U.N.T.S. 287 (entered into force Oct. 21, 1950, for the United States Feb. 2, 1956); Protocol Additional to the Geneva Conventions of 12 August 1949, and Relating to the Protection of Victims of International Armed Conflicts (Protocol I), June 8, 1977, 1125 U.N.T.S. 3; Protocol Additional to the Geneva Conventions of 12 August 1949, Relating to the Protection of Victims of Non-International Armed Conflicts (Protocol II), June 8, 1977, 1125 U.N.T.S. 609.

40. Interview with JAG officer #5 (Oct. 16, 2007).

41. Interview with JAG officer #4 (Oct. 16, 2007).

42. Convention Against Torture and Other Cruel, Inhuman or Degrading Treatment or Punishment art. 1, Dec. 10, 1984, S. Treaty Doc. No. 100-20 (1988), 1465 U.N.T.S. 85, 113–14, *available at* http://www2.ohchr.org/english/law/cat.htm.

43. *See generally* The Privatization of Health Care Reform: Legal and Regulatory Perspectives (M. Gregg Bloche ed., 2003); Simon Domberger & Paul Jensen, *Contracting Out by the Public Sector: Theory, Evidence, Prospects,* 13 Oxford Rev. Econ. Pol'y 67, 72–75 (1997) (arguing that privatization is efficient in a variety of contexts); F. Howard Nelson & Nancy Van Meter, *What Does Private Management Offer Public Education?,* 11 Stan. L. & Pol'y Rev. 271 (2000) (arguing for private management of "public" schools); Sharon Dolovich, *State Punishment and Private Prisons,* 55 Duke L.J. 437 (2005) (arguing that prison privatization undermines core public law values

of humanity and parsimony); Gillian E. Metzger, *Privatization as Delegation,* 103 Colum. L. Rev. 1367 (2003) (arguing that privatization can threaten public law values embodied in constitutional norms); Jody Freeman, *Extending Public Law Norms Through Privatization,* 116 Harv. L. Rev. 1285, 1300 (2003).

44. There are some exceptions. *See, e.g.,* Government by Contract, *supra* note 37; Verkuil, Outsourcing Sovereignty, *supra* note 33.

45. *See, e.g.,* Non-State Actors and Human Rights (Philip Alston ed., 2005); Math Noortman, *Non-State Actors in International Law, in* Non-State Actors in International Relations, at 59, 71–72 (Bas Arts et al. eds., 2001).

46. John Sifton, Remarks on Private Military Contractors at a Conference at Georgetown University Law Center (Apr. 2005).

47. *To Consider the Nomination of Lieutenant General David H. Petraeus, USA, to be General and Commander, Multi-National Forces-Iraq, Hearing Before the S. Armed Serv. Comm.,* 110th Congress (2007) (statement of Lt. Gen. David H. Petraeus, responding to a question from Sen. John McCain) ("[T]here are tens of thousands of contract security forces and ministerial security forces that do in fact guard facilities and secure institutions and so forth that our forces . . . would otherwise have to guard and secure, and so that does give me reason to believe that we can accomplish the mission in Baghdad.").

48. *See, e.g.,* Steven R. Ratner, *Corporations and Human Rights: A Theory of Legal Responsibility,* 111 Yale L.J. 443, 524–30 (2001) (arguing that more international law norms should be extended to bind corporations directly); *see also* David Weissbrodt & Muria Kruger, *Norms on the Responsibilities of Transnational Corporations and Other Business Enterprises with Regard to Human Rights,* 97 Am. J. Int'l L. 901 (2003) (same); Todd S. Milliard, *Overcoming Post-Colonial Myopia: A Call to Recognize and Regulate Private Military Companies,* 176 Mil. L. Rev. 1, 41–42 (2003) (same). *But see* Carlos M. Vázquez, *Direct vs. Indirect Obligations of Corporations Under International Law,* 43 Colum. J. Transnat'l L. 927 (2005) (urging caution).

49. *See, e.g.,* Michael Byers, Custom, Power and the Power of Rules: International Relations and Customary International Law 8 (1999) ("International relations scholars have traditionally . . . regarded international law as something of an epiphenomenon, with rules of international law being dependent on power, subject to short-term alteration by power-applying States, and therefore of little relevance to how States actually behave.").

50. *See* Memorandum from Alberto R. Gonzales, U.S. Att'y Gen., for President George W. Bush, Decision re Application of the Geneva Convention on Prisoners of War to the Conflict with Al Qaeda and the Taliban, at 2 (Jan. 25, 2002), *available at* http://www.gwu.edu/~nsarchiv/NSAEBB/NSAEBB127/02.01.25.pdf.

51. *Colin Powell Says Guantanamo Should Be Closed,* Reuters, Jun. 10, 2007, *available at* http://www.reuters.com/article/idUSN1043646920070610?feedType=RSS.

52. Madeleine K. Albright, Sec'y of State, Statement to the ASEAN Post-Ministerial Conference and Regional Forum, at 1 (July 28, 1997), *available at* http://www.disam.dsca.mil/pubs/Indexes/Vol%2020_1/Albright.pdf.

53. Proclamation No. 5686, 52 Fed. Reg. 28,959, 28,960 (July 31, 1987).

54. Press Release, U.S. Army, LOGCAP IV Logistics Contract Awarded Through Full and Open Competition (Apr. 17, 2008).

55. Office of the Special Inspector Gen. for Iraq Reconstruction, *Need to Enhance Oversight of Theater-Wide Internal Security Services Contracts, SIGIR-09-017,* at ii (2009), *available at* http://www.sigir.mil/reports/pdf/audits/09-017.pdf.

56. Jacques S. Gansler et al., Comm'n on Army Acquisition and Program Mgmt. in Expeditionary Operations, *Urgent Reform Required: Army Expeditionary Contracting* 3 (2007), *available at* http://www.army.mil/docs/Gansler_Commission _Report_Final_071031.pdf.

57. For example, the U.S. military strengthened its internal codes of conduct, updating the *U.S. Army Field Manual* so that, in addition to specifying prohibited acts, it emphasized that the main objective of wartime detention operations is "the implementation of the Geneva Conventions." James F. Gebhardt, *The Road to Abu Ghraib: U.S. Army Detainee Doctrine and Experience,* Mil. Rev. Jan.–Feb. 2005, at 44, 50. At the same time, the DOD dramatically stepped up training activities and gave military lawyers a greater role, *see* Frederic L. Borch, Judge Advocates in Combat: Army Lawyers in Military Operations from Vietnam to Haiti 30 (2001) [hereinafter Judge Advocates in Combat], by initiating a "law of war program," run primarily by the JAG Corps, designed to educate troops from all services in the law of war. *Id.* at 37; U.S. Dep't of Def., Dir. 5100.77, DOD Law of War Program (Nov. 5, 1974), *canceled by* U.S. Dep't of Def., Dir. 5100.77, DOD Law of War Program (Dec. 9, 1998) (reissuing 1974 directive "to update policy and responsibilities in the Department of Defense"). The JAG Corps also was given responsibility for helping to develop and review operations plans to ensure compliance with the law of war. Borch, Judge Advocates in Combat, *supra,* at 31.

58. Jones & Fay, *Investigation of the Abu Ghraib Detention Facility, supra* note 9, at 50–51.

2. Key Moments in U.S. Military and Security Outsourcing, from Vietnam to Iraq

1. George S. Prugh, Vietnam Studies, Law at War: Vietnam 1964–1973, at 88 (1975) [hereinafter Law at War].

2. In 1968–1969, the U.S. Army Procurement Agency awarded and administered contracts worth half a billion dollars that required contractors to employ more than fifty-two thousand people—a ratio of contractors to troops that more closely approaches one to ten. Joseph M. Heiser Jr., Vietnam Studies, Logistics Support 88 (1974) [hereinafter Logistics Support].

3. *Id.* at 45, 88–90, 139, 192.

4. Prugh, Law at War, *supra* note 1, at 96.

5. Heiser, Logistics Support, *supra* note 2, at 163. In the conclusion of his study, Heiser also notes that "the use of contractors to augment or supplement the military

forces is feasible and workable. Where contractors are to be supported by the Army logistical system, they can be better supported by depots than by direct support units. The Army supply system can obtain demand data for nonstandard commercial parts. However, the determination whether to support contractors from the Army's supply system or to have the contractor provide his own support should be the result of a careful analysis. The cost effectiveness and responsiveness of each method should be evaluated." *Id.* at 259.

6. Prugh, Law at War, *supra* note 1, at 99, 106–8.

7. *See* Francis J. Kelly, Vietnam Studies, U.S. Army Special Forces 1961–1971, at 7, 19–44 (1973) [hereinafter U.S. Army Special Forces].

8. *Green Berets, in War Since '62, Said to Be Pulling Out This Year,* N.Y. Times, July 12, 1970, at A4 [hereinafter *Green Berets, in War Since '62*].

9. Kelly, U.S. Army Special Forces, *supra* note 7, at preface, 30.

10. *Green Berets, in War Since '62, supra* note 8, at A4.

11. William Beecher, *Green Berets Weigh Cut in Force as Mission Shifts; A Small Reduction by 1969 in Vietnam Is Considered—Leader Describes Aims,* N.Y. Times, Aug. 3, 1968, at A8.

12. Kelly, U.S. Army Special Forces, *supra* note 7, at 96–133, 152–59.

13. *See U.S. Sends Lon Nol Mercenary Units; Force of 2,000 Well-Armed Cambodians Is Flown in from South Vietnam, U.S. Sends Lon Nol a Contingent of Mercenaries from Vietnam,* N.Y. Times, May 4, 1970, at A1.

14. *See, e.g., Siege Is Reported on 2d U.S. Outpost in South Vietnam; North Vietnamese Are Said to Hit Dakpek, a Camp 5 Miles from Laos Base Used for Patrols, At Least 3 Mercenaries at Special Forces Center Killed in Assault Siege Reported on 2d U.S. Camp Near Laotian Border in Vietnam,* N.Y. Times, Apr. 13, 1970, at A1 (reporting casualties sustained by "Montagnard tribesmen defenders who are paid, trained, and led by American Special Forces.").

15. Gene Roberts, *Green Berets Pleased by Renewed Attention; John Wayne Film and Recent Attacks to Their Camps Seems to Raise Spirits,* N.Y. Times, Aug. 31, 1968, at A4.

16. For an overview of Operation Phoenix that, while critical in some respects, is largely favorable, *see* Dale Andrade, Ashes to Ashes: The Phoenix Program and the Vietnam War (1990) [hereinafter Ashes to Ashes]. For a more critical view, *see, e.g.,* Wayne L. Cooper, *Operation Phoenix: A Vietnam Fiasco Seen from Within,* Wash. Post, June 18, 1972, at B1 [hereinafter *Operation Phoenix*]. Stuart Herrington has given a detailed account of his role as a Phoenix adviser *in* Stuart Herrington, Stalking the Vietcong (1982).

17. *See* Andrade, Ashes to Ashes, *supra* note 16; Cooper, *Operation Phoenix, supra* note 16.

18. Cooper, *Operation Phoenix, supra* note 16.

19. Andrade, Ashes to Ashes, *supra* note 16.

20. Cooper, *Operation Phoenix, supra* note 16; *see also* Peter R. Kann, *The Invisible Foe, New Intelligence Push Attempts to Wipe Out Vietcong Underground,* Wall St. J., Sept. 5, 1968, at A1.

21. Cooper, *Operation Phoenix, supra* note 16.

22. Peter R. Kann, *The Hidden War: Elite Phoenix Forces Hunt Vietcong Chiefs in an Isolated Village—Raid Prompted by Informers Finds, Most of Foe Gone and Natives Tight Lipped—Demolishing a VC Monument,* Wall St. J., May 25, 1969, at A1 [hereinafter *The Hidden War*].

23. *The Rise of Phoenix,* 75 Newsweek, No. 2, at 25 (Jan. 12, 1970).

24. Robert G. Kaiser Jr., *U.S. Aides in Vietnam Scorn Phoenix Project,* Wash. Post, Feb. 17, 1970, at A10.

25. Victor Marchetti & John D. Marks, The CIA and the Cult of Intelligence 245–46 (Alfred A. Knopf 1974).

26. Cooper, *Operation Phoenix, supra* note 16.

27. Kann, *The Hidden War, supra* note 22.

28. For a comprehensive discussion of the program, *see* Robert M. Blackburn, Mercenaries and Lyndon Johnson's "More Flags": The Hiring of Korean, Filipino, and Thai Soldiers in the War 145 (1994).

29. Philip Shabecoff, *Anti-U.S. Feelings Up in Philippines; American Troops' Misdeeds in Country Are Recalled,* N.Y. Times., Dec. 11, 1969 [hereinafter *Anti-U.S. Feelings Up in Philippines*].

30. *See, e.g.,* John W. Finney, *Manila War Role Is Issue in Capital: State Department Opposes Publication of Testimony,* N.Y. Times, Oct. 13, 1969, at A15; *see also* Shabecoff, *Anti-U.S. Feelings Up in Philippines, supra* note 29; James M. Naughton, *Agnew Tells the Thais to Ignore U.S. Critics,* N.Y. Times, Jan. 5, 1970, at A3.

31. S. Rep. No. 91-865, at 9–10 (1970), *reprinted in* 1970 U.S.C.C.A.N. 6054, 6054–6066. *See also* John W. Finney, *Long Debate Ends; Cooper-Church Limits on Cambodia Action Adopted, 58–73 Senate Passes Curb on War Power,* N.Y. Times, July 1, 1970.

32. Special Foreign Assistance Act of 1971, Pub. L. 91-652, §7(a)–(b), 84 Stat. 1942, 1943 (1971):

> (a) In line with the expressed intention of the President of the United States, none of the funds authorized or appropriated pursuant to this or any other Act may be used to finance the introduction of United States ground combat troops into Cambodia, or to provide United States advisers to or for Cambodian military forces in Cambodia.

> (b) Military and economic assistance provided by the United States to Cambodia and authorized or appropriated pursuant to this or any other Act shall not be construed as a commitment by the United States to Cambodia for its defense.

33. *See* Jay Price & Joseph Neff, *Army Molds a Future,* News & Observer (Raleigh, N.C.), July 27, 2004, at A1.

34. For an overview of this turn to privatization, *see generally* Jody Freeman, *Extending Public Law Norms Through Privatization,* 116 Harv. L. Rev. 1285 (2003) [hereinafter *Extending Private Law Norms*].

35. *See id.*

36. *See, e.g.,* Paul C. Light, The True Size of Government (1999).

37. *See* Freeman, *Extending Private Law Norms, supra* note 34 (describing studies).

38. Cong. Budget Office, U.S. Cong., *Contractors' Support of U.S. Operations in Iraq, Publ'n No. 3053,* at 13 (2008), *available at* http://www.cbo.gov/ftpdocs/96xx/doc9688/08-12-IraqContractors.pdf [hereinafter *Contractors' Support*].

39. *See* Steven Lee Meyers, *Pentagon to Trim Thousands of Jobs Held by Civilians,* N.Y. Times, Nov. 10, 1997, at A1 [hereinafter *Pentagon to Trim Thousands of Jobs*].

40. Press Release, Office of Assistant Sec'y of Def. (Pub. Affairs), U.S. Dep't of Def., Secretary Cohen Reshapes Defense for the Twenty-First Century (Nov. 10, 1997) *available at* http://www.fas.org/man/docs/dri/b11101997_bt605-97.html [hereinafter Secretary Cohen Reshapes Defense] (emphasis added).

41. *See* Bradley Graham, *Cohen Sets Major Pentagon Overhaul; Plan Includes Job Cuts, Consolidation, Putting Work Out for Bid,* Wash. Post, Nov. 10, 1997, at A1.

42. Office of Assistant Sec'y of Def. (Pub. Affairs), Secretary Cohen Reshapes Defense, *supra* note 40; *see also* Meyers, *Pentagon to Trim Thousands of Jobs, supra* note 39.

43. Interview with senior DOD official #1 (Oct. 24, 2007).

44. *See* National Defense Authorization Act for FY 1998, Pub. L. No. 105-85, § 912, 111 Stat. 1629 (1997).

45. Interview with senior DOD official #1, *supra* note 43.

46. *See* Steven L. Schooner, *Competitive Sourcing Policy: More Sail than Rudder?,* 33 Pub. Cont. L.J. 263 (2004).

47. Mark Calaguas, *Military Privatization: Efficiency or Anarchy?,* 6 Chi.-Kent J. Int'l & Comp. L. 58, 68 (2006).

48. P. W. Singer, Corporate Warriors: The Rise of the Privatized Military Industry 127, 131 (2003).

49. Ruta Nimkar, *From Bosnia to Baghdad: The Case for Regulating Private Military and Security Companies,* 20 J. of Pub. & Int'l Aff. 1, 9 (2009), *available at* http://www.princeton.edu/~jpia/pdf2009/chapter1.pdf.

50. Ken Silverstein, *Privatizing War: How Affairs of State Are Outsourced to Corporations Beyond Public Control,* Nation, July 28, 1997, at 14.

51. *See* Esther Schrader, *U.S. Companies Hired to Train Foreign Armies,* L.A. Times, Apr. 14, 2002, at A1; John Barry, *From Drug War to Dirty War: Plan Colombia and the U.S. Role in the Human Rights Violations in Colombia,* 12 Transnat'l L. & Contemp. Probs. 161, 191 (2002).

52. Interview with former Foreign Service officer (Mar. 26, 2006).

53. *See* Barry Yeoman, Op-Ed, *Need an Army? Just Pick Up the Phone,* N.Y. Times, Apr. 2, 2004, at A19.

54. Cong. Budget Office, *Contractors' Support, supra* note 38, at 12.

55. Program in Law and Publ. Affairs, Princeton Univ.'s Woodrow Wilson Sch. of Pub. and Int'l Affairs, *Summary of Meeting, Princeton Problem-Solving Workshop Series in Law and Security: A New Legal Framework for Military Contractors* 2 (2007) [hereinafter *A New Legal Framework*].

56. Interview with senior GAO official (Oct. 15, 2007).

57. Nicholas Parillo, *The De-Privatization of American Warfare: How the U.S. Government Used, Regulated and Ultimately Abandoned Privateering in the Nineteenth Century*, 19 Yale J.L. & Human. 1 (2007).

58. Program in Law and Publ. Affairs, *A New Legal Framework*, *supra* note 55.

59. *See, e.g.*, U.S. Gen. Accounting Office, *Defense Management: Challenges Facing DOD in Implementing Defense Reform Initiatives*, GAO/T-NSIAD/AIMD-98-122 *(1998)*; U.S. Gen. *Accounting* Office, *Defense Outsourcing: Better Data Needed to Support Overhead Rates for A-76 Studies*, GAO/NSIAD-98-62 (1998); U.S. Gen. Accounting Office, *Base Operations: Challenges Confronting DOD As It Renews Emphasis On Outsourcing*, GAO/NSIAD-97-86 (1997); U.S. Gen. Accounting Office, *Defense Outsourcing: Challenges Facing DOD As It Attempts to Save Billions in Infrastructure Costs*, GAO/NSIAD-97-110 (1997).

60. As a DOD report notes, "The increasing technical complexity of DoD weapons systems and equipment requires a level of specialized technical expertise, but of limited scope, that the DoD does not believe can be cost-effectively serviced and supported by a military force capability." U.S. Dep't of Def., *Report on DoD Program for Planning, Managing, and Accounting for Contractor Services and Contractor Personnel During Contingency Operations* 5 (2007), *available at* http://www.acq.osd.mil/log/PS/p_vault/Sec_815_report_Sec_854_interim_report_Oct07.pdf.

61. Interview with DOD official #2 (Nov. 7, 2007).

62. *See, e.*g., Memorandum from Stephen G. Bradbury, U.S. Assistant Att'y Gen., for John A. Rizzo, Senior Deputy Gen. Counsel, CIA, Re: Application of United States Obligations Under Article 16 of the Convention Against Torture to Certain Techniques That May Be Used in the Interrogation of High Value al Qaeda Detainees (May 30, 2005), *available at* http://luxmedia.vo.llnwd.net/o10/clients/aclu/olc_05302005_bradbury.pdf (advising that U.S. obligations under the Convention Against Torture would not apply outside U.S. territorial boundaries).

63. *What Went Wrong: Torture and the Office of Legal Counsel in the Bush Administration: Hearing Before the S. Subomm. on Admin. Oversight and the Cts.*, S. *Judiciary Comm.*, 111th Cong. (2009) (statement of Ali Soufan, CEO, The Soufan Group, LLC), *available at* http://judiciary.senate.gov/hearings/testimony.cfm?id=3842&wit_id=7906.

64. Anthony R. Jones & George R. Fay, Dep't of the Army, *AR 15–6 Investigation of the Abu Ghraib Detention Facility and 205th Military Intelligence Brigade* 50–51 (2004), *available at* http://fl1.findlaw.com/news.findlaw.com/hdocs/docs/dod/fay82504rpt.pdf.

65. Cong. Budget Office, *Contractors' Support*, *supra* note 38, at 12.

66. Interview with DOD official #2, *supra* note 61.

67. Interview with JAG officer #3 (Oct. 16, 2007).

68. Moshe Schwartz & Julia A. Tischuk, *Department of Defense Contractors in Iraq and Afghanistan: Background and Analysis*, R40764, at 7 (Cong. Research Serv., 2009), *available at* http://www.fas.org/sgp/crs/natsec/R40764.pdf.

69. Interview with DOD official #2, *supra* note 61.

70. U.S. Dep't of Def., *Report on DOD-Funded Service Contracts in Forward Areas* 5 (2007) [hereinafter *Report on DOD-Funded Service Contracts*].

71. A senior DOD official reported that the CENTCOM contractor census counts DOJ employees, of whom there were 248 as of July 2007, but does not count contractors from other agencies. Interview with DOD official #2, *supra* note 61.

72. The State Department and USAID reportedly do not keep uniform data on the numbers of contractors in Iraq, and the CIA figures, if they exist, are unavailable.

73. U.S. Dep't of Def., *Report on DOD-Funded Service Contracts, supra* note 70, at 3.

74. U.S. Dep't of Def., *2006 Quadrennial Defense Review* 75, 81 (2006).

75. Press Release, U.S. Army Sustainment Pub. Affairs, ASC Selects LOGCAP IV Contractors (June 28. 2007), *available at* http://www.army.mil/-news/2007/06/28/3836-asc-selects-logcap-iv-contractors/.

76. Assistant Deputy, Under Secretary of Defense, *Contractor Support of U.S. Operations in USCENTCOM AOR [US Central Command Area of Responsibility], Iraq, and Afghanistan,* Feb. 2010, *available at* http://www.acq.osd.mil/log/PS/hot_topics.html.

3. Too Many Gaps?

1. Anthony R. Jones & George R. Fay, Dep't of the Army, *AR 15-6 Investigation of the Abu Ghraib Detention Facility and 205th Military Intelligence Brigade* 51–52, 79 (2004), *available at* http://fl1.findlaw.com/news.findlaw.com/hdocs/docs/dod/fay82504rpt.pdf [hereinafter *Investigation of the Abu Ghraib Detention Facility*].

2. *Id.* at 79, 87.

3. U.S. Army Crim. Investigative Command, U.S. Dep't of Def., *Case Disposition on Case Number 0003-04-CID 149-83130, Report No. DODDOACID017333-018347,* at 207, 354 (2007), *available at* http://www.aclu.org/torturefoia/released/021109 .html (follow DODDOACID017333 hyperlink).

4. *See* Antonio M. Taguba, Dep't of the Army, *Article 15-6 Investigation of the 800th Military Police Brigade* 26, 36, 48 (2004), *available at* http://www.npr.org/iraq/2004/prison_abuse_report.pdf; Seymour M. Hersh, Chain of Command: The Road from 9/11 to Abu Ghraib 32–34, 61 (2004); Joel Brinkley & James Glanz, *Contractors in Sensitive Roles, Unchecked,* N.Y. Times, May 7, 2004, at A15, available at www .nytimes.com/2004/05/07/politics/07cont.html?scp=3+sq=brinkley%20glanz+st=cse.

5. Julian Borger, *Private Contractor Lifts the Lid on Systematic Failures at Abu Ghraib Jail,* Guardian, May 7, 2004, *available at* http://www.guardian.co.uk/world/2004/may/07/iraq.usa.

6. *See, e.g.,* P. W. Singer, *War, Profits, and the Vacuum of Law: Privatized Military Firms and International Law,* 42 Colum. J. Transnat'l L. 521, 545 (2004).

7. For a detailed survey of international and regional instruments concerning mercenaries, *see* Laura A. Dickinson, *Legal Regulation of Private Military Contractors, the New Mercenaries, in* International Criminal Law (M. Cherif Bassiouni ed., 2008).

8. Protocol Additional to the Geneva Conventions of 12 August 1949, and Relating to the Protection of Victims of International Armed Conflicts (Protocol I) art. 47, June 8, 1977, 1125 U.N.T.S. 3 [hereinafter Protocol I].

9. Protocol I defines a mercenary as a person who:

(a) is specially recruited locally or abroad in order to fight in an armed conflict;

(b) does, in fact, take direct part in hostilities;

(c) is motivated to take part in hostilities essentially by the desire for private gain, and in fact, is promised by or on behalf of a Party to the conflict, material compensation substantially in excess of that promised or paid to combatants of similar ranks and functions in the armed forces of that Party;

(d) is neither a national of a Party to the conflict nor a resident of territory controlled by a Party to the conflict;

(e) is not a member of the armed forces of a Party to the conflict; and

(f) has not been sent by a State which is not a Party to the conflict on official duty as a member of its armed forces.

Id. at art. 47(2)(a)–(f). These elements, in particular the motive requirement and the requirement that mercenaries must receive "compensation substantially in excess" of uniformed personnel, are difficult to prove, a point not lost on the U.S. representative at the diplomatic conference, who noted how easy it would be for any party to a conflict to avoid the impact of the Protocol. *See* Todd S. Milliard, *Overcoming Post-Colonial Myopia: A Call to Recognize and Regulate Private Military Companies,* 176 Mil. L. Rev. 1, 41–42 (2003).

10. International Convention Against the Recruitment, Use, Financing and Training of Mercenaries art. 4(b), G.A. Res. 44/34, U.N. GAOR, 44th Sess., Supp. No. 43, U.N. Doc A/RES/44/34 (Dec. 4, 1989) (entered into force Oct. 20, 2001), *available at* http://www.unwg.rapn.ru/en/conventions/Mercenary_Convention_-_English.pdf [hereinafter Mercenary Convention].

11. *Id.* The Mercenary Convention defines a mercenary as anyone who:

(a) Is specially recruited locally or abroad for the purpose of participating in a concerted act of violence aimed at:

(i) Overthrowing a government or otherwise undermining the constitutional order of a State; or

(ii) Undermining the territorial integrity of a State;

(b) Is motivated to take part therein essentially by the desire for significant private gain and is prompted by the promise or payment of material compensation;

(c) Is neither a national nor a resident of the State against which such an act is directed;

(d) Has not been sent by a state on official duty; and

(e) Is not a member of the armed forces of the State on whose territory the act is undertaken.

Id. at art. 1(2)(a)–(e).

12. Convention for the Amelioration of the Condition of the Wounded and Sick in Armed Forces in the Field, Aug. 12, 1949, 6 U.S.T. 3114, 75 U.N.T.S. 31 (entered

into force Oct. 21, 1950, for the United States Feb. 2, 1956) [hereinafter Geneva Convention I]; Convention for the Amelioration of the Condition of the Wounded, Sick, and Shipwrecked Members of Armed Forces at Sea, Aug. 12, 1949, 6 U.S.T. 3217, 75 U.N.T.S. 85 (entered into force Oct. 21, 1950, for the United States Feb. 2, 1956) [hereinafter Geneva Convention II]; Convention Relative to the Treatment of Prisoners of War, Aug. 12, 1949, 6 U.S.T. 3316, 75 U.N.T.S. 135 (entered into force Oct. 21, 1950, for the United States Feb. 2, 1956) [hereinafter Geneva Convention III]; Convention Relative to the Protection of Civilian Persons in Time of War, Aug. 12, 1949, 6 U.S.T. 3516, 75 U.N.T.S. 287 (entered into force Oct. 21, 1950, for the United States Feb. 2, 1956) [hereinafter Geneva Convention IV].

13. Protocol I, *supra* note 8; Protocol Additional to the Geneva Conventions of 12 August 1949, Relating to the Protection of Victims of Non-International Armed Conflicts (Protocol II), June 8, 1977, 1125 U.N.T.S. 609 [hereinafter Protocol II].

14. *See, e.g.,* Geneva Convention I, *supra* note 12, at art. 3(1)(a)–(d):

(a) Violence to life and person, in particular murder of all kinds, mutilation, cruel treatment and torture;

(b) Taking of hostages;

(c) Outrages upon personal dignity, in particular humiliating and degrading treatment;

(d) The passing of sentences and the carrying out of executions without previous judgment pronounced by a regularly constituted court, affording all the judicial guarantees which are recognized as indispensable by civilized peoples.

15. *Id.* The list of crimes in common article 3, applicable to internal armed conflict, is shorter than those prohibited in international armed conflict, termed "grave breaches," in each of the four conventions. *See, e.g.,* Geneva Convention I, *supra* note 12, at art. 50: "Grave breaches to which the preceding Article relates shall be those involving any of the following acts, if committed against persons or property protected by the Convention: willful killing, torture or inhuman treatment, including biological experiments, willfully causing great suffering or serious injury to body or health, and extensive destruction and appropriation of property, not justified by military necessity and carried out unlawfully and wantonly"; Geneva Convention II, *supra* note 12, at art. 51 (same language as Geneva Convention I); Geneva Convention III, *supra* note 12, at art. 130: "Grave breaches to which the preceding Article relates shall be those involving any of the following acts, if committed against persons or property protected by the Convention: willful killing, torture or inhuman treatment, including biological experiments, willfully causing great suffering or serious injury to body or health, compelling a prisoner of war to serve in the forces of the hostile Power, or willfully depriving a prisoner of war of the rights of fair and regular trial prescribed in this Convention"; Geneva Convention IV, *supra* note 12, at art. 147: "Grave breaches to which the preceding Article relates shall be those involving any of the following acts, if committed against persons or property protected by the present Convention: willful killing, torture or inhuman treatment, including biological experiments, willfully causing great suffering or serious injury to body or health,

unlawful deportation or transfer or unlawful confinement of a protected person, compelling a protected person to serve in the forces of a hostile Power, or willfully depriving a protected person of the rights of fair and regular trial prescribed in the present Convention, taking of hostages and extensive destruction and appropriation of property, not justified by military necessity and carried out unlawfully and wantonly."

16. *See, e.g.,* Sylvie Junod, *Additional Protocol II: History and Scope,* 33 Am. U. L. Rev. 29, 31–32 (1983).

17. Protocol II, *supra* note 13, at art. 1(1), art. 4 (emphasis added); *see also id.*

18. *See United States v. Krauch* (the "Farben Case"), 7 Trials of War Criminals Before the Nuremberg Military Tribunals Under Control Council Law No. 10 (1952); *United States v. Flick* ("The Flick Case"), 6 Trials of War Criminals Before the Nuremberg Military Tribunals Under Control Council Law No. 10 (1952); *United States v. Krupp* ("The Krupp Case"), 9 Trials of War Criminals Before the Nuremberg Military Tribunals Under Control Council Law No. 10 (1950).

19. *Prosecutor v. Kunarac,* Case No. IT-96–23-T & IT-96-23/1-T, Judgment, ¶ 496 (Feb. 22, 2001) [hereinafter Kunarac Trial Judgment], *available at* http://www.unhcr.org/cgi-bin/texis/vtx/refworld/rwmain?docid=3ae6b7560; *Prosecutor v. Kunarac,* IT-96-23 & IT-96-23/1-A, Appellate Judgment, ¶ 148 (June 12, 2002), *available at* http://www.unhcr.org/cgi-bin/texis/vtx/refworld/rwmain?docid=3debaafe4 [hereinafter Kunarac Appellate Judgment].

20. Alien Tort Statute, 28 U.S.C. 1350 (2000) [hereinafter ATS].

21. *Kadic v. Karadzic,* 70 F.3d 232, 239–40, 243 (2d Cir. 1995).

22. *In re XE Services Alien Tort Litigation,* 665 F. Supp. 2d 569 (E.D. Va. 2009).

23. The Convention on the Prevention and Punishment of the Crime of Genocide art. 4, Dec. 9, 1948, 102 Stat. 3045, 78 U.N.T.S. 277 (entered into force Jan. 12, 1951, for the United States Feb. 23, 1989) [hereinafter Genocide Convention] (emphasis added). The convention defines genocide as any of the following acts committed with intent to destroy, in whole or in part, a national, ethnical, racial or religious group, as such:

(a) Killing members of the group;

(b) Causing serious bodily or mental harm to members of the group;

(c) Deliberately inflicting on the group conditions of life calculated to bring about its physical destruction in whole or in part;

(d) Imposing measures intended to prevent births within the group;

(e) Forcibly transferring children of the group to another group.

Id. at art. 2(a)–(e).

24. Rome Statute of the International Criminal Court art. 7, July 17, 1998, 2187 U.N.T.S. 90 [hereinafter ICC Statute] (emphasis added).

25. See Carlos M. Vázquez, *Direct vs. Indirect Obligations of Corporations Under International Law,* 43 Colum. J. Transnat'l L. 927 (2005).

26. Convention Against Torture and Other Cruel, Inhuman or Degrading Treatment or Punishment art. 1, Dec. 10, 1984, S. Treaty Doc. No. 100-20 (1988), 1465 U.N.T.S. 85, 113–14, *available at* http://www2.ohchr.org/english/law/cat.htm

[hereinafter Torture Convention]. The complete definition of torture reads as follows: "For the purposes of this Convention, torture means any act by which severe pain or suffering, whether physical or mental, is intentionally inflicted on a person for such purposes as obtaining from him or a third person information or a confession, punishing him for an act he or a third person has committed or is suspected of having committed, or intimidating or coercing him or a third person, or for any reason based on discrimination of any kind, when such pain or suffering is inflicted by or at the instigation of or with the consent or acquiescence of a public official or other person acting in an official capacity. It does not include pain or suffering arising only from, inherent in or incidental to lawful sanctions." *Id*. at art. 1(1).

27. International Covenant on Civil and Political Rights arts. 7, 9, Dec. 16, 1966, 999 U.N.T.S. 171 (1966), *available at* http://www1.umn.edu/humanrts/instree/b3ccpr.htm [hereinafter ICCPR]. The language of article 7(1) does not, it is true, refer specifically to governmental misconduct alone: "Every human being has the inherent right to life. This right shall be protected by law. No one shall be arbitrarily deprived of his life." Yet because the treaty as a whole imposes obligations on states, *id*. at art. 2, commentators and courts have generally interpreted this provision as a protection against state execution without trial, rather than a general prohibition of murder by private parties. *See, e.g., Karadzic, supra* note 21, at 243 ("Summary execution—when not perpetrated in the course of genocide or war crimes—[is] proscribed by international law only when committed by state officials or under color of law.").

28. ICCPR, *supra* note 27, at art. 2.

29. *See, e.g.,* American Convention on Human Rights art. 1, Nov. 22, 1969, O.A.S.T.S. No. 36, 1144 U.N.T.S. 143 [hereinafter American Convention] ("The States Parties to this Convention undertake to respect the rights and freedoms recognized herein and to ensure to all persons subject to their jurisdiction the free and full exercise of those rights and freedoms.").

30. *See Velasquez Rodriguez Case,* 1988 Inter-Am. Ct. H.R. (ser. C) No. 4 (July 29, 1988).

31. *See McKesson Corp. v. Iran,* 52 F.3d 346, 351–52 (D.C. Cir. 1995) (holding Iran responsible for corporation over which it exercised control); *Foremost Tehran, Inc. v. Iran,* 10 Iran-U.S. Cl. Trib. Rep. 228, 241–42 (1987) (holding the same); *Maffezini v. Spain* (Rectification and Award), ICSID Case No. ARB/97/7 (Nov. 13, 2000, Jan. 31, 2001) (translation in English) (holding Spain responsible for the acts of its state entity); *Barcelona Traction, Light and Power Co.* (Belg. v. Spain) (Second Phase), 1970 I.C.J. 4, 39 (Feb. 5) ("Veil lifting . . . is admissible to play . . . a role in international law.").

32. *See, e.g.,* Int'l L. Comm'n, Draft Articles on Responsibility of States for Internationally Wrongful Acts, arts. 4, 8, *in* Report of the International Law Commission to the General Assembly, U.N. Doc. 56 U.N. GAOR Supp. (No. 10) at 43, U.N. Doc. A/56/10 (2001) (stating that the "conduct of any State organ shall be considered an act of that State under international law," and that a person's conduct shall be attributed to the state if he or she is acting on the state's instructions or under

the state's direction); *see also, e.g.,* Jordan J. Paust, *Human Rights Responsibilities of Private Corporations,* 35 Vand. J. Transnat'l L. 801 (2002).

33. *In re XE Services, supra* note 22 (corporations can be held liable under ATS for war crimes without showing of state action, while state summary execution claims require state action showing); *see also Bowoto v. Chevron Corp.,* 557 F. Supp. 2d 1080, 1095 (N.D. Cal. 2008). *But see Sinaltrainal v. Coca-Cola Co.,* 578 F.3d 1252 (11th Cir. 2009) (finding sufficient state action in ATS claims of torture and murder by paramilitaries and company defendant).

34. *See, e.g., Doe I v. Unocal Corp.,* 395 F.3d 932, 936 (9th Cir. 2002). Although the case ultimately settled out of court, the lawsuit is instructive. A group of Burmese citizens brought a class action under the ATS, *supra* note 20, against U.S. and French corporations that built a pipeline in Burma. The ATS confers jurisdiction on federal courts to consider "torts in violation of the law of nations" brought by noncitizens. *Id.* Plaintiffs alleged that the military forces committed multiple violations of international human rights through their conduct, including murder, rape, torture, and forced labor. The court concluded that the private corporations could be sued under a joint action approach if they were found to be willful participants in joint action with a state actor or its agents, here the Burmese military. In particular, there was "some evidence that Unocal could influence the army not to commit human rights violations, that the army might otherwise commit such violations, and that Unocal knew this." In reaching this decision, the court found the standard for aiding and abetting under the circumstances to be "knowing practical assistance or encouragement that has a substantial effect on the perpetration of the crime." *Unocal, supra,* at 936, 939, 947.

35. *See, e.g., Abdullahi v. Pfizer, Inc.,* 562 F.3d 163 (2d Cir. 2009); *Wiwa v. Royal Dutch Petroleum Co.,* No. 96 CIV-8386, 2002 WL 319887, at *3–4 (S.D.N.Y. Feb. 28, 2002), affirmed in relevant part, 226 F.3d 88 (2d Cir. 2009).

36. *Abdullahi, supra* note 35, at 187.

37. *Id.* at 188 (*quoting Brentwood Acad. v. Tenn. Secondary Sch. Athletic Ass'n,* 531 U.S. 288, 351 (internal quotations and citations omitted)).

38. *Id.* (*quoting Gorman-Bakos v. Cornell Coop. Extension,* 252 F. 3d. 545, 551–52 (2nd Cir. 2001) (internal quotations omitted)).

39. *Am. Mfrs. Mut. Ins. Co. v. Sullivan,* 526 U.S. 40, 50–55 (1999) (concluding that private insurance companies providing workers' compensation benefits were not state actors even though the government created and closely regulated the workers' compensation system and authorized benefits refusals prior to a hearing, because the government did not otherwise participate in the private insurers' refusals to pay benefits).

40. *Wiwa, supra* note 35, at *1–2, *6, *14 & n.15.

41. *See Sosa v. Alvarez-Machain,* 542 U.S. 692 (2004) (upholding the ATS as a tool for non-Americans to bring civil suits in U.S. courts, but only for violations of a relatively narrow class of norms).

42. *Ibrahim v. Titan Corp.,* 556 F. Supp. 2d 1 (D.D.C. 2007); *Saleh v. Titan Corp.,* 580 F.3d 1 (C.A.D.C., 2009); *cf. Tel-Oren v. Libyan Arab Republic,* 726 F.2d 774,

791–95 (D.C. Cir. 1984) (Opinion of Edwards, J.) (concluding that human rights claims brought by plaintiffs against the Palestine Liberation Organization could not be heard under the ATS, but nevertheless leaving open the possibility that claims could be brought under the ATS against nonstate actors so long as plaintiffs could demonstrate that the defendants have sufficient nexus to a state).

43. The U.S. Coalition Provisional Authority in Iraq, for example, sought to grant immunity for U.S. contractors, but the scope of this immunity is in question. *See* L. Paul Bremer, Coalition Provisional Auth., *Coalition Provisional Authority Order Number 17 (Revised): Status of the Coalition Provisional Authority, MNF-Iraq, Certain Missions and Personnel in Iraq* 4, § 2 (June 27, 2004), *available at* http://www .cpa-iraq.org/regulations/20040627_CPAORD_17_Status_of_Coalition__Rev__ with_Annex_A.pdf [hereinafter *CPA Order Number 17*] ("Unless provided otherwise herein, the MNF, the CPA, Foreign Liaison Missions, their Personnel, property, funds and assets, and all International Consultants shall be immune from Iraqi legal process."). In any event, the ability of Iraqi courts to function as a real check on abuses, even assuming they have jurisdiction, is also in question. *See, e.g.,* Robert F. Worth, *2 from Tribunal for Hussein Case Are Assassinated,* N.Y. Times, Mar. 2, 2005, at A8.

44. *See Kinsella v. United States ex rel. Singleton,* 361 U.S. 234, 248 (1960) (prohibiting military jurisdiction over civilian dependents in time of peace, regardless of whether the offense was capital or noncapital); *Grisham v. Hagan,* 361 U.S. 278, 280 (1960) (holding civilian employees committing capital offenses not amenable to military jurisdiction); *McElroy v. United States ex rel. Guagliardo,* 361 U.S. 281, 283–84 (1960) (expanding *Grisham* to include noncapital offenses); *Reid v. Covert,* 354 U.S. 1, 40–41 (1957) (holding that civilians in time of peace are not triable by court-martial for capital offenses).

45. Military Extraterritorial Jurisdiction Act of 2000, 18 U.S.C. §§ 3261–3267 (2000) [hereinafter MEJA].

46. Indeed, some commentators have argued that the George W. Bush administration exploited this loophole by assigning tasks to contractors under agreements with agencies other than the DOD. *See, e.g.,* M. Cherif Bassiouni, *The Institutionalization of Torture Under the Bush Administration,* 37 Case W. Res. J. Int'l L. 389, 411–16 (2006) [hereinafter *The Institutionalization of Torture*].

47. Ronald W. Reagan National Defense Authorization Act for Fiscal Year 2005, Pub. L. No. 108-375, § 1088 (2004) (codified as amended in MEJA, *supra* note 45, at § 3267 (1)(A)(2)).

48. MEJA Expansion and Enforcement Act of 2007, H.R. 2740, 110th Cong. (2007); *see also* David Johnston, *Immunity Deals Offered to Blackwater Guards,* N.Y. Times, Oct. 30, 2007, at A1.

49. *See* USA PATRIOT Act of 2001, Pub. L. No. 107-56, § 804, 115 Stat. 272 (2001) (amending 18 U.S.C. § 7 to include "the premises of United States diplomatic, consular, military or other United States Government missions or entities in foreign States" as well as "residences in foreign States . . . used for purposes of those

missions or entities or used by United States personnel assigned to those missions or entities"). Some commentators have suggested that Congress enacted this provision in order to allow for simpler prosecutions of terrorist suspects accused of attacking U.S. installations overseas. *See, e.g.*, John Sifton, *United States Military and Central Intelligence Agency Personnel Abroad: Plugging the Prosecutorial Gaps*, 43 Harv. J. on Legis. 487, 506 (2006) [hereinafter *Plugging the Prosecutorial Gaps*].

50. Scott Shane, *C.I.A. Contractor Guilty in Beating of Afghan Who Later Died*, N.Y. Times, Aug. 18, 2006, at A8 [hereinafter *C.I.A. Contractor Guilty*]; *see also* Sifton, *Plugging the Prosecutorial Gaps, supra* note 49, at 506.

51. War Crimes Act of 1996, 18 U.S.C. § 2441 (2006).

52. 18 U.S.C. § 2340A (2006). Ironically, the statutory amendments that expand the SMTJ to allow for a greater range of prosecution of domestic crimes committed overseas arguably limit the scope of torture prosecutions because such overseas abuse is no longer "extraterritorial." *See* Bassiouni, *The Institutionalization of Torture, supra* note 46, at 411–16.

53. 10 U.S.C. § 802(a)(10) (2006).

54. Section 552 of the John Warner National Defense Authorization Act for Fiscal Year 2007, Pub. L. 109-364, § 552, 120 Stat. 2083, 2089 (2005) (amending 10 U.S.C. § 802(a)(10)).

55. Griff Witte, *New Law Could Subject Civilians to Military Trial*, Wash. Post, Jan. 15, 2007, at A1.

56. *Ibrahim, supra* note 42 (dismissing plaintiffs' ATS, RICO, and federal contract law claims but preserving common law tort claims); *see also Saleh, supra* note 42 (same); *Al Shimari v. CACI Premier Tech., Inc.*, 657 F. Supp. 2d 700 (E.D. Va 2009) (same).

57. For a good overview of such cases, *see* Kateryna L. Rakowsky, Note, *Military Contractors and Civil Liability: Use of the Government Contractor Defense to Escape Allegations of Misconduct in Iraq and Afghanistan*, 2 Stan. J. Civ. Rts. & Civ. Liberties 365 (2006).

58. *In re Blackwater Security Consulting, LLC*, 460 F.3d 576 (4th Cir. 2006) (remanding case for further proceedings in state court).

59. *Lane v. Halliburton*, 529 F. 3d 548 (5th Cir. 2008) (remanding case for further proceedings in the district court); *Fisher v. Halliburton*, F. Supp. 2d (S.D. Tex. 2010) (ruling on remand that some claims could proceed).

60. *See Carmichael v. Kellogg, Brown & Root Servs., Inc.*, 450 F. Supp. 2d 1373 (N.D. Ga. 2006); *Lessin v. Kellogg, Brown & Root, Inc.*, 2006 WL 3940556 (S.D. Tex. 2006); *McMahon v. Presidential Airways, Inc.*, 460 F. Supp. 2d 1315 (M.D. Fla. 2006); *Harris v. Kellogg, Brown and Root Servs., Inc.*, 618 F. Supp. 2d 400 (W.D. Penn. 2009); *Potts v. DynCorp Int'l LLC*, 465 F. Supp. 2d 1245 (M.D. Ala. 2006); Al Shimari, *supra* note 56.

61. *See, e.g., Whitaker v. Kellogg, Brown & Root, Inc.*, 444 F. Supp. 2d 1277 (M.D. Ga. 2006); *Fisher v. Halliburton*, 454 F. Supp. 2d 637 (S.D. Texas, 2006) (dismissing case as raising a nonjusticiable political question). *Fisher* was reversed in *Lane v. Halliburton*, 529 F.3d 548 (5th Cir. 2008), but the court of appeals did not completely

reject use of the political question doctrine, instead reserving judgment on the question. *Lane, supra,* at 568 ("Permitting this matter to proceed now does not preclude the possibility that the district court will again need to decide whether a political question inextricably arises in this suit.").

62. *Japan Whaling Ass'n. v. Am. Cetacean Soc'y,* 478 U.S. 221, 230 (1986).

63. *McMahon, supra* note 60, at 1320–1321; *see also Harris, supra* note 60 (finding no political question bar to judicial review).

64. 28 U.S.C. 1346(b).

65. *See, e.g., Boyle v. United Tech. Corp.,* 487 U.S. 500, 512 (1988); *Harris, supra* note 60; *Al Shimari, supra* note 56.

66. *In re Agent Orange Prod. Liab. Litig.,* 373 F. Supp. 2d 7, 85–90 (E.D.N.Y. 2005).

67. *Cf. Jama v. Esmor Corr. Servs., Inc.,* 334 F. Supp. 2d 662, 688–89 (D.N.J. 2004) (rejecting government contractor defense for tort claims against private prison management corporation because contract did not specifically require or approve of corporation practices that led to abuse); *see also Ibrahim, supra* note 42 (refusing to dismiss case on contractor immunity grounds at early stage in proceedings); *Al Shimari, supra* note 56 (same).

68. *Ibrahim, supra* note 42, at 10–11, 19.

69. *Saleh, supra* note 42, at 9.

70. For an interesting discussion of this issue, *see* Susan Matthews, *Torture as Tort: Comparative Perspectives on the Development of Transnational Human Rights Litigation, in* Torture as Tort: Comparative Perspectives on the Development of Transnational Tort Litigation (Craig Scott ed., 2001).

71. *See, e.g., Al Shimari, supra* note 56, appeal docketed No. 09-1335 (4th Cir. Mar. 26, 2009); *Harris, supra* note 60, appeal docketed No. 09-2325 (3rd Cir. May 7, 2009); *see also Estate of Al-Razzaq et al. v. XE,* No. 3:09-cv-00626-LAB-BLM (S.D. Ca. filed Mar. 26, 2009); *Estate of Jarallah vs. XE,* No. 3:09-cv-00631-H-JMA (S.D. Ca. filed Mar. 27, 2009); *Estate of Abtan v. Prince,* No. 1:09-cv-617-LMB-TRJ (E.D. Va. filed June 2, 2009); *Estate Albazzaz v. Prince,* No. 1:09-cv-616-JCC-JFA (E.D. Va. filed June 2, 2009); *Estate of Sa'adoon v. Prince,* No. 1:09-cv-615-TSE-IDD (E.D. Va. filed June 2, 2009); *Estate of Rabea v. Prince,* No. 1:09-cv-00645 (E.D. Va. filed June 10, 2009).

72. Sources for the Passaro incident include Shane, *C.I.A. Contractor Guilty, supra* note 50; Andrea Weigl, *Passaro Convicted of Assaulting Afghan,* News & Observer (Raleigh, N.C.), Aug. 18, 2006, at A1, *available at* http://www.accessmylibrary.com/article-1G1-144400930/judge-sends-passaro-back.html; Andrea Weigl, *Passaro Will Serve 8 Years for Beating,* News & Observer (Raleigh, N.C.), Feb. 14, 2007, at B1, *available at* http://www.accessmylibrary.com/article-1G1-159285283/passaro-serve-8-years.html.

73. *United States v. Aaron Bridges Langston,* CR-07-210-PHX (D. Ariz., Indictment, Feb. 27, 2007).

74. Press Release, U.S. Attorney for the Eastern Dist. of Va., Military Contractor Sentenced for Possession of Child Pornography in Baghdad (May 25, 2007),

available at http://www.usdoj.gov/usao/vae/Pressreleases/05-MayPDFArchive/ 07/20070525khannr.html.

75. *U.S. v. Slough*, 677 F. Supp. 2d 112 (D.D.C., 2009).

76. Michael R. Gordon, *Military Role Overseeing Contractors Tested in Iraq*, N.Y. Times, Apr. 6, 2008, at A16, *available at* http://www.nytimes.com/2008/04/06/ world/middleeast/06contractor.html [hereinafter *Military Role Overseeing Contractors*].

77. Memorandum from the Majority Staff of the H.R. Comm. on Oversight and Gov't Reform to Members of the Comm. on Oversight and Gov't Reform, Additional Information on About Blackwater USA, at 2, 6–7 (Oct. 1, 2007), *available at* http:// www.scribd.com/doc/18951383/House-Oversight-Committees-Memorandum- on-Blackwater-October-2007 [hereinafter House Oversight Memorandum].

78. Interview with JAG officer #7 (Oct. 16, 2007).

79. Interview with JAG officer #8 (Oct. 16, 2007).

80. Human Rights First, *By the Numbers: Findings of the Detainee Abuse and Accountability Project* 3, 7 (2006), *available at* http://www.humanrightsfirst.info/ pdf/06425-etn-by-the-numbers.pdf.

81. A military jury convicted Sabrina Harman, an army reservist, on May 17, 2005, and sentenced her to six months in prison, to be followed by a dishonorable discharge. *Reservist Gets Six-Month Sentence for Abusing Iraqis at Abu Ghraib*, N.Y. Times, May 18, 2005, at A10. Among other acts that were the basis of the conviction, Harman had attached electric wires to a detainee and threatened him with execution if he stepped off a box on which he was standing. She also wrote "rapist" on a naked detainee's leg before he was forced to join a human pyramid. *See* T. R. Reid, *England to Plead Not Guilty in Second Trial: Judge Who Threw Out Army Private's Earlier Plea Will Preside over Court-Martial*, Wash. Post, July 8, 2005, at A7.

Sergeant Santos A. Cardona, who was assigned to a military police detachment, was convicted by a military jury of using a dog to torment a prisoner by letting the dog bark within inches of the prisoner's face. He was court-martialed at Fort Meade, Maryland, by a panel of four officers and three enlisted personnel, which found him guilty of aggravated assault and dereliction of duty. His military rank was reduced as part of his punishment, and his sentence included ninety days of hard labor and a $7,200 fine. Bureau of Int'l Info. Programs, U.S. Dep't of State, *Abu Ghraib Dog Handler Convicted, Sentenced to Hard Labor, Fined*, U.S. Fed, News, June 6, 2006, *available at* http://www.globalsecurity.org/intell/library/news/2006/intell- 060605-usia01.htm.

Captain Shawn Martin was found guilty in March 2005 of kicking detainees and staging the mock execution of a prisoner. He was sentenced to forty-five days in jail and fined $12,000. Eric Schmitt, *Iraq Abuse Trial Is Again Limited to Lower Ranks*, N.Y. Times, Mar. 23, 2006, at A1 [hereinafter *Iraq Abuse Trial*].

On Jan. 31, 2005, Sergeant Javal Davis pleaded guilty to battery, dereliction of duty, and making false statements. *Former Guard Pleads Guilty in Abuse Case*, N.Y. Times, Feb. 2, 2005, at A10. Specialist Meghan Ambuhl pleaded guilty to dereliction of duty, and on October 30, 2004, she was demoted and lost half a month's pay. Ivan

Frederick pleaded guilty to eight counts, including assault, indecent acts, and dereliction of duty. On October 21, 2004, he was sentenced to eight years in prison and forfeited pay. Roman Krol pleaded guilty to conspiracy and maltreating detainees, and was sentenced to ten months in prison. Schmitt, *Iraq Abuse Trial, supra.*

Specialist Armin Cruz pleaded guilty on September 11, 2004, to abusing prisoners at Abu Ghraib prison. He was sentenced to eight months in prison, demoted to the rank of private, and given a bad-conduct discharge. In May 2004, Specialist Jeremy Sivits pleaded guilty to abuse charges and was sentenced to the maximum of one year in prison, reduction in rank, and a bad-conduct discharge. Norimitsu Onishi, *Military Specialist Pleads Guilty to Abuse and Is Jailed,* N.Y. Times, Sept. 12, 2004, at A9.

For an overview of the response to the Abu Ghraib abuses, *see* Laura A. Dickinson, *Abu Ghraib: The Battle over Institutional Culture and Respect for International Law Within the U.S. Military, in* International Law Stories (John E. Noyes, Mark W. Janis & Laura A. Dickinson eds., 2007).

82. Jones & Fay, *Investigation of the Abu Ghraib Detention Facility, supra* note 1.

83. *See* Scott Horton, *Getting Closer to the Truth About the Blackwater Incident,* Harper's, Nov. 14, 2007, *available at* http://www.harpers.org/archive/2007/11/hbc-90001669.

84. *See, e.g.,* Alan M. Dershowitz, *Want to Torture? Get a Warrant,* S.F. Chron., Jan. 22, 2002.

85. *See* Peter Baker, David Johnston & Mark Mazzetti, *Abuse Issue Puts the CIA and Justice Dept. at Odds,* N.Y. Times, Aug. 27, 2009, *available at* http://www.nytimes.com/2009/08/28/us/politics/28intel.html?emc=eta1.

86. *See* Ewen MacAskill & Robert Booth, *Senior Bush Figures Could Be Prosecuted for Torture, Says Obama,* Guardian, Apr. 21, 2009, at http://www.guardian.co.uk/world/2009/apr/21/cheney-obama-cia-torture-memos (noting that although the president had indicated that there would be no prosecution of CIA employees, the president had left open the possibility of prosecuting senior Bush administration officials); *see also* Howard Fineman, *The Moral Burden: Obama's Ethical Certitude Has Wavered with the Torture Issue,* Newsweek, Apr. 22, 2009, *available at* http://www.newsweek.com/id/194888/page/1.

87. Program in Law and Publ. Affs., Princeton Univ.'s Woodrow Wilson Sch. of Pub. and Int'l Affairs, *Summary of Meeting, Princeton Problem-Solving Workshop Series in Law and Security: A New Legal Framework for Military Contractors* 2 (2007) (reporting speaker who emphasized that "contractors do not fall within the chain of command."); *id.* at 11 (reporting speaker who noted that "two separate formal chains of command exist because the U.S. government does not want a local commander to have the authority to order a contractor or a contract employee to do anything outside the scope of an existing contract.").

88. Interview with JAG officer #5 (Oct. 16, 2007).

89. *An Uneasy Relationship: U.S. Reliance on Private Security Firms in Overseas Operations: Hearing Before the S. Comm. on Homeland Sec. & Gov't Affs.,* 110th

Congress (2008) (statement of the Hon. P. Jackson Bell, Deputy Under Sec'y of Def. for Logistics and Material Readiness, U.S. Dep't of Def.), at 6 *available at* http://www.dod.mil/dodgc/olc/docs/testBell080227.pdf.

90. Human Rights First, *Private Security Contractors at War: Ending the Culture of Impunity* 10 (2008), *available at* http://www.humanrightsfirst.info/pdf/08115-usls-psc-final.pdf.

91. Sec'y of St.'s Panel on Personal Protective Services in Iraq, *Report of the Secretary of State's Panel on Personal Protective Services in Iraq* 6 (2007), *available at* http://merln.ndu.edu/archivepdf/iraq/State/94122.pdf. Panel members included Eric J. Boswell, George A. Joulwan, J. Stapleton Roy, and Patrick F. Kennedy.

92. House Oversight Memorandum, *supra* note 77, at 7.

93. Interview with JAG officer #5, *supra* note 88.

94. *Id.*

95. U.S. Army Crim. Investigation Command, U.S. Dep't of Def., *Case Disposition on Case Number 0003-04-CID 149-83130, Report DODDOACID014080-017333*, at 971, 1613, 1764 (2007) (reporting on investigation of abuse at Abu Ghraib prison in Iraq and noting that numerous contractors allegedly involved in the abuse could not be located).

96. Interview with JAG officer #10 (Oct. 16, 2007).

97. Interview with JAG officer #2 (Oct. 16, 2007).

98. *U.S. v. Slough,* 677 F. Supp. 2d 112 (D.D.C., 2009); David Johnston & John M. Broder, *F.B.I. Says Guards Killed 14 Iraqis Without Cause,* N.Y. Times, Nov. 14, 2007, *available at* http://www.nytimes.com/2007/11/14/world/middleeast/14blackwater.html.

99. Memorandum of Agreement (MOA) between the U.S. Dep't of Def. and the U.S. Dep't of State on USG Private Sec. Contractors (Dec. 5, 2007), *available at* http://www.defenselink.mil/pubs/pdfs/Signed%20MOA%20Dec%205%202007.pdf. [hereinafter MOA between State and DOD]; *see also* U.S. Gov't Accountability Office, *Rebuilding Iraq: DOD and State Department Have Improved Oversight and Coordination of Private Security Contractors in Iraq, but Further Actions Are Needed to Sustain Improvements* (2008), *available at* http://www.gao.gov/new.items/d08966.pdf [hereinafter *Rebuilding Iraq*]; Office of the Special Inspector Gen. for Iraq Reconstruction (SIGIR), *Opportunities to Improve Processes for Reporting, Investigating, and Remediating Serious Incidents Involving Private Security Contractors in Iraq, SIGIR-09-019* (2009) [hereinafter *Opportunities to Improve Processes*].

100. U. S. Gov't Accountability Office, *Rebuilding Iraq, supra* note 99.

101. SIGIR, *Opportunities to Improve Processes, supra* note 99.

102. *Id.;* 32 C.F.R. § 153.4 (2006); U.S. Dep't of Def. Instruction No. 5525.07 (June 18, 2007), *available at* http://www.dtic.mil/whs/directives/corres/pdf/552507p.pdf; MOA between State and DOD, *supra* note 99.

103. U. S. Gov't Accountability Office, *Rebuilding Iraq, supra* note 99, at 28 (*quoting* Secretary of Defense guidance); SIGIR, *Opportunities to Improve Processes,*

supra note 99, at 4–5, ("As a matter of policy, DoD has stated that it will give the Department of Justice an opportunity to prosecute in federal district court any alleged federal criminal offenses by civilians and will not initiate court-martial charges if the Department of Justice elects to prosecute those offenses." (*citing* Memorandum from Sec'y of Def. Robert Gates, to Sec'ys of the Military Dep'ts, et al., UCMJ Jurisdiction over DoD Civilian Employees, DoD Contractors, and Other Persons Serving with or Accompanying the Armed Forces Overseas During Declared War and in Contingency Operations (Mar.10, 2008), *available at* http://www.thespywhobilledme.com/Docs/UCMJ_Contractors.pdf.pdf)).

104. U.S. Gov't Accountability Office, *Rebuilding Iraq, supra* note 99, at 12 (note that the GAO emphasizes it has not independently verified these figures).

105. SIGIR, *Opportunities to Improve Processes, supra* note 99, at 12, 27.

106. In response, DOD officials asserted that they only track incidents that could have a strategic impact on missions. However, the SIGIR concluded that this definition "has the effect of narrowing the types of incidents [being tracked] and applying a narrower definition of serious incidents than that contained in the fragmentary order." *Id.* at 12–13.

107. The DOD and the State Department have had difficulty not only in tracking incidents but also in investigating and prosecuting them, even under the new system. The SIGIR found, for example, that the system is "not working as required." Specifically, the SIGIR concluded that the "requirements [specifying a process for military commanders to review and investigate serious incidents] are not being followed for the most serious incidents"—those involving death, serious injury, and property damage over $10,000. *Id.*

108. *Id.*

109. Michael R. Gordon, *Military Role Overseeing Contractors, supra* note 76.

110. *Reid v. Covert,* 354 U.S. 1 (1957) (holding unconstitutional the UCMJ's provisions extending military court jurisdiction to civilian dependants during peacetime); *Toth v. Quarles,* 350 U.S. 11 (1955) (holding unconstitutional court-martial jurisdiction over a former service member for crimes committed while on active duty); *Grisham v. Hagan,* 361 U.S. 278 (1960) (holding that civilian employees of the armed forces are not generally subject to UCMJ jurisdiction while overseas).

111. *See, e.g., United States v. Scheffer,* 523 U.S. 303 (1998). Indeed, in recent terrorism cases, the Court has cited the military justice system provided in the UCMJ favorably, in contrast to military commissions established to try terrorism suspects. *See, e.g., Hamdi v. Rumsfeld,* 542 U.S. 507 (2004); *Hamdan v. Rumsfeld,* 548 U.S. 557 (2006).

112. Department of Defense Memorandum on UCMJ Jurisdiction over DoD Civilian Employees, Mar. 10, 2008, *available at* http://www.dtic.mil/whs/directives/corres/pdf/sec080310ucmj.pdf.

113. James Risen, *Limbo for U.S. Women Reporting Iraq Assaults,* N.Y. Times, Feb. 13, 2008, at A1.

114. *Hamdan, supra* note 111.

115. Unless the Security Council authorizes a case to proceed, the ICC may exercise jurisdiction only when either the state in which the alleged crime occurred or the state of the nationality of the accused has consented to jurisdiction. ICC Statute, *supra* note 24, at art. 12(2). Neither the United States nor Iraq has consented to jurisdiction. *See* Coal. for the Int'l Criminal Court, Ratification of the Rome Statute, http://www.iccnow.org/?mod=romeratification (last visited Nov. 2, 2009).

116. Under the complementarity regime, the ICC may not consider a case if a state with jurisdiction is investigating or prosecuting the case, unless that state is "unwilling or unable genuinely to carry out the investigation or prosecution." ICC Statute, *supra* note 24, at art. 17.

117. ICCPR, *supra* note 27, at arts. 28–45. Iraq and the United States have both ratified the ICCPR. *See* Human Dev. Reports, Selected Conventions Related to Human Rights and Migration: Year of Ratification of the International Covenant on Civil and Political Rights, http://hdrstats.undp.org/en/indicators/69.html (last visited Dec. 11, 2009).

118. *See* Henry Steiner & Philip Alston, International Human Rights in Context: Law, Politics, Morals 776 (2d ed., Oxford U. Press 2000) (noting that no interstate complaint has ever been brought under any of the U.N. treaty-body procedures).

119. *See* Bremer, *CPA Order Number 17, supra* note 43, at § 2 ("Unless provided otherwise herein, the MNF, the CPA, Foreign Liaison Missions, their Personnel, property, funds and assets, and all International Consultants shall be immune from Iraqi legal process.").

120. *See* Press Release, White House, Text of Strategic Framework Agreement and Security Agreement Between the United States of America and the Republic of Iraq, http://georgewbush-whitehouse.archives.gov/news/releases/2008/11/20081127–2.html.

121. *See* Criminal Indictment Against U.S. Sec'y of Def. Donald Rumsfeld et al. for War Crimes Perpetrated Against Iraq Detainees at Abu Ghraib Detention Center (2003/2004), and in Guantánamo Bay Naval Station (Nov. 30, 2004), *available at* http://ccrjustice.org/ourcases/current-cases/german-war-crimes-complaint-against-donald-rumsfeld%2C-et-al.

122. *See German Prosecutor Rejects Investigation of Rumsfeld,* L.A. Times, Feb. 11, 2005, at A9.

4. The Unexplored Promise of Contract

1. Nora Bensahel et al., After Saddam: Prewar Planning and the Occupation of Iraq 138 (2008).

2. *An Oversight Hearing on Waste, Fraud, and Abuse in U.S. Government Contracting in Iraq: Hearing Before the S. Democratic Policy Comm.,* 109th Congress (2005) (statement of Franklin Willis, Former CPA Official), at 1, 2, *available at* http://dpc.senate.gov/hearings/hearing19/willis.pdf [hereinafter *2005 SDPC Hearing*].

3. *United States ex rel. DRC, Inc. v. Custer Battles, LLC,* 562 F.3d 295, 298 (4th Cir. 2009).

4. *2005 SDPC Hearing* (statement of Franklin Willis), *supra* note 2, at 2.

5. *Custer Battles, supra* note 3, at 300.

6. Id. at 299.

7. *See* Megan A. Kinsey, Note, *Transparency in Government Procurement: An International Consensus?,* 34 Pub. Cont. L.J. 155, 161–62 (2004).

8. 5 U.S.C. § 552(b)(c)(1) (2000).

9. 5 U.S.C. § 552(b)(c)(4) (2000).

10. *See* Maud Beelman et al., *Winning Contractors: U.S. Contractors Reap the Windfalls of Post-War Reconstruction,* Ctr. for Pub. Integrity, Oct. 30, 2003, available at http://www.commondreams.org/headlines03/1030-10.htm [hereinafter *Winning Contractors*].

11. Jacques S. Gansler et al., Comm'n on Army Acquisition and Program Mgmt. in Expeditionary Operations, *Urgent Reform Required: Army Expeditionary Contracting* 9 (2007), *available at* http://www.army.mil/docs/Gansler_Commission _Report_Final_071031.pdf. [hereinafter *Urgent Reform Required*].

12. *See* Jody Freeman, *Extending Public Law Norms Through Privatization,* 116 Harv. L. Rev. 1285 (2003) [hereinafter *Extending Public Law Norms*].

13. Jody Freeman, *The Private Role in Public Governance,* 75 N.Y.U. L. Rev. 543, 608, 634 (2000) [hereinafter *The Private Role*].

14. A notable exception is the joint initiative of the government of Switzerland and the International Committee of the Red Cross to craft standards for governments that hire contractors to perform military and security tasks. *See, e.g.,* Montreux Document on Pertinent International Legal Obligations and Good Practices for States Related to Operations of Private Military and Security Companies During Armed Conflict, Sept. 17, 2008, *available at* http://www.us-mission .ch/Press2008/September/Montreux%20Document.pdf [hereinafter Montreux Document].

15. For example, under the model contract for private prison management drafted by the Oklahoma Department of Corrections, contractors must comply with constitutional, federal, state, and private standards, including those established by the American Correctional Association. *See* Okla. Dep't of Corr., Correctional Services Contract, art. 1 [hereinafter Oklahoma Contract]. Other states' contracts with companies that manage private prisons contain similar provisions. *See, e.g.,* Fla. Corr. Privatization Comm'n, Correctional Services Contract with Corrections Corp. of America, § 5.1 [hereinafter Florida Contract]; Freeman, *The Private Role, supra* note 13, at 634 (*citing* Texas Dep't of Criminal Justice model contract); *see also* J. Michael Keating Jr., *Public over Private: Monitoring the Performance of Privately Operated Prisons and Jails, in* Private Prisons and the Public Interest, at 130, 138–41 (Douglas C. MacDonald ed., 1990); Requirements for Private Contractor, Miss. Code Ann. tit. 47, § 5-1211(2) (West 2009); Contract for Private Operation of Correctional Facility, Ohio Rev. Code Ann. § 9.06 (West 2009).

16. *See* Freeman, *The Private Role, supra* note 13, at 608 (discussing contractual hearing and oversight mechanisms in the nursing home context).

17. *See* Ctr. for Pub. Integrity, Contracts and Reports, http://projects.public integrity.org/wow/resources.aspx?act=resources (last visited Oct. 19, 2009) [hereinafter Contracts and Reports] (providing text of contracts).

18. To be sure, I relied only on the publicly available portions of the task orders and agreements. Thus, it is possible that some other portion of the agreement contained such terms. Nonetheless, as I discuss in the next chapter, if this is the case the lack of transparency on this point causes further problems.

19. *See* Agreement Between the Dep't of the Interior and CACI Premier Tech., Inc., Contract No. NBCHA010005 (2000), *available at* Contracts and Reports, *supra* note 17 (follow Contract Iraq Interrogation hyperlink) [hereinafter DOI-CACI].

20. Work Orders Nos. 000035D004, 000036D004, 000037D004, 000038D0004, 000064D004, 000067D004, 000070D004, 000071D004, 000072D004, 000073D004, and 000080D004, issued under DOI-CACI, *id.* [hereinafter Work Orders].

21. Work Order No. 000071/0001, *id.*

22. *See, e.g.,* OECD Convention on Combating Bribery of Foreign Public Officials in International Business Transactions art. 1, Dec. 18, 1997, 37 I.L.M. 1; False Claims Act, 31 U.S.C. § 3729 (2000).

23. 48 C.F.R. §§ 2.000 (2006).

24. *An Uneasy Relationship: U.S. Reliance on Private Security Firms in Overseas Operations: Hearing Before the S. Comm. on Homeland Sec. & Gov't Affs.,* 110th Congress (2008) (statement of the Hon. P. Jackson Bell, Deputy Under Sec'y of Def. for Logistics and Material Readiness, U.S. Dep't of Def.), at 2, *available at* http://www.dod.mil/dodgc/olc/docs/testBell080227.pdf.

25. *The State Department and the Iraq War: Hearing Before the H. Comm. on Oversight & Gov't Reform,* 110th Congress (2007) (statement of Condoleezza Rice, Sec'y of State, responding to question from Rep. John Sarbanes), *available at* http://frwebgate.access.gpo.gov/cgi-bin/getdoc.cgi?dbname=110_house_hearings&docid=f:47427.wais.

26. U.S. Dep't of Def., Instruction No. 3020.41, Contractor Personnel Authorized to Accompany the U.S. Armed Forces § 6.1 (Oct. 3, 2005) [hereinafter Instruction 3020.41].

27. Office of the Special Inspector Gen. for Iraq Reconstruction (SIGIR), *Opportunities to Improve Processes for Reporting, Investigating, and Remediating Serious Incidents Involving Private Security Contractors in Iraq, SIGIR-09-019,* at 3 (2009) (*citing* Joint Contracting Command-Iraq/Afghanistan, *Contracting Officer's Guide to Special Contract Requirements for Iraq/Afghanistan Theater Business Clearance* (2007)) [hereinafter *Opportunities to Improve Processes*], *available at* http://www.sigir.mil/files/audits/09-019.pdf. Moreover, all contracts not subject to DFAR Supp. 252.225-7040 exceeding $25,000 with contractors operating in the U.S. Central Command's area of responsibility but not authorized to accompany the U.S. armed forces deployed outside the United States, were required to include provisions

mandating the contractors and employees to comply with (1) U.S. and host country laws; (2) treaties and international agreements; (3) U.S. regulations, directives, instructions, policies, and procedures; and (4) force protection, security, health or safety orders, directives, and instructions issued by the combatant commander. *Id.*

28. Sec'y of State's Panel on Personal Protective Services in Iraq, *Report of the Secretary of State's Panel on Personal Protective Services in Iraq* 9 (2007), *available at* http://merln.ndu.edu/archivepdf/iraq/State/94122.pdf [hereinafter *Report*]. Panel members included Eric J. Boswell, George A. Joulwan, J. Stapleton Roy, and Patrick F. Kennedy.

29. Memorandum of Agreement (MOA) between the U.S. Dep't of Def. and the U.S. Dep't of State on USG Private Sec. Contractors (Dec. 5, 2007), *available at* http://www.defenselink.mil/pubs/pdfs/Signed%20MOA%20Dec%205%202007. pdf [hereinafter MOA between State and DOD].

30. U.S. Gov't Accountability Office, *Rebuilding Iraq: DOD and State Department Have Improved Oversight and Coordination of Private Security Contractors in Iraq, but Further Actions Are Needed to Sustain Improvements* (2008), *available at* http://www.gao.gov/new.items/d08966.pdf [hereinafter *Rebuilding Iraq*].

31. *See, e.g.,* SIGIR, *Opportunities to Improve Processes, supra* note 27, at 1.

32. Convention Against Torture and Other Cruel, Inhuman or Degrading Treatment or Punishment art. 1, Dec. 10, 1984, S. Treaty Doc. No. 100-20 (1988), 1456 U.N.T.S. 85 (1984) [hereinafter Torture Convention].

33. *See, e.g.,* Oklahoma Contract, *supra* note 15, § 6.4; Florida Contract, *supra* note 15, § 6.5; Freeman, *The Private Role, supra* note 13, at 634 (describing model contract for private prison management drafted by the Texas Dep't of Criminal Justice).

34. *See, e.g.,* Work Order No. 000071/0001, *supra* note 20 (statement of work) (requiring that human intelligence adviser must have at least "10 years of experience" and must be "knowledgeable of Army/Joint Interrogation procedures."). Notably, this work order does not require the contractor to provide any training. *See id.*

35. *See* Agreement Between the U.S. Dep't of Def. and Chugach McKinley, Inc., Professional Skills, Contract No. DASW01-03-D-0025 (July 3, 2003), *available at* http://projects.publicintegrity.org/docs/wow/ChugachMcKinley-Iraq.pdf.

36. *See, e.g.,* Work Order No. 000071/0001, *supra* note 20.

37. Statement under oath of Torin Nelson, Sept. 9, 2005, *Saleh v. Titan,* Case No. 1:05cv-1165, at 16.

38. Anthony R. Jones & George R. Fay, Dep't of the Army, *AR 15-6 Investigation of the Abu Ghraib Detention Facility and 205th Military Intelligence Brigade* 18, 50, 85 (2004), *available at* http://fl1.findlaw.com/news.findlaw.com/hdocs/docs/dod/fay82504rpt.pdf [hereinafter *Investigation of the Abu Ghraib Detention Facility*]. Indeed, General Fay concluded that the best approach would be for the contracts to require that the contract interrogators receive training, including training in the Geneva Conventions and other applicable legal rules, within existing government training programs. At a minimum, prior to deployment, "all contractor linguists or interrogators should receive training in the Geneva Conventions standards for the treatment of detainees/prisoners." Furthermore, if the contract allows training that is

"equivalent" to the training that government interrogators receive, "the Contracting Officer, with the assistance of technical personnel, must evaluate and assess the offer-ors'/contractor's written rationale as to why it believes the employee has 'equivalent' training. It appears that under the CACI contract, no one was monitoring the contractor's decisions as to what was considered 'equivalent.'" *Id.*

39. *See, e.g.*, Interview with JAG officer #2 (Oct. 16, 2007).

40. U.S. Dep't of Def., Instruction 3020.41, *supra* note 26, at § 6.3.5.3.4.

41. Sec'y of State's Panel on Personal Protective Services in Iraq, *Report, supra* note 28, at 6.

42. U.S. Dep't of State, the Broad. Bd. of Governors Office of Inspector Gen., & the Office of the Special Inspector Gen. for Iraq Reconstruction (SIGIR), *Joint Audit of Blackwater Contract and Task Orders for Worldwide Personal Protective Services in Iraq, AUD/IQO-09-16, SIGIR-09-21,* at 22 (2009), *available at* http://www.dtic .mil/cgi-bin/GetTRDoc?AD=ADA508739&Location=U2&doc=GetTRDoc.pdf [hereinafter *Joint Audit of Blackwater*].

43. Out of 180 countries (with 180 as the worst), Iraq ranks 178th. Transparency Int'l, *Corruption Perceptions Index 2008* (2008), *available at* http://www .transparency.org/policy_research/surveys_indices/cpi/2008.

44. Jones & Fay, *Investigation of the Abu Ghraib Detention Facility, supra* note 38, at 52.

45. Freeman, *The Private Role, supra* note 13, at 608–9.

46. *See* Office of Inspector Gen., Dep't of Health and Human Servs., *The External Review of Hospital Quality: A Call for Greater Accountability* 1–2 (1999), *available at* http://oig.hhs.gov/oei/reports/oei-01-97-00050.pdf; *see also* Office of Inspector Gen., Dep't of Health and Human Servs., *The External Review of Hospital Quality: The Role of Accreditation* 6–7 (1999), *available at* http://oig.hhs.gove/oei/reports/oei-01-97-00051.pdf [hereinafter *The External Review of Hospital Quality*] (detailing lack of accountability and quality oversight in accredited hospitals).

47. *See, e.g.*, U.S. Dept. of Health and Human Servs., *Nursing Home Compare,* http://www.medicare.gov/NHCompare/Home.asp (last visited Dec. 11, 2009) (database includes information on nursing homes certified by Medicare or Medicaid).

48. *See* Eleanor D. Kinney, *Private Accreditation as a Substitute for Direct Government Regulation in Public Health Insurance Programs: When Is It Appropriate?,* 57 Law & Contemp. Probs. 47, 52 (1994) [hereinafter *Private Accreditation as a Substitute for Direct Government*].

49. Inspector General oversight arises from the Inspector General (IG) Act, codified as amended at 5 U.S.C. app. 3, §§ 1–12 (1994). "The IG Act authorized the creation of offices whose mission is to detect and prevent fraud, waste, and abuse in their respective departments and agencies across the executive branch." Michael R. Bromwich, *Running Special Investigations: The Inspector General Model,* 86 Geo. L.J. 2027, 2027 (1998). For an analysis of the role that inspectors general play in various agencies, *see id.*

50. *See* Office of Inspector Gen., USAID, *Semiannual Report to the Congress* 13 (2004), *available at* http://www.usaid.gov/oig/public/semiann/sarc0409.pdf.

51. For a searing indictment of the government's failure to oversee military contractors and that failure's role in the Abu Ghraib atrocities, *see* Steven L. Schooner, *Contractor Atrocities at Abu Ghraib: Compromised Accountability in a Streamlined, Outsourced Government,* 16 Stan. L. & Pol'y Rev. 549 (2005) [hereinafter *Contractor Atrocities at Abu Ghraib*].

52. *See* USAID, *Assistance for Iraq: Contracts and Grants* (2005), *available at* http://www.usaid.gov/iraq/activities.html [hereinafter *Assistance for Iraq*].

53. *See* Shane Harris, *AID Plans to Contract Out Oversight of Iraq Contracts,* Gov-Exec.Com, May 20, 2003, http://www.govexec.com/dailyfed/0503/052003h1.htm.

54. Office of the Inspector Gen., U.S. Dep't of Def., *Acquisition: Contracts Awarded for the Coalition Provisional Authority by the Defense Contracting Command-Washington (D-2004-057),* at 24 (2004), *available at* http://www.dodig.mil/audit/reports/fy04/04-057.pdf.

55. Comptroller Gen., U.S. Gen. Accounting Office, *Sourcing and Acquisition, Rep. No. GAO-03-771R,* at 1 (2003); *see also* Laura Peterson, *Outsourcing Government: Service Contracting Has Risen Dramatically in the Last Decade,* Ctr. for Pub. Integrity, Oct. 30, 2003, *available at* http://projects.publicintegrity.org/WOW/report.aspx?aid=68 [hereinafter *Outsourcing Government*]. For a detailed discussion of the depletion of the acquisition workforce, *see* David A. Whiteford, *Negotiated Procurements: Squandering the Benefit of the Bargain,* 32 Pub. Cont. L.J. 509, 555–57 (2003).

56. Gansler, *Urgent Reform Required, supra* note 11; *see also Defense Management: Actions Needed to Overcome Long-Standing Challenges with Weapon Systems Acquisition and Service Contract Management: Hearing Before the H. Subcomm. on Def., Comm. on Appropriations,* 111th Congress (2009) (statement of Gene L. Dodaro, Acting Comptroller Gen. of the U.S.), at 16, *available at* http://www.gao.gov/new.items/d09362t.pdf.

57. *See* P. W. Singer, Corporate Warriors: The Rise of the Privatized Military Industry 123–24 (2003).

58. In practice, one way these requirements are avoided is through the use of blanket purchase order agreements, in which task orders can be issued under preexisting contracts. *See* Maud Beelman et al., *Winning Contractors, supra* note 10, and accompanying text. For criticism of the lack of open bidding on the Iraq contracts, *see* Ctr. for Responsive Politics, *Rebuilding Iraq—The Contractors* (2003). For an opposing view, *see* Jeffrey Marburg-Goodman, *USAID's Procurement Contracts: Insider's View,* 39 Procurement L, 10 (2003), *available at* http://pdf.usaid.gov/pdf_docs/PCAAB390.pdf.

59. Federal Acquisition Regulation, 48 C.F.R. §§ 16.301–16.307 (2006).

60. Under the cost-plus system, companies have an incentive to inflate the costs of services so that their fee, typically measured as a percentage of this cost, is as high as possible, *see* Laura Peterson, *Outsourcing Government, supra* note 55, although such

contracts do contain a cost ceiling that cannot be exceeded without the contracting officer's approval. 48 C.F.R. § 16.301-1 (2005). Under the Federal Acquisition Regulations (FAR), these contracts can only be utilized when costs cannot be estimated with sufficient accuracy. *Id.* § 16.301-2.

61. Presidential Memorandum on Improving Government Acquisition 2 (July 29, 2009), *available at* http://www.whitehouse.gov/omb/assets/memoranda_fy2009/m-09-25.pdf.

62. Jones & Fay, *Investigation of the Abu Ghraib Detention Facility, supra* note 38, at 50, 52, 86.

63. Ed Harriman, *Where Has All the Money Gone?*, 27 London Rev. of Books 3, 4, 5 (2005), *available at* http://www.lrb.co.uk/v27/n13/harr04_.html.

64. *2005 SDPC Hearing* (statement of Franklin Willis), *supra* note 2, at 4.

65. *See generally, id.* Of course, the lack of oversight may have a more cynical explanation: it permits private contractors (who may have powerful connections within government) to reap profits without significant constraints.

66. After a scandal, however, such as the uproar surrounding revelations of abuse at Abu Ghraib prison, ombudspersons may be enlisted to investigate such problems.

67. Jones & Fay, *Investigation of the Abu Ghraib Detention Facility, supra* note 38, at 50.

68. A model for this type of oversight might be the role that the International Committee on the Red Cross (ICRC) currently plays in monitoring the conduct of governmental actors during armed conflict. The Geneva Conventions require state parties to allow ICRC representatives to visit military detention centers to ensure that detainees are treated in accord with the principles of international human rights and humanitarian law. Geneva Convention Relative to the Treatment of Prisoners of War art. 126, Aug. 12, 1949, 6 U.S.T. 3316, 75 U.N.T.S. 135; Geneva Convention Relative to the Protection of Civilian Persons in Time of War arts. 76, 143, Aug. 12, 1949, 6 U.S.T. 3516, 75 U.N.T.S. 287. Yet, it is at best ambiguous whether the ICRC would be empowered to play a similar role with respect to private security contractors. The contracts could make this role explicit.

69. Jones & Fay, *Investigation of the Abu Ghraib Detention Facility, supra* note 38, at 19.

70. U.S. Gov't Accountability Office, *Rebuilding Iraq, supra* note 30, at 1, 4, 9.

71. *Id.* at 4, 16.

72. U.S. Dep't of State, the Broad. Bd. of Governors Office of Inspector Gen., & the Office of the SIGIR, *Joint Audit of Blackwater, supra* note 42, at 32.

73. Elise Castelli, *How DoD Will Add 20,000 Acquisition Officers*, Defense News, April 13, 2009, *available at* http://www.defensenews.com/story.php?i=4035334.

74. Maud Beelman et al., *Winning Contractors, supra* note 10. For example, the DOD has taken more and more control over reconstruction and emergency relief functions, normally the province of USAID. The State Department, meanwhile, manages the contract with DynCorp to provide Iraqi police training. *See* Ctr. for Pub. Integrity, Contracts and Reports, *supra* note 17. And the State Department's Bureau

of Population, Refugees, and Migration (PRM) manages refugee assistance funds. *See* http://www.state.gov/g/prm/c25756.htm.

75. Schooner, *Contractor Atrocities at Abu Ghraib, supra* note 51, at 564–70.

76. *Id.*

77. Sec'y of State's Panel on Personal Protective Services in Iraq, *Report, supra* note 28, at 5, 6.

78. U.S. Gov't Accountability Office, *Rebuilding Iraq, supra* note 30, at 14.

79. MOA between State and DOD, *supra* note 29.

80. *See, e.g.,* Harry P. Hatry, Urban Inst., Performance Measurement: Getting Results 3–10 (Urban Inst. Press, 1999).

81. William D. Eggers, *Performance-Based Contracting: Designing State-of-the-Art Contract Administration and Monitoring Systems* 1, 2 (1997), *available at* http://reason.org/files/e0f57a04efae97a83b33c7520dc65dc8.pdf [hereinafter *Performance-Based Contracting*].

82. *See, e.g.,* Oklahoma Contract, *supra* note 15, §§ 5, 6.3–6.4.

83. *See* Freeman, *The Private Role, supra* note 13, at 634–35 (describing contract between private corporation and state of Texas).

84. *See* Performance-based Standards, *Performance-Based Standards for Juvenile Correction and Detention Facilities,* Pbstandards.org (last visited Oct. 19, 2009); *see also* Geoffrey F. Segal & Adrian T. Moore, Weighing the Watchmen: Evaluating the Costs and Benefits of Outsourcing Correctional Services 15–16 (2002).

85. *A Tale of Two Systems: Cost, Quality, and Accountability in Private Prisons,* 115 Harv. L. Rev. 1868, 1889–90 (2002) [hereinafter *Tale of Two Systems*].

86. 42 U.S.C. § 604a(a)(1)(A) (2000).

87. *See* Pamela Winston et al., *Privatization of Welfare Services: A Review of the Literature, Reference No. 8834-002,* at 3–6 (2002), *available at* http://aspe.hhs.gov/hsp/privatization02/report.pdf.

88. *See* Mary Bryna Sanger, The Welfare Marketplace: Privatization and Welfare Reform 28–48 (2003) [hereinafter The Welfare Marketplace] (discussing issues raised by performance contracting for welfare services); Sheena McConnell et al., *Privatization in Practice: Case Studies of Contracting for TANF Case Management, Reference No. 8834-008,* at 39–51 (2003), *available at* http://www.mathematica-mpr.com/PDFs/privatize.pdf (discussing use of performance measures in welfare contracts).

89. *See* Gillian E. Metzger, *Privatization as Delegation,* 103 Colum. L. Rev. 1367, 1387–88 (2003) [hereinafter *Privatization as Delegation*].

90. *See, e.g., 2005 SDPC Hearing* (statement of Franklin Willis), *supra* note 2, at 3–4.

91. For example, the CACI agreement was an ID/IQ contract. *Cf.* Schooner, *Contractor Atrocities at Abu Ghraib, supra* note 51, at 569 (using the "Abu Ghraib experience" as an illustration of the dangers of ID/IQ contracts).

92. ID/IQ contracts are governed by 48 C.F.R. § 16.500-6 (2005). For a discussion of ID/IQ contracts, *see* Karen DaPonte Thornton, *Fine-Tuning Acquisition*

Reform's Favorite Procurement Vehicle, the Indefinite Delivery Contract, 31 Pub. Cont. L.J. 383 (2002) [hereinafter *Fine-Tuning Acquisition Reform*].

93. *See* 48 C.F.R. § 16.504 (2005); *see also* Schooner, *Contractor Atrocities at Abu Ghraib, supra* note 51, at 565.

94. *See* Thornton, *Fine-Tuning Acquisition Reform, supra* note 92, at 387.

95. *See, e.g.,* Schooner, *Contractor Atrocities at Abu Ghraib, supra* note 51, at 563.

96. Agreement Between the Dep't. of Def. and Military Professional Resources Inc., Iraq Interpreters, Contract No. GS-23F-9814H (Apr. 28, 2003), *available at* http://projects.publicintegrity.org/docs/wow/MPRI_Linguists.pdf.

97. Work Order No. 000071D004, *supra* note 20, at 6.

98. *See, e.g.,* Nestor Davidson, *Relational Contracts in the Privatization of Social Welfare: The Case of Housing,* 24 Yale L. & Pol'y Rev. 263, 264 (2006) [hereinafter *Relational Contracts*] (arguing for a "relational" approach to contracting that "shifts the locus of efficiency and accountability efforts from contractual specificity and enforcement to encouraging flexibility and fostering mutual responsibility for program goals"); Metzger, *Privatization as Delegation, supra* note 89, at 1388 ("[T]he operational flexibility of private providers can make them better able to improve staff performance and tailor their programs to meet the needs of particular participants or employers."); Martha Minow, *Public and Private Partnerships: Accounting for the New Religion,* 116 Harv. L. Rev. 1229, 1262 (2003) ("Rigid standards could force private providers to behave like government and lose their potential for innovation, efficiency, and flexibility.").

99. *See* Eggers, *Performance-Based Contracting, supra* note 81, at 2.

100. *See* Sanger, The Welfare Marketplace, *supra* note 88, at 21–22, 42–43, 68–69, 104–6.

101. *See generally* Michael Power, The Audit Society: Rituals of Verification (1999).

102. *See* Ian Smillie, *At Sea in a Sieve? Trends and Issues in the Relationship Between Northern NGOs and Northern Governments, in* Stakeholders: Government-NGO Partnerships for International Development, at 10–11 (Ian Smillie & Henny Helmich eds., 1999).

103. *See, e.g.,* Davidson, *Relational Contracts, supra* note 98 and accompanying text (discussing important benefits of discretion).

104. *See id.*

105. *See* Freeman, *The Private Role, supra* note 13, at 634–635 (describing contract between private corporation and the Texas Dep't of Criminal Justice).

106. *See, e.g.,* Nat'l Comm. for Quality Assurance, What Does NCQA Review When It Accredits an HMO?, http://www.ncqa.org/tabid/689/Default.aspx (then follow 2010 NQCA Health Plan Accreditation Requirements hyperlink under "In-Depth Health Plan Accreditation Information").

107. *See* Ctr. for Pub. Integrity, Contracts and Reports, *supra* note 17.

108. Freeman, *The Private Role, supra* note 13, at 608.

109. Although NCQA's accreditation program is voluntary, almost half the HMOs in the nation, covering three-quarters of all HMO enrollees, are currently involved in

the NCQA accreditation process. Significantly, employers increasingly require or request NCQA accreditation of the plans with which they do business. *See* Nat'l Comm. for Quality Assurance (NCQA), The Basics: Assessing Quality, http://www.ncqa .org/tabid/440/Default.aspx.

110. Freeman, *The Private Role, supra* note 13, at 618–19; *see also* J. Robert Lilly & Paul Knepper, *The Corrections-Commercial Complex,* 39 Crime & Delinq. 150, 156–57 (1993).

111. *See* 42. U.S.C. §§ 1395w-28(f).

112. *See, e.g.,* Oklahoma Contract, *supra* note 15; Freeman, *The Private Role, supra* note 13, at 634 (describing model contract for private prison management drafted by the Texas Dep't of Criminal Justice that contains such a requirement).

113. Freeman, *The Private Role, supra* note 13, at 628–29. Freeman notes that, "[t]hroughout its history, the ACA has fostered professionalism in prison administration through the development of standards and promoted progressive reforms such as rehabilitation." *Id.* at 629.

114. *See, e.g.,* Florida Contract, *supra* note 15, at § 5.21 (requiring prison to maintain accreditation); Oklahoma Contract, *supra* note 15, at § 5.2.

115. *See* Malcolm M. Feeley & Edward L. Rubin, Judicial Policy Making and the Modern State: How the Courts Reformed America's Prisons 162–64 (1998).

116. Freeman, *The Private Role, supra* note 13, at 629.

117. *See* Isabel V. Sawhill & Shannon L. Smith, *Vouchers for Elementary and Secondary Education, in* Vouchers and the Provision of Public Services, at 263 (C. Eugene Steuerle et al. eds., 2000).

118. *See Accreditation: What Does It Mean?,* Parent Power!, Dec. 2000, at 2–3, *available at* http://www.edreform.com/_upload/00dec.pdf#ppArt75.

119. Stephen D. Sugarman & Emlei M. Kuboyama, *Approving Charter Schools: The Gate-Keeper Function,* 53 Admin. L. Rev. 869, 937 (2001).

120. Freeman, *The Private Role, supra* note 13, at 612–613; *see also* Kinney, *Private Accreditation as a Substitute for Direct Government, supra* note 48, at 65. As Freeman observes, in the prison context "the ACA, rather than government agencies, may effectively establish correctional standards." Other private organizations—such as the American Medical Association, the National Sheriffs' Association, the American Public Health Association, and the National Fire Protection Association, all of which have published guidelines or standards governing "such things as medical care, sanitation, and safety in prisons"—play a similar role. In the health care context, the Joint Commission on Accreditation of Healthcare Organizations also develops industry standards, through "a committee that includes representatives of professional and industry groups, as well as government representatives from" the Health Care Financing Administration. Freeman, *The Private Role, supra* note 13, at 610, 612, 629.

121. Because ACA officials are generally chosen from the ranks of experienced corrections officials, for example, "personal and professional relationships between ACA overseers and prison management are not uncommon, creating a common sympathy and sense of purpose that tells against both more meaningful standards and more

rigorous enforcement." Sharon Dolovich, *State Punishment and Private Prisons,* 55 Duke L.J. 439, 492 (2005) [hereinafter *State Punishment and Private Prisons*]. Moreover, Dolovich argues that because the institutions pay for accreditation, thereby "providing income on which the ACA is dependent for its survival . . . a degree of capture is likely." *Id.* (citation omitted).

122. *Id.* at 490–91 (acknowledging benefits of ACA accreditation of prisons); Kinney, *Private Accreditation as a Substitute for Direct Government, supra* note 48, at 65 (acknowledging benefits of JCAHO accreditation of hospitals).

123. To be sure, the Federal Acquisition Regulation does require the evaluation of all contracts in excess of $1,000,000, 48 C.F.R. § 42.1502 (2006), and also requires contract officers to take into account the past performance of contractors in all competitively negotiated acquisitions expected to exceed $1,000,000. 48 C.F.R. § 15.304(c)(3) (2006). Thus, in theory, an internal "blacklist" of rogue contractors could be created to guard against repeat abuses. But such an internal system hardly substitutes for independent accreditation.

124. *See, e.g.,* Overview of the U.N. Global Compact, UN.org, http://www .unglobalcompact.org/abouttheGC/index.html (last modified June 30, 2009) (program, launched by U.N. secretary-general Kofi Annan, to encourage corporations to agree voluntarily to respect nine principles, including the protection of human rights and the environment); David Stout, *Oil and Mining Leaders Agree to Protect Rights in Remote Areas,* N.Y. Times, Dec. 21, 2000, at A9 (describing agreement among oil and mining companies, the British and U.S. governments, and human rights organizations, providing that companies will voluntarily comply with human rights standards). For broader discussion of this "transnational new governance" trend, see, e.g., Kenneth W. Abbott & Duncan Snidal, *Strengthening International Regulation Through Transnational New Governance: Overcoming the Orchestration Deficit,* 42 Vand. J. Transnational L. 501 (2009).

125. *See* Sphere Project, *Humanitarian Charter and Minimum Standards in Disaster Response* (2004), *available at* http://www.wpro.who.int/internet/files/eha/ toolkit/web/Technical%20References/Handbooks%20and%20Manuals/Sphere%20 Handbook.pdf [hereinafter *Humanitarian Charter*].

126. *See* Int'l Peace Operations Assoc., IPOA Code of Conduct 12, http:// ipoaworld.org/eng/codeofconduct/87-codecodeofconductv12enghtml.html (last visited Dec. 11, 2009).

127. *See* Work Orders, *supra* note 20.

128. *See* Agreement Between U.S. Dep't of State and DynCorp Int'l Inc., Iraq Law Enforcement, Contract No. SLMAQM-03-C-0028 (Apr. 18, 2003), *available at* http://projects.publicintegrity.org/docs/wow/DynCorp.pdf.

129. *See* Sphere Project, *Humanitarian Charter, supra* note 125. Although SPHERE itself is a project of the not-for-profit sector, *see* http://www.sphereproject .org (listing representatives of not-for-profits and governments as board members), nothing prevents contracting agencies from requiring for-profit entities as well to follow SPHERE guidelines in fulfilling contracts.

130. *See, e.g.*, Dolovich, *State Punishment and Private Prisons, supra* note 121.

131. *See, e.g.*, Freeman, *Extending Public Law Norms, supra* note 12, at 1317.

132. For example, section 313(2) of the Restatement (Second) of Contracts provides: "A promisor who contracts with a government or governmental agency to do an act for or render a service to the public is not subject to contractual liability to a member of the public for consequential damages resulting from performance or failure to perform unless (a) the terms of the promise provide for such liability; or (b) the promisee is subject to liability to the member of the public for the damages and a direct action against the promisor is consistent with the terms of the contract and with the policy of the law authorizing the contract and prescribing remedies for its breach." Restatement (Second) of Contracts § 313(2) (1981). For further discussion of third-party beneficiary suits involving government contracts, *see* Melvin Aron Eisenberg, *Third-Party Beneficiaries*, 92 Colum. L. Rev. 1358, 1406–1412 (1992).

133. 5 U.S.C. § 2302 (1989). While it is true that such employees could bring a qui tam action for fraud, 31 U.S.C. § 3730(b)(1), (c), (d), (h) (2000), such a suit would do nothing to protect the employee from being fired.

134. 31 U.S.C. § 3730(h) (2009).

135. 31 U.S.C. § 3730(c) (2009).

136. *2005 SDPC Hearing* (statement of Franklin Willis), *supra* note 2, at 4.

137. *Id.* at 3.

138. *Id.* at 3, 4.

139. *Id.* at 3.

140. *United States ex rel. DRC, Inc. v. Custer Battles, LLC*, 562 F.3d 295, 308–9 (4th Cir. 2009).

141. *See, e.g.*, Jack M. Sabatino, *Privatization and Punitives: Should Government Contractors Share the Sovereign's Immunities from Exemplary Damages?*, 58 Ohio St. L.J. 175, 191 (1997) (expressing concern that litigation and administrative costs could "siphon away public resources that could have been devoted to, among other things, the effective implementation and oversight of the contractors' work.")

142. *See* Metzger, *Privatization as Delegation, supra* note 89, at 1404–1405.

143. *See, e.g.*, William E. Kovacic, *The Civil False Claims Act as a Deterrent to Participation in Government Procurement Markets*, 6 Sup. Ct. Econ. Rev. 201, 205 (1998) (reporting contractors' concerns that the specter of qui tam suits is "a costly, substantial burden of doing business with the government").

144. See Stephen L. Schooner, *Fear of Oversight: The Fundamental Failure of Businesslike Government*, 50 Am. U. L. Rev. 627, 668 n.137 (2001).

145. *See, e.g.*, Montreux Document, *supra* note 14.

146. Indeed, as Bradley Karkkainen has pointed out, the Toxics Release Inventory (TRI), 42 U.S.C. § 11023 (2000), which requires that industrial facilities report the release and transfer of specific chemicals, has had a significant impact on pollution emissions. *See* Bradley C. Karkkainen, *Information as Environmental Regulation: TRI and Performance Benchmarking, Precursor to a New Paradigm?*, 89 Geo. L.J. 257, 287–88 (2001).

According to Karkkainen, the TRI, because it creates a performance metric, "both compels and enables facilities and firms to monitor their own environmental performance" and "encourages them to compare, rank, and track performance among production processes, facilities, operating units, and peer or competitor firms." In addition, Karkkainen argues that the TRI data "subjects the environmental performance of facilities and firms to an unprecedented degree of scrutiny by their peers, competitors, investors, employees, consumers, community residents, environmental organizations, activists, elected officials, regulators, and the public in general." As a result, this transparency scheme "unleashes, strengthens, and exploits multiple pressures, all tending to push in the direction of continuous improvement as facilities and firms endeavor to leapfrog over their peers to receive credit for larger improvements or superior performance." In addition, administrators—whether within companies or in government bureaucracies monitoring contract compliance—have a management incentive to improve transparency. *Id*. at 261–63, 295–305. Thus, although information by itself does not provide accountability, *see id*. at 338–43 (noting that some small firms may be unconcerned about the mere release of information), it can enable other accountability mechanisms.

5. Public Participation / Private Contract

1. Press Release, DynCorp Int'l Inc., DynCorp Int'l Inc. Reports Fourth Quarter and Fiscal 2008 Year-End Fin. Results (May 28, 2008), *available at* http://ir.dyn-intl.com/releasedetail.cfm?ReleaseID=312738.

2. *See* Press Release, DynCorp Int'l Inc., DynCorp Int'l Awarded Extension of Iraq Police Training (Sept. 5, 2006); Press Release, DynCorp Int'l Inc., DynCorp Int'l Awarded Contract to Train Afghan Police (Sept. 7, 2005).

3. *See, e.g.*, Howard J. Krongard & Thomas F. Gimble, *U.S. Dep't of State & U.S. Dep't of Def., Interagency Assessment of Afghanistan Police Training and Readiness* 1 (2006), *available at* http://oig.state.gov/documents/organization/76103.pdf [hereinafter *Interagency Assessment of Afghanistan Police Training*] (concluding that the "U.S.-funded program to train and equip the Afghan National Police (ANP) is generally well conceived and well executed.").

4. Office of the Special Inspector Gen. for Iraq Reconstruction (SIGIR), *Review of DynCorp International, LLC, Contract S-LMAQM-04-C-0030, Task Order 0338, for the Iraqi Police Training Program Support, SIGIR06-029, DOS-OIG-AUD/IQO-07-20*, at ii, 12, 18 (2007), *available at* http://www.sigir.mil/reports/pdf/audits/06-029.pdf [hereinafter *Review of DynCorp International*].

5. *Interagency Assessment of Afghanistan Police Training, supra* note 3, at 11, 16, 45. To be sure, police training is difficult in this context. For example, many of the Afghani recruits were illiterate, and the force was plagued by "a history of low pay and pervasive corruption, in an insecure environment." *Id*. at 1. Indeed, police chiefs regularly took bribes to allow drugs to pass along routes they controlled, and they frequently engaged in skimming money received. Seth G. Jones, Nat'l Research Def. Inst., *Counterinsurgency in Afghanistan* 69 (2008), *available at* http://www.rand

.org/pubs/monographs/2008/RAND_MG595.pdf [hereinafter *Counterinsurgency in Afghanistan*].

6. Robert Perito, Michael Dzidzic & Beth DeGrasse, *Building Civilian Capacity for U.S. Stability Operations: The Rule of Law Component,* U.S. Inst. of Peace Special Report No. 118, at 1, 4 (2004), *available at* http://www.usip.org/files/resources/sr118.pdf [hereinafter *Building Civilian Capacity*].

7. Jones, *Counterinsurgency in Afghanistan,* supra note 5, at 69, 71.

8. James Glanz & David Rohde, *U.S.-Trained Afghan Police Force Is Failing, Report Says,* N.Y. Times, Dec. 4, 2006, *available at* http://www.nytimes.com/2006/12/03/world/asia/03iht-kabul.3763052.html?pagewanted=all.

9. Indeed, at the time of the report, there was "still confusion at CSTC-A and in the embassy's INL office over what is contained in the Department of State contract and its numerous modifications." Krongard & Gimble, *Interagency Assessment of Afghanistan Police Training, supra* note 3, at 35.

10. As discussed in Chapter 1, *accountability* refers to post hoc mechanisms that allow actors to hold other actors to a set of standards, to judge whether they have fulfilled their responsibilities in light of these standards, and to impose sanctions if they determine that these responsibilities have not been met. Because the disciplining power of public participation does not always take the form of post hoc sanctions, however (unless a decision maker is subsequently voted out of office), we must think more broadly not just about mechanisms of accountability but also about mechanisms of *constraint.* Thus, actors may be disciplined through processes that don't necessarily result in formal sanctions after the fact but that may nevertheless effectively limit the scope of discretion wielded by those actors.

11. To be sure, as the classic "tyranny of the majority" concept illustrates, democratic participation does not always check against abuses of fundamental human dignity or other rights, as when large popular majorities support limiting those rights. *See generally* Russell Hardin, *The Street-Level Epistemology of Democratic Participation,* 10 J. of Pol. Phil. 212 (2002).

12. *See, e.g.,* Benedict Kingsbury, Nico Krisch & Richard B. Stewart, *The Emergence of Global Administrative Law,* 68 Law & Contemp. Probs. 15 (2005) [hereinafter *Global Administrative Law*]; Alfred C. Aman Jr., The Democracy Deficit, Taming Globalization Through Law Reform 154–55 (2004) [hereinafter The Democracy Deficit]; Peter H. Schuck, *Introduction, in* Foundations of Administrative Law, at 4 (Peter H. Schuck ed., 1994).

13. *See, e.g.,* Jonathan Turley, *The Military Pocket Republic,* 97 Nw. U. L. Rev. 1, 72 (2002) ("This layer of agencies creates obvious problems for theories of democracy that emphasize the ability of citizens to influence their government through participatory action or deliberative process."). *But see* Mark Seidenfeld, *A Civic Republican Justification for the Bureaucratic State,* 105 Harv. L. Rev. 1511, 1542 (1992) (arguing that agencies, because they fall between the extremes of a "politically overresponsive Congress and the over-insulated courts," may be best situated to institute a civic republican model of policy making).

14. 5 U.S.C. § 552 (2000).

15. 5 U.S.C. app. § 2 (2000) (requiring that critical regulatory meetings be announced in advance and be made open to the public).

16. Inspector general oversight arises from the Inspector General (IG) Act, codified as amended at 5 U.S.C. app. 3 §§ 1–12 (1994). The IG Act authorized the creation of offices whose mission is to detect and prevent fraud, waste, and abuse in their respective departments and agencies across the executive branch. *Id.* For an analysis of the role that inspectors general play in various agencies, *see* Michael R. Bromwich, *Running Special Investigations: The Inspector General Model,* 86 Geo. L. Rev. 2027 (1998).

17. *See, e.g.,* Civil Service Reform Act of 1978, Pub. L. 95-454, 92 Stat. 1111 (codified as amended in scattered sections of 5 U.S.C.). *See generally* Thomas M. Devine, *The Whistleblower Protection Act of 1989: Foundation for the Modern Law of Employee Dissent,* 51 Admin. L. Rev. 531 (1999) (analyzing the act's provisions). Since enactment of the landmark Civil Service Reform Act in 1978, hundreds of state statutes have also been passed to protect whistleblowers. *See* Robert G. Vaughn, *State Whistleblower Statutes and the Future of Whistleblower Protection,* 51 Admin. L. Rev. 581, 582–83 (1999) (collecting whistleblower statutes).

18. For a description of the civil service rules generally, *see* Ronald N. Johnson & Gary D. Libecap, The Federal Civil Service and the Problem of Bureaucracy: The Economics and Politics of Institutional Change (1994).

19. *See* Administrative Procedure Act, 5 U.S.C. § 553(c) (2000) [hereinafter APA].

20. 5 U.S.C. §§ 551–59, 701–6 (2000); *see, e.g., Motor Vehicle Mfrs. Ass'n v. State Farm Mut. Auto. Ins. Co.,* 463 U.S. 29, 48–49 (1983) (requiring that regulators provide reasons for their policies and base their decisions on an administrative record that is publicly available).

21. *See, e.g., Detroit Free Press v. Ashcroft,* 303 F.3d 681, 683 (6th Cir. 2002) ("The Framers of the First Amendment . . . protected the people against secret government.").

22. *See* Jack M. Beermann, *Privatization and Political Accountability,* 28 Fordham Urb. L.J. 1507, 1509 (2001) ("Political accountability should be understood to include the democratic character of decision-making, the clarity of responsibility for an action or policy within the political system, and the ability of the body politic to obtain accurate information about a governmental policy or action.").

23. Cary Coglianese, *Administrative Law, in* International Encyclopedia of Social & Behavioral Sciences, at 85–88 (Neil J. Smelser & Paul B. Bates eds., 2001) ("Transparent procedures and opportunities for public input give organized interests an ability to represent themselves, and their constituencies, in the administrative process. . . . These procedures may also protect against regulatory capture. . . ."); Thomas W. Merrill, *Capture Theory and the Courts: 1967–1983,* 72 Chi.-Kent L. Rev. 1039, 1043 (1997) (noting the judicial thrust toward "changing the procedural rules that govern agency decisionmaking . . . [to] force agencies to open their doors—and their minds—to formerly unrepresented points of view, with the result that capture would be eliminated or at least reduced.")

24. *See, e.g.,* Mariano-Florentino Cuéllar, *Rethinking Regulatory Democracy,* 57 Admin. L. Rev. 411 (2005). On the other hand, some argue that the focus on transparency can at times impede the ability of regulators to secure much-needed information from the industries they regulate. *See* Cary Coglianese, Richard Zeckhauser & Edward Parson, *Seeking Truth for Power: Informational Strategy and Regulatory Policymaking,* 89 Minn. L. Rev. 277, 280 (2004) ("We conclude that regulators' need to secure information from those they regulate provides a reason for preserving some degree of opacity in an otherwise transparent and accountable regulatory process.").

25. *See, e.g.,* Robert A. Dahl, *Can International Organizations Be Democratic? A Skeptic's View, in* Democracy's Edges, at 19 (Ian Shapiro & Casiano Hacker-Cordón eds., 1999).

26. Richard Falk & Andrew Strauss, *On the Creation of a Global People's Assembly: Legitimacy and the Power of Popular Sovereignty,* 36 Stan. J. Int'l L. 191 (2000); Richard Falk & Andrew Strauss, *Bridging the Globalization Gap: Toward a Global Parliament,* 80 Foreign Affs. 212 (2001).

27. *See* Ruth W. Grant & Robert O. Keohane, *Accountability and Abuses of Power in World Politics,* 99 Am. Pol. Sci. Rev. 29, 32, 33 (2005) [hereinafter *Accountability and Abuses of Power*] (*citing* Benedict Anderson, *Imagined Communities: Reflections on the Origin and Spread of Nationalism* (rev. ed. 1991) [hereinafter *Imagined Communities*]).

28. Kingsbury, Krisch & Stewart, *Global Administrative Law, supra* note 12, at 16, 61.

29. *See* Peter L. Lindseth, *Agents Without Principals: Delegation in an Age of Diffuse and Fragmented Governance, in* Reframing Self-Regulation in European Private Law (Fabrizio Cafaggi, ed., 2006); Gillian Metzger, *Private Delegations, Due Process, and the Duty to Supervise, in* Government by Contract: Outsourcing and American Democracy (Jody Freeman & Martha Minow eds., 2009) [hereinafter *Private Delegations*]; Paul R. Verkuil, Outsourcing Sovereignty: Why Privatization of Government Functions Threatens Democracy and What We Can Do About It (2007).

30. *See* Mary L. Heen, *Congress, Public Values, and the Financing of Private Choice,* 65 Ohio St. L.J. 853, 868 (2004) ("Politics offer a process for preference formation through the protection of voting rights and procedures for political deliberation, including open proceedings and constitutional protections for public discussion and criticism. Private firms have fewer obligations to provide access to information about their operations or the reasons for their decisions."). *Cf.* Paul Starr, *The Case for Skepticism, in* Privatization and Its Alternatives 25, 27–29 (William T. Gormley Jr. ed., 1991) (expressing concerns about privatization). For example, federal contracting measures are generally exempt from notice and comment requirements. *See Am. Hosp. Ass'n v. Bowen,* 834 F.2d 1037, 1053 (D.C. Cir. 1987) (ruling that a federal request for proposals and subsequent contract did not implicate the rulemaking processes of § 553 of the APA, *supra* note 19). Similarly, the Model Procurement Code for State and Local Governments allows a review of contracts only at the request of a bidder, not the public. Model Procurement Code for State and Local

Governments (1979). *See also* Matthew Diller, *The Revolution in Welfare Administration: Rules, Discretion, and Entrepreneurial Government,* 75 N.Y.U. L. Rev. 1121, 1198 (2000) (*citing* Model Procurement Code for State and Local Governments, *supra,* at § 9-101).

31. *See* Laura A. Dickinson, *Government for Hire: Privatizing Foreign Affairs and the Problem of Accountability Under International Law,* 47 Wm. & Mary L. Rev. 135, 193 (2005).

32. *See* Sharon Dolovich, *State Punishment and Private Prisons,* 55 Duke L.J. 437 (2005).

33. National Defense Authorization Act for Fiscal Year 2008, H.R. 4986, 110th Cong, § 861 (2008) [hereinafter 2008 Defense Authorization Act].

34. *See* GAO Report, *Contingency Contracting: DOD, State, and USAID Continue to Face Challenges in Tracking Contractor Personnel and Contracts in Iraq and Afghanistan* 8–15 (Oct. 2009), available at http://www.gao.gov/new.items/d101.pdfh.

35. *See* Renae Merle, *Census Counts 100,000 Contractors in Iraq,* Wash. Post, Dec. 5, 2006, at D1.

36. Joe Sterling, *Waxman: Contractor's Re-Hiring Raises "Serious Questions,"* CNN Politics.com, Oct. 5, 2007, *available at* http://www.cnn.com/2007/POLITICS/10/05/waxman.blackwater/index.html.

37. Eric Schmitt, *Report Details Shooting by Drunken Blackwater Worker,* N.Y. Times, Oct. 2, 2007, at A10 [hereinafter *Shooting by Drunken Blackwater Worker*].

38. Memorandum from the Majority Staff of the H.R. Comm. on Oversight and Gov't Reform to Members of the Comm. on Oversight and Gov't Reform, Additional Information on About Blackwater USA, at 9 (Oct. 1, 2007), *available at* http://www.scribd.com/doc/18951383/House-Oversight-Committees-Memorandum-on-Blackwater-October-2007 [hereinafter House Oversight Memorandum].

39. Schmitt, *Shooting by Drunken Blackwater Worker, supra* note 37.

40. Justine Redman & Mike Mount, *Contractor Involved in Iraq Shooting Got Job in Kuwait,* CNN Politics.com, Oct. 4, 2007, *available at* http://www.cnn.com/2007/POLITICS/10/04/blackwater.contractor/index.html.

41. Human Rights First, *Private Security Contractors at War: Ending the Culture of Impunity* 9 (2008) [hereinafter *Private Security Contractors at War*], *available at* http://www.humanrightsfirst.info/pdf/08115-usls-psc-final.pdf. Under a three-year, $293 million contract awarded in 2004, Aegis provided a range of security and intelligence services to the DOD through management of the Iraq Reconstruction Operation Centers (ROCs). These centers coordinated military-contractor activity and collected "serious incident reports" on cases in which contractors discharge weapons. *Id.* at 9–10.

42. Office of the Special Inspector Gen. for Iraq Reconstruction, *Compliance with Contract No. W911S0-04-C-0003 Awarded to Aegis Defence Services Limited, Report Number 05-005,* at 7, 8 (2005).

43. Human Rights First, *Private Security Contractors at War, supra* note 41, at 9.

44. Current ROC director Major Kent Lightner has said that "only a handful" of the roughly thirty DOD contractors have reported "weapons discharges," and he emphasizes that these companies are not necessarily the ones implicated in the worst incidents. Former ROC head Colonel Timothy Clapp has similarly asserted that only a few firms regularly report "discharge of firearms" incidents, most notably Aegis and Armorgroup. "In their contracts, it says [DOD contractors] are supposed to report, but whether they do or not is up to them." Colonel Clapp also noted that "you have to take it with a grain of salt. Some of the companies clearly underreport." In addition, because the ROCs only keep track of DOD contractors, many contractors (for example, Blackwater security guards working under State Department contracts) do not participate in the reporting system at all. *Id.* at 9, 13, 14.

45. *Id.* at 14.

46. *Id.* at 10. Indeed, while the reports paint a stark picture of the dangers that contractors face, they "often contain[] cursory incident descriptions and no follow-up on potential civilian casualties," demonstrating "the SIR system to be ill-suited for accountability purposes." *Id.*

47. Freedom of Information Act, 5 U.S.C. § 552(a)(4)(B) (2006) [hereinafter FOIA].

48. *Id.* at §§ 552(b)(1), 552(b)(3).

49. For example, in 2003, a consortium of rights groups including the American Civil Liberties Union, the New York Civil Liberties Union, the Center for Constitutional Rights, Physicians for Human Rights, Veterans for Common Sense, and Veterans for Peace filed a FOIA request for records concerning the treatment of prisoners in U.S. custody abroad. As of 2008, the government had released more than a hundred thousand pages of documents. Press Release, Am. Civil Liberties Union, Justice Dep't Report Reveals Senior Gov't Officials Knew Early on of Interrogation Abuse but Did Not Stop It (May 20, 2008). The impact of these disclosures is perhaps most apparent in the debate about U.S. interrogation practices. In one recent case, documents released to the ACLU have provided gruesome details about the deaths of some prisoners in custody as well as a fierce internal discussion within the government over the legitimacy of abusive tactics. Press Release, Am. Civil Liberties Union, Latest Government Documents Show Army Command Approved and Encouraged Abuse of Detainees, ACLU Says (Apr. 19, 2005). One of the prisoners, Farhad Mohamed, had contusions under his eyes and the bottom of his chin, a swollen nose, cuts, and large bumps on his forehead when he died in Mosul in 2004. Another document reveals questions the Army Criminal Investigation Task Force (CITF) raised about harsh interrogation methods applied to Guantánamo prisoners. One memo drafted in September 2002 identifies "unacceptable methods" involving "threats," "discomfort," and "sensory deprivation," strongly suggesting that CITF expressed disapproval of abusive methods as far back as September 2002. CITF commander Brittain Mallow instructed his unit not to participate in "any questionable interrogation techniques at the facility." These documents not only highlight questionable practices but also show that U.S. authorities were internally divided about the use of these techniques. Press

Release, Am. Civil Liberties Union, ACLU Obtains Def. Dep't Documents About Prisoner Deaths and Interrogations (May 14, 2008).

50. Whistleblower Protection Act of 1989, 5 U.S.C. §§ 1201, 1222, 2302.

51. Notification and Federal Employee Antidiscrimination and Retaliation Act of 2002, 5 U.S.C. § 2302(b)(8) (2006).

52. *See* Bruce D. Fisher, *The Whistleblower Protection Act of 1989: A False Hope for Whistleblowers,* 43 Rutgers L. Rev. 355, 376, 407–8, 415 (1991) [hereinafter *The Whistleblower Protection Act of 1989*].

53. False Claims Act, 31 U.S.C. §§ 3230(b), 3729(a) (2006).

54. Pratap Chatterjee, *Halliburton Hearing Unearths New Abuse,* CorpWatch, June 27, 2005, *available at* http://www.corpwatch.org/article.php?id=12476.

55. *An Oversight Hearing on Waste, Fraud, and Abuse in U.S. Government Contracting in Iraq: Hearing Before the S. Democratic Policy Comm.,* 109th Congress (2005) (statement of Bunnatine Greenhouse, U.S. Army Corps of Engineers), at 1, 2, 3 *available at* http://dpc.senate.gov/hearings/hearing22/greenhouse.pdf [hereinafter *2005 SDPC Hearing*].

56. Neely Tucker, *A Web of Truth,* Wash. Post, Oct. 19, 2005, at C1.

57. Assoc. Press, *FBI Probes Halliburton's Pentagon Contracts,* Newsday, Oct. 28, 2004.

58. Erik Eckholm, *Halliburton Case Is Referred to Justice Dept., Senator Says,* N.Y. Times, Nov. 19, 2005.

59. Jennifer K. Elsea, Moshe Schwartz & Kennon H. Nakamura, *Private Security Contractors in Iraq: Background, Legal Status, and Other Issues, RL 32419,* at 1 (Cong. Research Serv., 2008).

60. FOIA, *supra* note 47, at § 552(b)(4).

61. The Center for Public Integrity requested contract terms on a wide range of reconstruction and security contractors in Iraq. Maud Beelman et al., *Winning Contractors: U.S. Contractors Reap the Windfalls of Post-War Reconstruction,* Ctr. for Pub. Integrity, Oct. 30, 2003, available at http://www.commondreams.org/headlines03/1030-10.htm. Journalists such as David Isenberg have requested terms of specific contracts, such as the State Department's Worldwide Services Protection Contract with Blackwater. David Isenberg, *The Rules of Contract Based Warfare,* United Press Int'l, Sept. 5, 2008. The *Los Angeles Times* and Human Rights First used FOIA to request information about the Aegis contract to monitor incidents in which contractors have discharged their weapons. See Human Rights First, *Private Security Contractors at War, supra* note 41. Yet the confidential business exception makes more terms off limits than the national security exception alone, reducing the scope of FOIA as it applies to contractors. For example, the *Dallas Morning News* used FOIA to request unclassified information about a 2005 State Department audit of a DynCorp contract. Tod Robberson, *DynCorp Has Big Role, Little Oversight in War Efforts,* Dallas Morning News, Feb. 9, 2007, *available at* http://www.txcn.com/sharedcontent/dws/news/world/stories/122406dnintldyncorp.32c4b08.html [hereinafter *DynCorp has Big Role*]. Although the State Department

regularly audits DynCorp and other contractors, it limits public access to the findings. The State Department initially rejected the newspaper's request, stating: "We need permission from DynCorp to release this because it may contain proprietary information." *DynCorp Has Big Role, supra.* Ultimately, the State Department did release the report, which revealed that the company had overbilled the government by more than $1.8 million. *Id.*

62. Robberson, *DynCorp Has Big Role, supra* note 61.

63. 41 U.S.C. § 265(a) (2009).

64. Notification and Federal Employee Antidiscrimination and Retaliation Act of 2002, *supra* note 51, at § 2302(b)(8).

65. *See id.*

66. The Whistleblower Protections for Contractor Employees Act, Pub. L. 110-181, § 846 (2008), improves protections for contractor whistleblowers to some degree but still leaves them without sufficient rights. Army contractor employees now may disclose information about government wrongdoing to a slightly broader group—including not only members of Congress but also congressional committees, the inspector general, the GAO, and DOD employees responsible for contract oversight—though they may not make disclosures to the general public. They may also disclose information that evidences gross misconduct and not merely a substantial violation of law, and the employee need only reasonably believe that misconduct has occurred. Furthermore, the statute gives such employees the right to challenge retaliation in federal court if the agency takes no action or decides the matter adversely. *Id.* Yet these expanded provisions only apply to a narrow category of DOD contractors and don't protect contractors who come forward to the public at large.

67. 10 U.S.C. § 2409(b) (2009).

68. Fisher, *The Whistleblower Protection Act of 1989, supra* note 52, at 415.

69. 31 U.S.C. 3730 (2009).

70. Robert Capps, *Sex-Slave Whistle-Blowers Vindicated,* Salon.com, Aug. 6, 2002, http://dir.salon.com/story/news/feature/2002/08/06/dyncorp/index.html [hereinafter *Sex-Slave Whistle-Blowers Vindicated*].

71. Mark Fineman, *U.S. Firms Secretly Bid to Uphold Law in Iraq,* L.A. Times, Apr. 18, 2003.

72. Robert Capps, *Outside the Law,* Salon.com, Nov. 29, 2009, http://dir.salon.com/news/feature/2002/06/26/bosnia/index.html [hereinafter *Outside the Law*].

73. *Id.* (*quoting* Human Rights Watch researcher Martina Vandenberg).

74. Antony Barnett & Solomon Hughes, *British Firm Accused in UN "Sex Scandal,"* Observer, July 29, 2001, *available at* http://www.guardian.co.uk/world/2001/jul/29/unitednations.

75. Capps, *Outside the Law, supra* note 72.

76. Human Rights Watch, *Hopes Betrayed: Trafficking of Women and Girls to Post-Conflict Bosnia and Herzegovina for Forced Prostitution* 67 (2002) [hereinafter *Hopes Betrayed*] (*citing* Deposition of Benjamin Dean Johnston, *Johnston v. DynCorp, Inc.,* Dist. Court, Tarrant County, Texas, Mar. 20, 2001, pp. 50–52).

77. Leslie Wayne, *America's For-Profit Secret Army*, N.Y. Times, Oct. 13, 2002, at C1.

78. The U.S. Army's Criminal Investigative Command followed up on Johnston's claims and eventually implicated at least two DynCorp employees in wrongdoing involving local prostitutes. Capps, *Sex-Slave Whistle-Blowers Vindicated, supra* note 70. According to the Army report, one source reported that "several members of DynCorp . . . purchased women from local brothels and had them live in their residences for sexual and domestic purposes. . . . [T]he individuals purchased the women from local 'mafia' and, when tired of the women would sell them back." Human Rights Watch, *Hopes Betrayed, supra* note 76, at 63 (*quoting* U.S. Army Crim. Investigation Div., *Agents Investigation Report, ROI. 0075-00-CID597-49891*). Although none has faced criminal prosecution, at least thirteen DynCorp employees were sent home from Bosnia, and at least seven fired, for purchasing women or participating in other prostitution-related activities. Capps, *Sex-Slave Whistle-Blowers Vindicated, supra* note 70.

79. Capps, *Sex-Slave Whistle-Blowers Vindicated, supra* note 70.

80. Tod Robberson, *Employees Not Convinced Whistle-Blowers Are Safe*, Dallas Morning News, Feb. 9, 2007, *available at* http://www.contractormisconduct.org/ass/contractors/59/cases/690/761/veritas-capital-dyncorp-in-bosnia_dmn.pdf [hereinafter *Employees Not Convinced Whistle-Blowers Are Safe*].

81. 10 U.S.C. § 2409(b) (2009).

82. Kelly Patricia O'Meara, *DynCorp Disgrace, Insight*, Jan. 14, 2002, *available at* http://www.corpwatch.org/article.php?id=11119.

83. Robberson, *Employees Not Convinced Whistle-Blowers Are Safe, supra* note 80.

84. Assoc. Press, *Iraq Fraud Whistleblowers Vilified*, MSNBC.com, Aug. 25, 2007, http://www.msnbc.msn.com/id/20430153/print/1/displaymode/1098/ [hereinafter *Iraq Fraud Whistleblowers Vilified*].

85. *An Oversight Hearing on Accountability for Contracting Abuses in Iraq: Hearing Before S. Democratic Policy Comm.*, 109th Congress (2006) (statement of Julie McBride, Former KBR/Halliburton Employee), *available at* http://www.halliburtonwatch.org/reports/mcbride.pdf; *see also* Assoc. Press, *Iraq Fraud Whistleblowers Vilified, supra* note 84.

86. Doug Swanson, *Accountant Says She Was Fired After Finding DynCorp Fraud*, Dallas Morning News, Dec. 24, 2006, *available at* http://www.dallasnews.com/sharedcontent/dws/news/world/stories/DN-DynCorplongest_24int.ART.State.Edition1.3deb8be.html.

87. *See, e.g.*, 18 U.S.C. § 207 (2010).

88. *See, e.g., id.*; Honest Leadership and Open Government Act of 2007, Pub. L. No. 110-181 121 Stat. 735.

89. 18 U.S.C. § 207 (2010).

90. 41 U.S.C. § 423(d) (2007).

91. 41 U.S.C. § 423(d)(1) (2007).

92. 48 C.F.R. § 6.302–2 (2005).

93. Jarrett Murphy, *Cheney's Halliburton Ties Remain,* CBSNEWS.com, Sept. 26, 2003, http://www.cbsnews.com/stories/2003/09/26/politics/main 575356.shtml.

94. *See, e.g.,* Scott Harris & Charlie Cray, *War Profiteering and Halliburton,* Global Policy Forum, May 20, 2003, http://www.globalpolicy.org/component/content/ article/168/34798.html.

95. Robert Bryce & Julian Borger, *Cheney Is Still Paid by Pentagon Contractor,* Guardian, Mar. 12, 2003.

96. Leslie Wayne, *Pentagon Brass and Military Contractors' Gold,* N.Y. Times, June 29, 2004, at C1 [hereinafter *Pentagon Brass*].

97. William D. Hartung & Michelle Ciarrocca, World Policy Inst., *The Ties That Bind: Arms Industry Influence in the Bush Administration and Beyond* (2004).

98. Wayne, *Pentagon Brass, supra* note 96.

99. The examples are numerous. DynCorp International boasts two retired generals, General Barry R. McCaffrey and General Peter J. Schoomaker of the U.S. Army, and two retired admirals, Admiral Leighton W. Smith Jr. and Admiral Joseph W. Prueher, on its Board of Directors. DynCorp Int'l Inc., *Board of Directors,* http:// www.dyn-intl.com/board-of-directors.aspx (last visited Dec. 4, 2009).

The three members of Triple Canopy's Board of Directors, Tom Katis, Matt Mann, and Ignacio Balderas, as well as the company's CEO, Lee Van Arsdale, all served for extensive periods in the U.S. Army's special forces. Triple Canopy Inc., *Leadership,* http://www.triplecanopy.com/triplecanopy/en/about/leadership.php (last visited Dec. 4, 2009); Press Release, Triple Canopy Inc., Triple Canopy Announces Change of Command (Nov. 15, 2005), *available at* http://www.triplecanopy.com/ triplecanopy/en/news/20051115.php.

The founder and CEO of Blackwater Worldwide, Erik Prince, is a former member of the Navy Seals. Evan Thomas & Mark Hosenball, *The Man Behind Blackwater,* Newsweek, Oct. 22, 2007.

The management ranks of British security firms draw from a similar pool of experienced military professionals. For example, Erinys International Chief Executive Officer Jonathan Garratt served for ten years with the British Army in counterterrorism, and Non-Executive Chairman Alastair Morrison served in the United Kingdom's Special Forces, available at http://www.erinys.net/#/management/4531407400. At ArmorGroup, Noel Philp and Christopher Beese, the chief operating officer and the chief administrative officer, respectively, both served for many years in the British Army. ArmorGroup Int'l, *Protecting People and Infrastructure Around the World, Annual Report and Accounts 2004,* at 22, 23 (2004).

And the logistics and postconflict reconstruction contract firms are no less starstudded at top management levels. For example, a former commander of the Space and Missile Systems Center of the U.S. Air Force, Lester L. Lyles, serves on the board of Kellogg, Brown & Root, Inc. KBR, Inc., *Board of Directors,* http://www.kbr .com/corporate/corporate_governance/board_of_directors/index.aspx (last visited Dec. 4, 2009). Retired General Richard B. Myers of the U.S. Air Force serves on the

Board of Directors of Northrop Grumman. Northrop Grumman, *Board of Directors,* http://www.northropgrumman.com/leadership/board/index.html (last visited Dec. 4, 2009).

100. U.S. Gov't Accountability Office, *Defense Contracting: Post-Government Employment of Former DOD Officials Needs Greater Transparency, GAO-08-485,* at 4 (2008). Moreover, because Congress repealed a statute requiring DOD to report on turnover numbers, it was difficult for the GAO to obtain information. And the contractors appeared to underreport the statistics: contractors reported hiring 1,263 individuals who matched GAO criteria as former DOD senior and acquisition officials. But the IRS showed that the contract firms had actually hired 2,435 such employees—nearly twice as many. *Id.* at 2, 5.

101. Wayne, *Pentagon Brass, supra* note 96.

102. *Id.*

103. Staff of the H.R. Comm. on Gov't Reform—Minority Staff Special Investigations Div. and the Staff of the S. Dem. Policy Comm., 108th Cong., Joint Report Prepared for Sen. Byron L. Dorgan, Rep. Henry A. Waxman, Sen. Ron Wyden & Rep. John D. Dingell, *Contractors Overseeing Contractors, Conflicts of Interest Undermine Accountability in Iraq* i, 1, 3 (2004).

104. *Cf.* David Cole, *Enemy Aliens,* 54 Stan. L. Rev. 953, 957 (2002) (arguing that "[i]n the wake of September 11, citizens and their elected representatives have repeatedly chosen to sacrifice the liberties of noncitizens in furtherance of the citizenry's purported security . . . [b]ecause noncitizens have no vote, and thus no direct voice in the democratic process" and are therefore "a particularly vulnerable minority.").

105. Perito, Dzidzic & DeGrasse, *Building Civilian Capacity, supra* note 6, at 6.

106. U.S. Dep't of State, Human Rights, http://www.state.gov/g/drl/rls/hrrpt/ (last visited Dec. 2, 2009).

107. U.S. Dep't of State, Trafficking in Persons Report, http://www.state.gov/g/tip/rls/tiprpt/index.htm (last visited Dec. 2, 2009).

108. The National Defense Authorization Act for Fiscal Year 2008, Pub. L. No. 110-181, §§ 842, 843, 845, 846, 122 Stat. 3.

109. 41 U.S.C. § 423(d) (2007).

110. 2008 Defense Authorization Act, *supra* note 33, at §847.

111. *See* Grant & Keohane, *Accountability and Abuses of Power, supra* note 27, at 32.

112. The World Bank, for example, has moved in this direction, *see* Lori Udall, *The World Bank and Public Accountability: Has Anything Changed?, in* The Struggle for Accountability: The World Bank, NGOs, and Grassroots Movements, at 391–393 (Jonathan A. Fox & L. David Brown eds., 1998) [hereinafter *The World Bank and Public Accountability*], as has UNHCR, *see* Tania Kaiser, *Participation or Consultation? Reflections on a "Beneficiary Based" Evaluation of UNHCR's Programme for Sierra Leonean and Liberian Refugees in Guinea,* June–July 2000, 17 J. Refugee Stud. 185, 186 (2004) [hereinafter *Participation or Consultation?*].

113. For a critical account of efforts to promote democracy in developing countries, *see* Balakrishnan Rajagopal, International Law from Below: Development, Social Movements, and Third World Resistance 135–62 (2003).

114. *Cf.* Anderson, Imagined Communities, *supra* note 27, at 372–73 (assuming, in the context of arguing against the democratic legitimacy of NGOs, that individuals possess democratic entitlements only *within* a particular state or policy).

115. Jody Freeman, for example, has observed that, in order to protect public law values, "interested individuals, or representative groups should be entitled to participate in contract negotiation." Jody Freeman, *The Private Role in Public Governance,* 75 N.Y.U. L. Rev. 543, 668 (2000) [hereinafter *The Private Role*].

116. Aman, The Democracy Deficit, *supra* note 12, at 154–55.

117. *See* Freeman, *The Private Role, supra* note 115, at 624–25.

118. Mont. Code Ann. § 2-8-302 (2005).

119. For a discussion of such provisions, *see* Aman, The Democracy Deficit, *supra* note 12, at 154–56.

120. *See* Ctr. for Pub. Integrity, Contracts and Reports, http://projects.public integrity.org/wow/resources.aspx?act=resources (last visited Oct. 19, 2009) [hereinafter Contracts and Reports] (providing text of contracts).

121. Agreement Between U.S. Army Engineering and Tetra Tech. Inc., Contract No. W912DY-04-D-0011, at § C.4.5.23 (Apr. 8, 2004), *available at* http://projects. publicintegrity.org/docs/wow/TetraTech-Munitions.pdf.

122. Agreement Between U.S. Army Engineering and Zapata Engineering, Contract No. W912DY-04-D-0007, at § C.4.5.23 (Feb. 27, 2004), *available at* http:// projects.publicintegrity.org/docs/wow/Zapata-Munitions.pdf("PublicInvolvement. Assist in responsiveness summaries, public meetings, restoration advisory boards, community restoration planning, administrative record establishment and maintenance, and other stakeholder forums that facilitate public involvement.").

123. Agreement Between U.S. Army Engineering and Wash. Group Int'l, Contract No. W905S-04-D-0010, at §2.2.8 (Mar. 12, 2004), *available at* http://projects .publicintegrity.org/docs/wow/WashingtonGroup-Iraq_electrical.pdf.

124. *See generally* Kaiser, *Participation or Consultation?, supra* note 112, at 186 (discussing ways to facilitate measuring the impact of aid programs).

125. *See* Metzger, *Private Delegations, supra* note 29, at 1494.

126. Fla. Corr. Privatization Comm'n, Correctional Services Contract with Corrections Corp. of America § 5.24; Okla. Dep't of Corr., Correctional Services Contract § 5.15; Freeman, *The Private Role, supra* note 115, at 634 (*citing* Texas Dep't of Criminal Justice Model Contract).

127. 42 U.S.C. § 1395mm(c)(5)(A).

128. UNHCR, *NGO Partnerships in Refugee Protection: Questions & Answers* 16 (2004), *available at* http://www.un-ngls.org/orf/HCR-NGO-partnerships.pdf.

129. *See* Lori Udall, *The World Bank and Public Accountability, supra* note 112, at 392–93.

130. David Hunter, *Using the World Bank Inspection Panel to Defend the Interests of Project-Affected People,* 4 Chi. J. Int'l L. 201 (2003) [hereinafter *Using the World Bank Inspection Panel*].

131. Dana L. Clark, *The World Bank and Human Rights: The Need for Greater Accountability,* 15 Harv. Hum. Rts. J. 205, 207 (2002).

132. *See* International Bank for Reconstruction and Development, Res. No. 93-10 (1993) and International Development Association, Res. No. IDA 93-6 (1993), *reprinted in* 34 ILM 520 (1995) [hereinafter Inspection Panel Resolutions]; *see also* Hunter, *Using the World Bank Inspection Panel, supra* note 130.

133. *See* Richard B. Stewart, *U.S. Administrative Law: A Model for Global Administrative Law?*, 68 Law & Contemp. Probs. 63, 95 (2005) [hereinafter *U.S. Administrative Law*].

134. Inspection Panel Resolutions, *supra* note 132, at ¶¶ 2–3.

135. World Bank, *The World Bank Operations Manual* § 17.55 (1999), *available at* http://siteresources.worldbank.org/OPSMANUAL/Resources/EntireOpManual External.pdf [hereinafter *World Bank Operations Manual*].

136. Stewart, *U.S. Administrative Law, supra* note 133, at 95.

137. World Bank Inspection Panel, Cases by Request Number, http://web .worldbank.org/WBSITE/EXTERNAL/EXTINSPECTIONPANEL/0,,content MDK:20221606~menuPK:64129250~pagePK:64129751~piPK:64128378~theSit ePK:380794,00.html.

138. For an excellent analysis of inspection panel complaints through 2004, *see* Daniel D. Bradlow, *Private Complainants and International Organizations: A Comparative Study of the Independent Inspection Mechanisms in International Financial Institutions*, 36 Geo. J. Int'l L. 403 (2005); *see also* Michael B. Likosky, Law, Infrastructure, and Human Rights (2006); Sigrun I. Skogly, The Human Rights Obligations of the World Bank and the International Monetary Fund (2001).

139. Ben Dysart, Tim Murphy & Antonia Chayes, *Beyond Compliance? An External Review Team Report on the Compliance Advisor/Ombudsman Office of the IFC and MIGA*, at iii (2003).

140. *See generally* Compliance Advisor Ombudsman, *CAO Operational Guidelines* (2007), *available at* http://www.cao-ombudsman.org/about/whoweare/ documents/EnglishCAOGuidelines06.08.07Web.pdf.

141. Compliance Advisor Ombudsman, *A Retrospective Analysis of CAO Interventions, Trends, Outcomes, and Effectiveness* (2006). An internal IFC study of sixteen complaints, based on interviews with relevant stakeholders, concluded that the process was excellent or good in eleven cases and poor in five cases. Measures of quality included whether the process disclosed important public information, fostered public participation, and satisfied complainants. *Id.*

142. *See* Stewart, *U.S. Administrative Law, supra* note 133, at 95 ("There are only a few examples of such arrangements, but their number might grow with the intensification of global regulation and demands by affected non-state actors for administrative law protections and methods for securing greater accountability for the decision of global regulatory administrative bodies.").

143. *See* John H. Langbein, *The Contractarian Basis of the Law of Trusts*, 105 Yale L.J. 625 (1995) [hereinafter *Contractarian Basis of the Law of Trusts*].

144. *See generally* Austin Wakeman Scott & William Franklin Fratcher, The Law of Trusts (4th ed. 1987) [hereinafter Law of Trusts].

145. *See* Grant & Keohane, *Accountability and Abuses of Power, supra* note 27, at 33.

146. The Covenant of the League of Nations art. 22, June 28, 1919, U.N. Doc. A/297 (1947).

147. U.N. Charter ch. XII.

148. Richard Caplan, International Governance of War-Torn Territories: Rule and Reconstruction 31–32 (2005) [hereinafter International Governance of War-Torn Territories].

149. Ruth Gordon, *Saving Failed States: Sometimes a Neocolonialist Notion,* 12 Am. U. J. Int'l L. & Pol'y 903, 941–42, 950 (1997).

150. U.N. Charter art. 76(b).

151. U.N., Trusteeship Council, http://www.un.org/en/mainbodies/trusteeship/ (last visited Dec. 2, 2009).

152. *See, e.g.* Int'l Comm'n on Intervention & State Sovereignty, *The Responsibility to Protect* (2001), *available at* http://www.iciss.ca/pdf/Commission-Report.pdf; Saira Mohamed, Note, *From Keeping Peace to Building Peace: A Proposal for a Revitalized United Nations Trusteeship Council,* 105 Colum. L. Rev. 809 (2005); Gerald B. Helman & Steven R. Ratner, *Saving Failed States,* 89 Foreign Pol'y 3 (1992).

153. Steven R. Ratner, The New UN Peacekeeping: Building Peace in Lands of Conflict after the Cold War (1995).

154. Caplan, International Governance of War-Torn Territories, *supra* note 148, at 33–41. Caplan notes that a key distinction between the new forms of administration and the old League Mandates or U.N. Trusteeships is the multiplicity of actors— multiple states, international organizations and NGOs—involved. *Id.* at 33.

155. Rosa Ehrenreich Brooks, *Failed States, or the State as Failure?,* 72 U. Chi. L. Rev. 1159 (2005).

156. Noah Feldman, What We Owe Iraq: War and the Ethics of Nation-Building 52–91 (2004).

157. Scott & Fratcher, Law of Trusts, *supra* note 144.

158. For an argument that an agency costs approach derived from theories of the firm might yield useful solutions to problems in trust law, *see* Robert H. Sitkoff, *An Agency Costs Theory of Trust Law,* 89 Cornell L. Rev. 621 (2004) [hereinafter *An Agency Costs Theory*].

159. Langbein, *Contractarian Basis of the Law of Trusts, supra* note 143.

160. *See* Nestor M. Davidson, *Relational Contracts in the Privatization of Social Welfare: The Case of Housing,* 24 Yale L. & Pol'y Rev. 263 (2006).

161. Frank H. Easterbrook & Daniel R. Fischel, *The Corporate Contract,* 89 Colum. L. Rev. 1416 (1989) (noting that the usefulness of fiduciary duties in the corporate context is limited by their open-ended nature).

162. Sitkoff, *An Agency Costs Theory, supra* note 158, at 680.

163. David Luban, *Faculty Pro Bono and the Question of Identity,* 49 J. Leg. Educ. 58 (1999).

164. Ann L. MacNaughton & Jay G. Martin, *Practical Impacts of Sustainable Development on Energy Law,* 19 Nat. Resources & Env't 33, 37 (2004) (describing the

Bank's effort as: "An unprecedented effort in socioeconomic planning and public consultation over a ten-year period that began in 1993, engaging tens of thousands of citizens in nearly two thousand meetings for input into the planning of the 660-mile underground pipeline that now transports Doba crude oil from three hundred wells in southwestern Chad to the coast of Cameroon for international export."). *Id.*

165. Luc Lamprière, unpublished report, at 14.

166. *Id.*

167. Meredith Kruger, Oliver Ksionski & Maria Jacques, *Chad: History Before, During, and After Oil Development, in* Greasing the Wheels of Development? The World Bank, Human Rights, and Chad's Oil, at 21 (2006) [hereinafter *Greasing the Wheels*].

168. For a discussion of NGO concerns, *see Greasing the Wheels, supra* note 167, at 13–16.

169. Lamprière, *supra* note 165, at 17.

170. DynCorp Int'l Inc., *Annual Report 2009,* at 2, 4, 5, 14, 15 (2009), *available at* http://files.shareholder.com/downloads/DCP/780764076x0x210767/B1EE7D80-69C3-46C8-9390-EC2330719CC9/DY211_061608_AnnualReport_final.pdf [hereinafter *2009 DynCorp Annual Report*].

171. *Id.*

172. Andrew Wander, *Firm Training ISF Has Had Trouble Elsewhere,* Daily Star, Sept. 20, 2008.

173. *2009 DynCorp Annual Report, supra* note 170, at 15.

174. *DynCorp International Selected to Continue Police Training in Afghanistan,* Bus. Wire, Aug. 5, 2008, *available at* http://findarticles.com/p/articles/mi_m0EIN/is_/ai_n27969652; Press Release, DynCorp Int'l Inc., DynCorp Int'l Awarded Police Training Work in Haiti and Liberia (Mar. 31, 2008), *available at* http://ir.dyn-intl.com/releasedetail.cfm?ReleaseID=302437. [hereinafter DynCorp in Haiti and Liberia].

175. DynCorp in Haiti and Liberia, *supra* note 174.

176. Tod Robberson, *Afghanistan Deal Could Net DynCorp over $2.1B,* Dallas Morning News, Dec. 23, 2006 [hereinafter *Afghanistan Deal*].

177. *See Privatizing the Drug War,* Wash. Post, May 31, 2001, http://www.washingtonpost.com/wp srv/liveonline/01/world/world_schakowsky0531.htm.

178. *2009 DynCorp Annual Report, supra* note 170, at 4, 8.

179. As discussed earlier, the firm is one of the three primary contractors that protects State Department diplomats and sites. Spencer Ackerman, *Blackwater Heir Wants to Keep State Dept. Security Contract,* Wash. Independent, Aug. 10, 2009. At the same time, the firm is one of three companies that recently won the lucrative LOGCAP IV contract to provide logistics support to the U.S. military worldwide, with a special emphasis on troops deployed in the Middle East. *2009 DynCorp Annual Report, supra* note 170, at 8. The contract has a term of up to ten years and a ceiling of $5 billion per year per contractor. *Id.* at 5. The firm is winning other

logistics contracts as well. For example, in 2008 the U.S. Army Corps of Engineers awarded DynCorp a construction contract in Afghanistan that has a potential value of $1.8 billion, SIGIR, *Review of DynCorp International, supra* note 4, at 2, and a separate contract totaling more than $100 million for new Afghan National Army garrisons in Jalalabad and Kunduz to house up to four thousand Afghan troops. DynCorp Int'l Inc., *Annual Report 2008,* at 3 (2008), *available at* http://www .annualreports.com/HostedData/AnnualReports/PDFArchive/dcp2008.pdf. In related work, the firm provides translators to the U.S. Army Intelligence and Security Command. *Id.* at 7.

180. Perito, Dzidzic & DeGrasse, *Building Civilian Capacity, supra* note 6, at 4; John M. Broder & David Rohde, *State Dept. use of Contractors Leaps in 4 Years,* N.Y. Times, Oct. 24, 2007, at A1. The stories of DynCorp recruits are interesting. For example, after nine years as police chief in Austin, Stan Knee decided to work for DynCorp as a mentor to senior Afghan law-enforcement officials. Mr. Knee told the *Dallas Morning News* that he took the job because he wanted to support the rule of law. "This is about more than a paycheck . . . [i]t is about building a country." Mr. Knee further observed that, after coordinating cross-border operations with Mexican counterparts for many years, "I became convinced that police are police, no matter where you go in the world . . . I think people that get into police work, in general, have good hearts and want to protect the innocent and weak against the bullies of the world." Denise Nelson, who served as a police officer in Katy and Oak Cliff, Texas, began work in September 2005 as a police trainer in Kunduz, Afghanistan, because, she told the *Dallas Morning News,* "I was looking for a new experience." She noted that some of the Afghani recruits found it difficult to take orders from a woman, and believed that it's O.K. to beat women. But she noted, "They don't dare do that to us. . . . They know we have guns. We know how to shoot." Tod Robberson, *Many Reasons Given for Taking Risky Jobs,* Dallas Morning News, Dec. 24, 2006.

181. Jones, *Counterinsurgency in Afghanistan, supra* note 5, at 69.

182. Krongard & Gimble, *Interagency Assessment of Afghanistan Police Training, supra* note 3, at 8.

183. *Id.* at 35.

184. SIGIR, *Review of DynCorp International, supra* note 4, at iv.

185. Robberson, *Afghanistan Deal, supra* note 176.

186. *Id.*

187. Perito, Dzidzic & DeGrasse, *Building Civilian Capacity, supra* note 6, at 4.

6. Uniformed Military Lawyers, Organizational Structure and Culture, and the Impact of Privatization

1. Interview with JAG officer #10 (Oct. 16, 2007).

2. I interviewed twenty judge advocates, most of whom had served in either Iraq or Afghanistan, or in both, during the previous five years. I received permission

from the Army JAG school in Virginia, and many of the interviews were conducted at the school in April 2007. Most of the interviewees had been judge advocates for approximately eight years and were at the school for their second round of training. Several additional judge advocates were identified for interview through the so-called snowball method: they were mentioned by one or more of the initial interviewees. A few had served in other conflicts, including the first Persian Gulf War and the conflict in the Balkans in the 1990s. As noted in the text, most of the judge advocates interviewed were part of the Army JAG Corps, though some were judge advocates in other services. Of course, the organizational structure and culture of the judge advocates may vary somewhat from service to service, and it is beyond the scope of this study to fully explore the possible impact of those differences on the compliance issues I discuss.

3. *See, e.g.,* Organization Theory: From Chester Barnard to the Present and Beyond (Oliver E. Williamson ed., 1995) [hereinafter Organization Theory]; James G. March, Decisions and Organizations (1988) [hereinafter Decisions and Organizations]; James G. March & Herbert Simon, Organizations (2d ed. 1958) [hereinafter Organizations]; W. Richard Scott, Organizations: Rational, Natural, and Open Systems (2d ed. 1987) [hereinafter Open Systems]; Herbert A. Simon, Administrative Behavior: A Study of the Decision-Making Process in Administrative Organization (2d ed. 1957) [hereinafter Administrative Behavior]; Serge Taylor, Making Bureaucracies Think: The Environmental Impact Statement Strategy of Administrative Reform (1984) hereinafter Making Bureaucracies Think]; Organizational Environments: Ritual and Rationality (John W. Meyer & W. Richard Scott eds., 1983) [hereinafter Organizational Environments]; The New Institutionalism in Organizational Analysis (Walter W. Powell & Paul J. Dimaggio eds., 1991) [hereinafter New Institutionalism]; Edward L. Rubin, *Images of Organizations and Consequences of Regulation,* 6 Theoretical Inq. L. 347 (2005) [hereinafter *Images of Organizations*].

4. *See, e.g.,* Rubin, *Images of Organizations, supra* note 3. In law, organization theory is most associated with scholars who study the role of professionalization and professional organizations on the activity of lawyers. *See, e.g.,* Ethics in Practice: Lawyers' Roles, Responsibilities, and Regulation (Deborah L. Rhode ed., 2000); Richard L. Abel, American Lawyers (2000).

5. *See, e.g.,* Douglass C. North, Institutions, Institutional Change, and Economic Performance (1990) [hereinafter Institutional Change]; Oliver E. Williamson, The Mechanics of Governance (1996) [hereinafter Mechanics of Governance].

6. *See, e.g.,* John W. Meyer, *Institutionalization and the Rationality of Formal Organizational Structure, in* Organizational Environments, *supra* note 3, at 261.

7. *See, e.g.,* Terry M. Moe, *The Politics of Structural Choice: Toward a Theory of Public Bureaucracy,* in Organization Theory, *supra* note 3, at 116.

8. *See, e.g.,* Mary Douglas, *Converging on Autonomy: Anthropology and Institutional Economics, in* Organizational Theory, *supra* note 3, at 98 [hereinafter *Converging on Autonomy*].

9. *See, e.g.*, Oliver Hart, *An Economist's Perspective on the Theory of the Firm, in* Organization Theory, *supra* note 3, at 154; Edward B. Rock & Michael L. Wachter, *Islands of Conscious Power: Law, Norms, and the Self-Governing Corporation*, 149 U. Pa. L. Rev. 1619 (2001).

10. *See, e.g.*, Abel, American Lawyers, *supra* note 4.

11. *See, e.g.*, Marshall W. Meyer, Change in Public Bureaucracies (2008).

12. Rubin, *Images of Organizations, supra* note 3, at 349–66.

13. Armen A. Alchian & Harold Demsetz, *Production, Information Costs, and Economic Organization*, 62 Am. Econ. Rev. 777 (1972); Michael C. Jensen & William H. Meckling, *Theory of the Firm: Managerial Behavior, Agency Costs and Ownership Structure*, 3 J. Fin. Econ. 305 (1976).

14. March, Decisions and Organizations, *supra* note 3; March & Simon, Organizations, *supra* note 3; Scott, Open Systems, *supra* note 3; Simon, Administrative Behavior, *supra* note 3.

15. North, Institutional Change, *supra* note 5; Williamson, The Mechanics of Governance, *supra* note 5.

16. W. Richard Scott, *Symbols and Organizations: From Barnard to the Institutionalists, in* Organization Theory, *supra* note 3, at 38, 39 (quoting Chester I. Barnard, *The Functions of the Executive* 6 (1938)).

17. Sally S. Simpson, Corporate Crime, Law and Social Control 116–51 (2002).

18. Rubin, *Images of Organizations, supra* note 3, at 373.

19. Taylor, Making Bureaucracies Think, *supra* note 3.

20. Rubin, *Images of Organizations, supra* note 3, at 374.

21. Scott, *supra* note 16, at 39, 43 (citing Barnard, *supra* note 16, at 122–23).

22. Douglas, *Converging on Autonomy, supra* note 8, at 98, 102.

23. Organizational Environments, *supra* note 3; New Institutionalism, *supra* note 3.

24. *See, e.g.*, Richard Tanner Pascale & Anthony G. Athos, The Art of Japanese Management: Applications for American Executives (1981); Peter Tasker, A Major Exploration of Modern Japan (1987); David G. Litt et al., *Politics, Bureaucracies and Financial Markets: Bank Entry into Commercial Paper Underwriting in Japan and the United States*, 139 U. Pa. L. Rev. 369 (1990).

25. John W. Meyer, *Institutionalization and the Rationality of Formal Organizational Structure, in* Organizational Environments, *supra* note 3, at 261; John W. Meyer & Brian Rowan, *Institutionalized Organizations: Formal Structure as Myth and Ceremony, in* New Institutionalism, *supra* note 3, at 41. For example, states (at least prior to the No Child Left Behind Act) tended to deem schools successful on the basis of their teachers' fulfillment of certain professional requirements rather than by evaluating the quality of education in particular classrooms. Aaron Benavot, Yun-Kyung Cha, David Kamens, John W. Meyer, & Suk-Ying Wong, *Knowledge for the Masses: World Models and National Curricula, 1920–1986*, 56 Am. Soc. Rev. 85 (1991).

26. *Id.* at 145.

27. Ryan Goodman & Derek Jinks, *How to Influence States: Socialization and International Human Rights Law,* 54 Duke L.J. 621 (2004).

28. For a broader argument along these lines, see Paul Schiff Berman, *Seeing Beyond the Limits of International Law*, 84 Texas L. Rev. 1265 (2006).

29. Talcott Parsons, The Social System (1951).

30. Niklas Luhmann, Social Systems 6 (John Bednarz Jr. & Dirk Baecker trans., Stan. U. Press 1995) (1984).

31. *See generally* Ludwig von Bertalanffy, General System Theory: Foundations, Development and Applications (1968); Walter Buckley, Sociology and Modern Systems Theory (1967); Jay Galbraith, Organization Design (1977); Toward a Unified Theory of Human Behavior: An Introduction to General Systems Theory (Roy Grinker ed., 1956) [hereinafter Toward a Unified Theory of Human Behavior]; George J. Klir, An Approach to General Systems Theory (1969); Alfred Kuhn, The Logic of Social Systems: A Unified, Deductive, System-Based Approach to Social Science (1974).

32. Gunther Teubner, *Corporate Fiduciary Duties and Their Beneficiaries: A Functional Approach to the Legal Institutionalization of Corporate Responsibility, in* Corporate Governance and Director Liabilities: Legal, Economic and Sociological Analyses of Corporate Social Responsibility, at 149 (Klaus J. Hopt & Gunther Teubner eds., 1985); Gunther Teubner, *Juridification: Concepts, Aspects, Limits, Solutions, in* Juridification of the Social Spheres: A Comparative Analysis of the Areas of Labor, Corporate, Antitrust and Social Welfare Law, at 3 (Gunther Teubner ed., 1987).

33. See, e.g., Lauren B. Edelman & Mark C. Suchman, *When the "Haves" Hold Court: Speculations on the Organizational Internalization of Law*, 33 Law & Soc'y Rev. 941 (1999).

34. Though not stated there in these terms, these factors are drawn from Rubin, *Images of Organizations, supra* note 3, and Taylor, Making Bureaucracies Think, *supra* note 3.

35. *See, e.g.,* Simpson, *supra* note 17.

36. *See* Elizabeth Chambliss, *MDPs: Toward an Institutional Strategy for Entity Regulation,* 4 Legal Ethics 45, 56–64 (2002) (criticizing the ABA's command-and-control approach to entity regulation and calling for more institutional support for in-house compliance specialists); Elizabeth Chambliss & David B. Wilkins, *A New Framework for Law Firm Discipline,* 16 Geo. J. Legal Ethics 335 (2003) (proposing that law firms be encouraged to invest in in-house compliance specialists); *see also* Ian Ayres & John Braithwaite, Responsive Regulation: Transcending the Deregulation Debate 125–28 (1992) ("An independent internal compliance group is essential to the success of an enforced self-regulation scheme").

37. *See* Elizabeth Chambliss & David B. Wilkins, *The Emerging Role of Ethics Advisors, General Counsel, and Other Compliance Specialists at Large Law Firms,* 44 Ariz. L. Rev. 559 (2002).

38. *See* Taylor, Making Bureaucracies Think, *supra* note 3, at 252; Chambliss & Wilkins, *A New Framework for Law Firm Discipline*, *supra* note 36, at 588–89.

39. U.S. War Dep't, *Instructions for the Government of Armies of the United States in the Field*, General Orders No. 100 (Apr. 24, 1863), *reprinted in* The Laws of Armed Conflicts 3 (Dietrich Schindler & Jiří Toman eds., 3d rev. ed. 1988), *available at* http://www.civilwarhome.com/liebercode.htm.

40. *See* Theodor Meron, *Francis Lieber's Code and Principles of Humanity, in* Politics, Values, and Functions: International Law in the 21st Century, at 249 (Jonathan I. Charney et al. eds., 1997). *See also* Thomas G. Barnes, *Introduction, in* Lieber's Code and the Law of War, at 3 (Richard Shelly Hartigan ed., 1995); Theodor Meron, *The Humanization of Humanitarian Law,* 94 Am. J. Int'l L. 239 (2000).

41. *See* generally Samuel P. Huntington, The Soldier and the State: The Theory and Politics of Civil-Military Relations (1957).

42. *See* Patrick Finnegan, *The Study of Law as a Foundation of Leadership and Command: The History of Law Instruction at the United States Military Academy at West Point,* 181 Mil. L. Rev. 112 (2004).

43. U.S. Dep't of the Army, *Report of the Department of the Army Review of the Preliminary Investigations into the My Lai Incident* (1970), *available at* http://www.loc.gov/rr/frd/Military_Law/pdf/RDAR-Vol-I.pdf.

44. James F. Gebhardt, *The Road to Abu Ghraib: U.S. Army Detainee Doctrine and Experience,* Mil. Rev., Jan.–Feb. 2005, at 44, 50.

45. Frederic L. Borch, Judge Advocates in Combat: Army Lawyers in Military Operations from Vietnam to Haiti 30, 37 (2001) [hereinafter Judge Advocates in Combat]; U.S. Dep't of Def., Dir. 5100.77, DOD Law of War Program (Nov. 5, 1974), *canceled by* U.S. Dep't of Def., Dir. 5100.77, DOD Law of War Program (Dec. 9, 1998), *available at* http://www.au.af.mil/au/awc/awcgate/dod/d510077p.txt (reissuing 1974 directive "to update policy and responsibilities in the Department of Defense").

46. Borch, Judge Advocates in Combat, *supra* note 45, at 31.

47. Interview with JAG officer #14 (Oct. 18, 2007).

48. Interview with JAG officer #16 (Oct. 18, 2007).

49. Interview with JAG officer #14, *supra* note 47.

50. Borch, Judge Advocates in Combat, *supra* note 45, at 81.

51. Interview with JAG officer #12 (Oct. 18, 2007).

52. Int'l and Operational Law Dep't, Judge Advocate Gen. Legal Ctr. & Sch., U.S. Army, *Operational Law Handbook* (2008).

53. Borch, Judge Advocates in Combat, *supra* note 45, at 240.

54. *Id.*

55. Interview with JAG officer #20 (Oct. 16, 2007).

56. W. Hays Parks, Assistant Gen. Counsel to the Dep't of Def., Remarks, in panel discussion regarding military contractors, sponsored by the University of Virginia School of Law and the Judge Advocate General's School (Oct. 15, 2007). For

information regarding the panel, see *Law Regarding Civilian Combatants, Contractors Murky, Say Experts* (Nov. 20, 2007), *at* http://www.law.virginia.edu/html/news/2007_fall/civiliancombat.htm.

57. For a further discussion, *see* Laura A. Dickinson, *Abu Ghraib, in* International Law Stories (John Noyes, Mark Janis & Laura Dickinson eds., 2007) [hereinafter *Abu Ghraib*].

58. David Luban, *Lawfare and Legal Ethics in Guantánamo,* 60 Stan. L. Rev. 1981 (2008).

59. Tim Golden, *After Terror, a Secret Rewriting of Military Law,* N.Y. Times, Oct. 24, 2004, at A1 [hereinafter *After Terror*].

60. William Glaberson, *Tribunal v. Court-Martial: A Matter of Perception,* N.Y. Times, Dec. 2, 2001, at B6 [hereinafter *Matter of Perception*] (*citing* Edward Sherman, former army lawyer and former dean of Tulane Law School); *see also* Golden, *After Terror, supra* note 59.

61. Glaberson, *Matter of Perception, supra* note 60 (*citing* John S. Cooke, a retired army judge who was chair of the American Bar Association Section on Armed Forces Law); Golden, *After Terror, supra* note 59.

62. Neil A. Lewis, *Rules on Tribunal Require Unanimity on Death Penalty,* N.Y. Times, Dec. 28, 2001, at A1.

63. Neil A. Lewis, *Lawyer Says Detainees Face Unfair System,* N.Y. Times, Jan. 22, 2004, at A25; Jonathan Mahler, *Commander Swift Objects,* N.Y. Times Mag., June 13, 2004, at 42.

64. Mark Mazzetti & Neil A. Lewis, *Military Lawyers Caught in Middle on Tribunals,* N.Y. Times, Sept. 16, 2006, at A1.

65. Neil A. Lewis, *Military's Opposition to Harsh Interrogation is Outlined,* N.Y. Times, July 28, 2005, at A21.

66. *Id.*

67. V. Adm. Albert T. Church III, *Review of Department of Defense Detention Operations and Detainee Interrogation Techniques* 8 (Mar. 11, 2005), *available at* http:// www.dod.gov/pubs/foi/detainees/church_report_l.pdf.

68. Jeannie Shawl, *New US Army Interrogation Manual Mandates Geneva Rules,* Jurist, Sept. 6, 2006. Congress, however, subsequently exempted CIA operatives from the requirements of the *Field Manual,* except when operating under DOD control or within a DOD facility. *See* Detainee Treatment Act of 2005, § 1002(a), 10 U.S.C. §801 (2006).

69. For an argument about the role that military culture can play in deterring war crimes, *see generally* Mark J. Osiel, Obeying Orders: Atrocity, Military Discipline, and the Law of War (1999).

70. Interview with JAG officer #7 (Oct. 16, 2007).

71. Interview with JAG officer #1 (Oct. 16, 2007).

72. Interview with JAG officer #4 (Oct. 16, 2007).

73. Interview with JAG officer #7, *supra* note 70.

74. iCasualties.org, Operation Iraqi Freedom (2009), *available at* http://icasualties.org/Iraq/Index.aspx.

75. Interview with JAG officer #7, *supra* note 70.

76. Interview with JAG officer #8 (Oct. 16, 2007).

77. *Id.*

78. Interview with JAG officer #7, *supra* note 70.

79. Interview with JAG officer #8, *supra* note 76.

80. Interview with JAG officer #7, *supra* note 70.

81. Interview with JAG officer #8, *supra* note 76.

82. Interview with JAG officer #2 (Oct. 16, 2007).

83. Interview with JAG officer #7, *supra* note 70.

84. Interview with JAG officer #8, *supra* note 76.

85. *Id.*

86. Human Rights First, *Private Security Contractors at War: Ending the Culture of Impunity* 17 (2008) (quoting Lieutenant General Peter Chiarelli), *available at* http://www.humanrightsfirst.info/pdf/08115-usls-psc-final.pdf.

87. *Id.*

88. Interview with JAG officer #6 (Oct. 16, 2007).

89. Interview with JAG officer #8, *supra* note 76.

90. Interview with JAG officer #5 (Oct. 16, 2007).

91. Interview with JAG officer #2, *supra* note 82.

92. *Id.*

93. Interview with JAG officer #5, *supra* note 90.

94. Interview with JAG officer #8, *supra* note 76.

95. *Id.*

96. *Id.*

97. Interview with JAG officer #5, *supra* note 90.

98. Interview with JAG officer #2, *supra* note 82.

99. Interview with JAG officer #18 (Feb. 12, 2007).

100. Interview with JAG officer #6, *supra* note 88.

101. *Id.*

102. Interview with JAG officer #8, *supra* note 76.

103. *Id.*

104. Interview with JAG officer #2, *supra* note 82.

105. Interview with JAG officer #3 (Oct. 16, 2007).

106. Interview with JAG officer #6, *supra* note 88.

107. Interview with JAG officer #2, *supra* note 82.

108. Interview with JAG officer #6, *supra* note 88.

109. Interview with JAG officer #3, *supra* note 105.

110. Interview with JAG officer #2, *supra* note 82.

111. Interview with JAG officer #5, *supra* note 90.

112. Interview with JAG officer #2, *supra* note 82.

113. Interview with JAG officer #8, *supra* note 76.

114. Interview with JAG officer #4, *supra* note 72.

115. Interview with JAG officer #5, *supra* note 90.

116. Interview with JAG officer #4, *supra* note 72.

117. Interview with JAG officer #8, *supra* note 76.

118. Interview with JAG officer #6, *supra* note 88.

119. Interview with JAG officer #12, *supra* note 51.

120. Interview with JAG officer #5, *supra* note 90.

121. Interview with JAG officer #6, *supra* note 88.

122. Interview with JAG officer #7, *supra* note 70.

123. Interview with JAG officer #6, *supra* note 88.

124. Interview with JAG officer #2, *supra* note 82.

125. Interview with JAG officer #7, *supra* note 70.

126. Interview with JAG officer #5, *supra* note 90.

127. *Id.*

128. Interview with JAG officer #7, *supra* note 70.

129. Interview with JAG officer #1, *supra* note 71.

130. Interview with JAG officer #7 *supra* note 70.

131. The Uniform Code of Military Justice, 10 U.S.C. §§ 801–946 (2006), provides that soldiers may be punished for many such acts. *See, e.g.,* 10 U.S.C. § 889 (2006) (disrespect toward superior commissioned officer); 10 U.S.C. § 892 (2006) (failure to obey order or regulation); 10 U.S.C. § 912 (2006) (drunk on duty); 10 U.S.C. § 915 (2006) (malingering); 10 U.S.C. § 933 (2006) (disrespect toward a superior commanding officer).

132. *See* 10 U.S.C. § 815 (2006).

133. *See* 10 U.S.C. §§ 856a, 858a (2006).

134. *See* Interview with JAG officer #7, *supra* note 70.

135. Interview with JAG officer #2, *supra* note 82.

136. Interview with JAG officer #4, *supra* note 72.

137. Interview with JAG officer #1, *supra* note 71.

138. Interview with JAG officer #3, *supra* note 105.

139. Interview with JAG officer #5, *supra* note 90.

140. Paul von Zeilbauer, *Marines' Trials in Iraq Killings Are Withering,* N.Y. Times, Aug. 30, 2007, at A1. Interview with JAG officer #5, *supra* note 90.

141. Interview with JAG officer #2, *supra* note 82.

142. Interview with JAG officer #5, *supra* note 90.

143. *Id.*

144. *Id.*

145. Interview with JAG officer #2, *supra* note 82.

146. Human Rights First, *By the Numbers: Findings of the Detainee Abuse and Accountability Project* 3, 7 (2006), *available at* http://www.humanrightsfirst.info/pdf/06425-etn-by-the-numbers.pdf.

147. For a discussion of the ways in which a military culture steeped in rules of law proved resistant to Bush administration initiatives, *see* Dickinson, *Abu Ghraib, supra* note 57.

148. Jess Bravin, *Two Prosecutors at Guantanamo Quit in Protest,* Wall St. J., Aug. 1, 2005, at B1.

149. Peter Finn, *Guantanamo Prosecutor Quits, Says Evidence Was Withheld,* Wash. Post, Sept. 25, 2008, at A6.

150. Interview with JAG officer #2, *supra* note 82.

151. Interview with JAG officer #5, *supra* note 90.

152. *See, e.g.,* Interview with JAG officer #3, *supra* note 105.

153. *See, e.g., id.*

154. Interview with JAG officer #5, *supra* note 90.

155. Interview with JAG officer #4, *supra* note 72.

156. Interview with JAG officer #8, *supra* note 76.

157. Interview with JAG officer #4, supra note 72.

158. Interview with JAG officer #3, *supra* note 105.

159. Interview with JAG officer #5, *supra* note 90.

160. Interview with JAG officer #2, *supra* note 82.

161. Interview with JAG officer #7, *supra* note 70.

162. Interview with JAG officer #8, *supra* note 76.

163. Interview with JAG officer #5, *supra* note 90.

164. Interview with JAG officer #2, *supra* note 82.

165. Interview with JAG officer #7, *supra* note 70.

166. Interview with JAG officer #2, *supra* note 82.

167. Interview with JAG officer #7, *supra* note 70.

168. *See* Laura A. Dickinson, *Mercenarism and Private Military Contractors, in* International Criminal Law 355, 369–75 (M. Cherif Bassiouni ed., 3d ed., 2008); *see also* my Chapter 3 in the present book.

169. Interview with JAG officer #2, *supra* note 82.

170. Interview with JAG officer #3, *supra* note 105.

171. Interview with JAG officer #8, *supra* note 76.

172. Interview with JAG officer #3, *supra* note 105.

173. Interview with JAG officer #2, *supra* note 82.

174. Interview with JAG officer #1, *supra* note 71.

175. Interview with JAG officer #5, *supra* note 90.

176. Interview with JAG officer #1, *supra* note 71.

177. Interview with JAG officer #8, *supra* note 76.

178. Interview with JAG officer #3, *supra* note 105.

179. Interview with JAG officer #5, *supra* note 90.

180. Tom Jackman, *Security Contractor Cleared in Two Firings,* Wash. Post, Aug. 2, 2007, at A15 (*quoting* jury forewoman Lea C. Overby).

181. *Id.*

182. *See* Blackwater USA: Hearing Before the H. Comm. on Oversight and Government Reform, 110th Cong. 97 (2007) (testimony of Erik Prince) ("Our men are not serving members of the U.S. military. . . . And I believe that is why they extended [the Uniform Code of Military Justice], not just to wars that were declared but also to contingency operations as well.").

183. Steve Fainaru, *Four Hired Guns in an Armored Truck, Bullets Flying, and a Pickup and a Taxi Brought to a Halt. Who did the Shooting and Why*, Wash. Post, Apr. 15, 2007, at A1.

184. Anthony R. Jones & George R. Fay, Dep't of the Army, *AR 15-6 Investigation of the Abu Ghraib Detention Facility and 205th Military Intelligence Brigade* 50–51 (2004), *available at* http://fl1.findlaw.com/news.findlaw.com/hdocs/docs/dod/fay82504rpt.pdf.

185. Office of the Special Inspector Gen. for Iraq Reconstruction, *Compliance with Contract No. W911S0-04-C-0003 Awarded to Aegis Defence Services Limited, Report Number 05-005*, at 5 (2005), *available at* http:// www.globalsecurity.org/military/library/report/2005/sigir-apr05_report.pdf.

186. *See* Jennifer K. Elsea, Moshe Schwartz & Kennon H. Nakamura, *Private Security Contractors in Iraq: Background, Legal Status, and Other Issues, RL 32419*, at 9–11 (Cong. Research Svc., 2008) [hereinafter *Private Security Contractors in Iraq*], *available at* http:// fas.org/sgp/crs/natsec/RL32419.pdf. A government report indicates that as of 2009 only 5 percent of the employees of private security contractors employed in Iraq by the DOD are U.S. citizens, and fully 77 percent are not Iraqi either. Moshe Schwartz, *Department of Defense's Use of Private Security Contractors in Iraq and Afghanistan: Background, Analysis, and Options for Congress* 6 (Cong. Research Svc., 2010), *available at* http://www.fas.org/sgp/crs/natsec/R40835.pdf.

Of the roughly 8,600 security contractors directly employed by the DOD and State Department in Iraq as of May 2008—a figure that does not include subcontractors hired to protect reconstruction contractors or security contractors working for other agencies—7,503 were not U.S. citizens. Likewise, of the 1,400 security contractors working directly for the State Department in Iraq, 759 were not U.S. citizens, and 6,744 of the security contractors hired by the DOD were not U.S. citizens, 5,061 of whom were third-country nationals—citizens of neither the United States nor Iraq. Elsea, Schwartz & Nakamura, *Private Security Contractors in Iraq, supra*, at 9–11.

Latin America is a major source for such labor. As of 2008, there were 1,200 Peruvians in Iraq, mostly guarding sites in Baghdad's Green Zone. Patrick J. McDonnell, *Iraq Contractors Recruit Latin America's Needy*, L.A. Times, Jan. 28, 2008, at A1 [hereinafter *Latin America's Needy*]. Many other Latin Americans have also served there, with reports indicating that as of 2007, there were 1,200 Chileans, 700 Salvadorans, and hundreds of others from Colombia, Honduras, and other countries. Kristina Mani, *Latin America's Hidden War in Iraq*, Foreign Policy, Oct. 2007, *available at* http://www.foreignpolicy.com/story/cms.php?story_id=3984.

Triple Canopy, in particular, recruits heavily in the region, for example hiring employees in Honduras through its subsidiary Your Solutions and in Peru through its affiliates 3dGlobal Solutions and Gesecur SAC. Dario Bermudez, *Unknown Chapters of Chilean Mercenaries in Honduras*, El Nacional, Sept. 25, 2005. According to the Honduran newspaper *La Tribuna*, in one day in July 2005, Your Solutions shipped 108 Hondurans, 88 Chileans, and 16 Nicaraguans to Iraq. *Group of 88 Chileans Trained in Honduras Was Able to Travel to Iraq*, http://www.cooperativa.cl/prontus _nots/site/artic/20051007/pags/20051007133322.html.

Other countries where security firms have recruited labor have included Nepal, Fiji, Uganda, and South Africa. Eric Stoner, *Outsourcing the Iraq War: Mercenary Recruiters Turn to Latin America, NACLA Report on the Americas* (2008), *available at* https://nacla.org/node/4805. Indeed, as of 2007, security firms in Iraq had hired approximately 1,500 Ugandan guards, Guy Raz, *US Contractors in Iraq Rely on Third-World Labor*, Nat'l Pub. Radio, Oct. 10, 2007 [hereinafter *Third-World Labor*], employed primarily by the firm SOC-SMG, and between 2,000 and 4,000 South Africans, many of whom were hired by DynCorp to guard police officers training local Iraqi police. Nir Rosen, *Security Contractors: Riding Shotgun with Our Shadow Army in Iraq*, Mother Jones, Apr. 23, 2007; Stephanie Haines, *Private Security Contractors Look to Africa for Recruits*, Christian Sci. Monitor, Jan. 8, 2008.

187. Tim Weiner, *A Security Contractor Defends His Team, Which, He Says, Is Not a Private Army*, N.Y. Times, Apr. 29, 2007, at Week in Review 4, available at http:// www.nytimes.com/2007/04/29/weekinreview/29reading.html? scp=1&sq=A%20 Security%C20Contractor%C20Defends%C20his%20Team&st=cse (quoting an interview by R. J. Hillhouse of Gary Jackson).

188. Interview with senior director of government affairs for a private security firm, granted on condition of anonymity.

189. Mike Hager, *Chile's Iraq Mercenaries Under Investigation by U.N. Group*, Santiago Times, July 9, 2007, available at http:// latinoinsurgent.blogspot.com/ 2007/07/santiago-times-chiles-iraq-mercenaries.html.

190. For example, in a 2004 attack on the Shaheen Hotel, one of the security contractors killed was the South African Frans Strydom, a member of Koevoet (Afrikaans for crowbar), a counterinsurgency group that paid bounties for the bodies of blacks seeking majority rule during the 1980s. Another South African security contractor who sustained serious injuries, Deon Gouws, was a former police officer who belonged to the notorious Vlakplaas death squad that terrorized blacks under the apartheid regime. The South African Truth and Reconciliations Commission granted amnesty to both Strydom and Gouws after they had confessed to killing blacks and terrorizing anti-apartheid activists. Both men had been working for the firm Erinys, which had an $80 million contract to protect oil installations. Louis Nevaer, *Hired Guns in Iraq May Have War Crimes Pasts*, Pacific News Serv., May 3, 2004, available at http:// news.pacificnews.org/news/view_article.html?article_id=68c393b4 db74f12d009eab2321704610.

191. Jonathan Franklin, *US Contractor Recruits Guards for Iraq in Chile,* Guardian, Mar. 5, 2004, at 14, available at http:// www.guardian.co.uk/world/2004/mar/05/iraq.chile/print.

192. The typical salary for Peruvians, for example, is $1,000 a month (or $33 per day), compared to the $500 per day that top-end guards from Great Britain, the United States, or Australia might earn. To be sure, the salary often far exceeds what the workers might earn domestically, and some employees are enthusiastic about their experiences and the pay. One father of two from Peru who earns about $200 per month has said, "Iraq was a good time for me. . . . I just wish I could go back. . . . I never ate so much!" And the work of the TCNs typically differs from that of their higher-paid northern and western counterparts: rather than guarding diplomats as they travel throughout the country, the TCNs from developing countries typically perform "static" security, "staffing checkpoints and guard towers, searching visitors, and keeping alert." McDonnell, *Latin America's Needy, supra* note 186. Yet for Ugandan security guards working for the firm SOC-SMG, the pay disparities between them ($3.33 per hour) and their American employees are problematic. A number of Ugandans have sued the company in Uganda, claiming that they were misled about their contract terms. Raz, *Third-World Labor, supra* note 186.

193. The 2007 National Defense Authorization Act extends the jurisdiction of the Uniform Code of Military Justice, 10 U.S.C. § 801-946 ("UCMJ"), to apply "[i]n time of declared war or a contingency operation" to "persons serving with or accompanying an armed force in the field." Pub. L. No. 109-364, § 552, 120 Stat. 2217 (codified as amended at 10 U.S.C. § 802(a)(10) (2007)). A "contingency operation" is defined more broadly than a declared war and includes, for example, a military operation designated by the secretary of defense as an operation in which the Armed Forces may become involved in hostilities or military actions against an enemy of the United States or against an opposing military force, or that results in a call or order to, or retention on, active duty members of the uniformed services by the president during a time of war or national emergency. 10 U.S.C. § 101(a)(13) (2007). Thus, contractors can now be subject to prosecution by court-martial for violating the UCMJ if they serve with or accompany an armed force in the field in a contingency operation, such as Operation Iraqi Freedom or Operation Enduring Freedom in Afghanistan.

194. *See* Michael R. Gordon, *Military Role Overseeing Contractors Tested in Iraq,* N.Y. Times, Apr. 6, 2008, at A16, available at http:// www.nytimes.com/2008/04/06/world/middleeast/06contractor.html (noting that in 2006 Congress granted the military authority to charge contractors accompanying the armed forces into the field).

195. *See* John Stafford & David Goodwin, *Revised Rules for Battlefield Contractors,* Nat'l Def. Mag., Aug. 2008, http:// www.nationaldefensemagazine.org/archive/2008/August/Pages/RevisedRulesforBattlefieldContractors.as ("[The Military Extraterritorial Jurisdiction Act], which applied only to Defense Department contractors when first enacted in 2000, was later expanded . . . [in fiscal year 2005] to apply to contractors of all federal agencies supporting the Defense Department").

196. Kara M. Sacilotto, *DoD Issues Final Rule on Law of War Training and Disclosure Obligations,* Wiley Rein, LLP, Jan. 16, 2009, http://www.wileyrein.com/publications.cfm?sp=articles&id=4878.

197. U.S. Gov't Accountability Office, *Rebuilding Iraq: DOD and State Department Have Improved Oversight and Coordination of Private Security Contractors in Iraq, but Further Actions Are Needed to Sustain Improvements* 4 (2008) (noting that the State Department now requires one diplomatic security agent to ride in each security contractor motorcade).

198. The devil is, as always, in the details. For example, even trying to figure out what the appropriate norms should be is likely to become tangled in the difficulties of interagency coordination among agencies whose own organizational cultures stand far apart.

7. Conclusion

1. Karen DeYoung & Scott Wilson, *34,000 Troops Will Be Sent to Afghanistan,* Wash. Post, Dec. 1, 2009.

2. Office of the Under Sec'y of Def. for Acquisition, Tech. and Logistics, U.S. Dep't of Def., *Contractor Support of U.S. Operations in USCENTCOM AOR, Iraq, and Afghanistan* 1 (2009), *available at* http://www.acq.osd.mil/log/PS/hot_topics.html.

INDEX

Aaron, Harold R., 26

Abdullahi v. Pfizer (2009), 47–48

Abu Ghraib abuse scandal: accountability of CACI and Titan, 65–68; civilian vs. military prosecutions, 57; contractors involved in, 2, 40–41; monitoring and oversight role in, 84, 85; and organizational culture, 156–157; political will to prosecute cases, 58; tort litigation resulting from, 52–53; and training of interrogators, 80

Accountability: for Abu Ghraib abuses, 40, 65–68; and chain of command, 20; contract design as mechanism for, 13, 18; delegation as path for, 121; legal framework as mechanism for, 18; mechanisms for, 12–13, 18; of military vs. contractors, 179–180; monitoring and oversight as mechanism for, 13, 14; and organizational structure and culture, 13, 19, 185–187; public participation as mechanism for, 13, 19; sanctions as, 146, 152, 160, 171–172

Accreditation: contract provisions for, 73, 92–95; NGOs' role in, 94, 100, 195; and performance benchmarks, 88; recommendations for, 193

Adjudication mechanisms. *See* Grievance mechanisms; Internal compliance programs

Administrative law: and contract law, 73; globalization of, 106; and public participation, 104, 105

Administrative Procedure Act of 1946, 105

Administrative sanctions, 171–172

Aegis Corporation, 59, 109–110, 183–184

Afghanistan War: Combined Security Transition Command, 138, 140; Joint Contracting Command, 77; troop levels for, 189; Vietnam War compared to, 29–30. *See also specific contractors*

African Union, 138

Agency proliferation: and contractor tracking, 192; effect of, 107–110. *See also specific agencies*

Albright, Madeleine, 16

Alien Tort Statute (ATS), 45, 47–48, 191

Aman, Fred, 125

American Correctional Association, 88, 92

American Manufacturers Mutual Insurance Co. v. Sullivan (1999), 48

Anticorruption training, 81

Armed Contractor Oversight Division, 61, 62, 85

Army Corps of Engineers, 112, 126

Army Criminal Investigative Division, 60

Article 15 proceedings, 171–172